Introduction to
Social Welfare Policy

Introduction to Social Welfare Policy:
Power, Scarcity and Common Human Needs

W. Joseph Heffernan
THE UNIVERSITY OF TEXAS AT AUSTIN

F. E. PEACOCK PUBLISHERS, INC.
ITASCA, ILLINOIS 60143

CONTENTS

PREFACE

This book does not offer any settled conclusions on social welfare policy. Rather it introduces the student to a few of the central conceptual tools available for the analysis of complex social welfare problems. It is hoped this work will assist the social worker to think more critically about the responsiveness (and the lack thereof) of the body politic to the social problems of the late 20th century.

The work draws from economics, political science, and social work. During the period of its writing, the author was associated with the Poverty Institute, the Center for the Study of Public Policy, and the School of Social Work, all at the University of Wisconsin, Madison. From my colleagues at all three places I learned a great deal about economics, politics, and social welfare. Some of my colleagues taught me more than others. All of them could have taught me more had I been a more able student.

This volume would surely not exist except for the fine quality of typing and first editorship by Priscilla Fortier. She typed more drafts and provided more incisive criticism than either of us likes to recall. Her ingenuity and resourcefulness saved the manuscript from extinction on more than one occasion. I appreciate the assistance of Mary Tittel and Barbara Turman in the final proofreading stage of production. Other persons have read and commented on various chapters. Among these Dennis Dresang, Irv Garfinkel, Sheldon Danziger, Michael Sossin, John Tropman, Judith Casset-ty, and Robert Lampman deserve special thanks. Needless to say, the book would have been improved had I had the time and energy to incorporate all of their suggestions. Finally, the staff of F. E. Peacock Publishers was supportive and helpful. Of these I would like to specifically thank Tom LaMarre, Gloria Reardon and Joyce Usher.

My first instructor in the politics and economics of welfare was my grandfather, Judge Henry Dannehl. He taught me the contra-dictions inherent in a capitalistic-democratic society trying to care for its poor. My wife, Charlene, and our daughters Katy, Kristi, and Amy each know their own unique contributions to this work, and I shall not embarrass them by an inadequate effort to say thanks.

W. Joseph Heffernan
Austin, Texas

PART I

A LOGIC OF
PUBLIC SOCIAL WELFARE POLICY

CHAPTER 1

THE SCOPE OF
SOCIAL WELFARE PROGRAMS

Intro.

A broad range of social welfare programs explicitly designed to promote the economic security and social well-being of individual citizens has been adopted by national, state, and local governments in the United States. Collectively, these programs now cost more than $300 billion dollars a year. There has been, especially in very recent years, an expansion of public social programs to respond to the problems of poverty, income insecurity, unemployment, ill health, mental illness, juvenile delinquency, developmental disabilities, and family discord and disruptions.

Since 1972 the rate of increase in public spending for social programs has far outstripped the growth of the public sector in other areas.[1] The propriety of this expansion, the effectiveness of the programs which comprise it, and the lessons it holds for future social welfare policy are issues of prime concern to professional social workers, recipient groups, taxpayer alliances, public officeholders, and political candidates. The expansion has moved forward at a very uneven rate; some programs receive generous public support, while others seem to be ignored by those who hold public office. This unevenness has puzzled not only scholars and public officials but the general public as well.

Public awareness and official response to a wide variety of social problems are critically influenced by such things as changes in economic conditions, the character of political leadership, and protest movements, as well as other highly unique and idiosyncratic events. Because of the multiple factors influencing choice, the government often appears to respond to the problems of need in a curious, disjointed manner. This nation has a comprehensive program to respond to temporary unemployment, but virtually no program at all for those more permanently estranged from the labor force. If psychiatric problems are diagnosed, eligibility is established for a wide variety of governmentally sponsored medical and paramedical services, but nagging problems of personal adjustment often elicit no public response. The factors which link a *personal problem* to a *public response* constitute the central concerns in a study of the politics of social welfare.

We all enter the political arena with some set notions about the proper role of government and some hazy notions of which set of policies is likely to be the most effective. Ideally, we would be willing to modify these conceptions as evidence and new experiences change the nature of the choices before us. To filter out questions, a framework of analysis is a critical necessity. The search for an effective framework of analysis must begin with a limitation of concerns, so the questions can be posed in an answerable form.

BOUNDARIES OF CONCERN

Establishing the boundaries of intellectual concern is an important undertaking. Without it, inquiry is likely to lose any sense of order and form. Purposeful and serious inquiry into any complex social problem requires specialization so that each new task can draw upon the accumulated wisdom of past problem solving. Within academic institutions, this specialization, or division of labor into departments such as political science, economics, sociology, is based on reasonably well-established distinguishing characteristics of each discipline. The disciplines, and even subunits within disciplines, have developed not only separate subject matter specialties, but also distinct methodologies, traditions, and conceptual frameworks. Their distinctiveness has had a clearly positive impact on teaching and learning and a somewhat more ambiguous, but generally positive, consequence for basic research. While the boundaries were drawn in the spirit of encouraging rigor in analysis, they also have had the impact of reducing the opportunities to ask broader questions about the social process.[2]

Professions, unlike disciplines, tend to evolve around a group of conceptually unrelated but functionally integrated tasks.[3] Each profession, such as law, medicine, and the ministry, has a reasonably distinct functional role to play in the social process. The professions also develop distinctiveness in the way they are organized for the delivery of their specialized function. This distinctiveness has enormously facilitated the structure of the professional marketplace. Professional boundaries, while drawn to encourage the highest level of relevant competence at the level of interaction between client and professional, have paradoxically had the impact of reducing a conceptually rigorous approach to the specific problems with which the professional deals.

Social welfare professionals have inherited the problems (and the promise) of the professions and of the disciplines. The level of scholarly rigor must not be so demanding that the social worker is unwilling to act. Unlike the scholar, who has a detached responsibility, the professional social worker must intervene in a way that is relevant to the expectations of the community. That is to say, they must perform with a reasonable level of certainty that the interventions they recommend and perform will indeed produce the expected results,[4] and these results will have been sanctioned by their source of authority.

The student of social welfare seeking to acquire the necessary delicate balance between knowledge and skill is likely to be frustrated by what appear to be conflicting demands. Of course, this awareness is only an early recognition of a critical dilemma to which there is no final resolution. There is, on the one side, a need for arbitrary abstractions and precise definitions in order to categorize and limit what would otherwise be a limitless area of study. On the other side, there is the recognition that social problems do not come to us in neat disciplinary or legal boxes. Poverty, for example, is a political, social, and economic problem simultaneously. Poverty and its problems impact upon decisions at all levels of government, from the White House to the county courthouse. Both the public and the private sectors of the economy are involved. In the face of such frustration, the place to begin is with an attempt to limit the parameters of concern.

Despite the great bulk of social welfare literature, and perhaps even because of it, there is no precise statement of the definition of social welfare institutions. This is a natural development, since the term, used to refer to a specific set of programs, is developed only in connection with the social problems of a specific time and place. There is, nonetheless, a more general notion around which a consensus has emerged: The basic tenets and programs of any social welfare system reflect the dominant and enduring values of a society.[5]

As an example of the definitions often used, three are cited here. The *NASW Encyclopedia of Social Work* says:

> "Social welfare" generally denotes the full range of orga-
> nized activities of voluntary and governmental agencies that
> seek to prevent, alleviate, or contribute to the solution of
> recognized social problems, or to improve the well-being of
> individuals, groups, or communities. Such activities use a
> wide variety of professional personnel such as physicians,
> nurses, lawyers, educators, engineers, ministers, social
> workers, and paraprofessional counterparts of each.[6]

Walter Friedlander defines social welfare as:

> ... the organized system of social services and institutions,
> designed to aid individuals and groups to attain satisfying
> standards of life and health, and personal and social relation-
> ships which permit them to develop their full capacities and
> to promote their well-being in harmony with the needs of
> their families and community.[7]

The U.S. Committee Report at the 1974 International Conference on Social Welfare, authored by John Turner, considers the term *social welfare* to include:

1. The wide range of services designed to attain ways of life acceptable to individuals and the community, sometimes thought of collectively as the "social aspects of develop-ment" and including services designed to strengthen the individual confronted with economic, physical, mental, or social disabilities, together with
2. those aimed at influencing the remedy of conditions lead-ing to dependency.[8]

The adoption of a specific program requires a more or less precise articulation of values and assumptions. Articulated values which are codified into a specific public program do not develop in a vacuum but are shaped by both the economic context and the political structures in which the social welfare choices are made. In the pages to follow, this text will attempt to provide a frame of reference for understanding the diverse pathways that lead to public social welfare programs.

The diversity of responses or causal paths of choice cannot be used as an excuse for the lack of a specific statement of focus. As E. E. Schattschneider has written in regard to a similar problem:

There is something strange about the feeling of scholars that a definition is not necessary. Inevitably there is a lack of focus in the discipline because it is difficult to see things that are undefined. People who cannot define the object of their studies do not know what they are looking for, and if they do not know what they are looking for, how can they tell when they have found it?[9]

In order to emphasize the central themes of this text, two central concepts are reviewed at the outset.

CENTRAL CONCEPTS

Two central concepts will shape this investigation of social welfare policy: political power and economic scarcity. The definitions of these central concepts will be dealt with in the next chapter; here we will establish some parameters of concern. We will not be dealing with the whole of the political economy, but only the part of it that is relevant to the domestic social policy of social welfare. The politics of social welfare is similar to and different from politics in general; it is, simply put, a subset of politics. Correspondingly, the economics of social welfare is similar to and different from economics in general; it is a subset of economics. In both cases the subset is bounded by an area of concern, in this case, the boundary of social welfare. Social welfare itself contains dimensions that are not within either of these subsets. Diagrammatically, the area of concern in this text is the double-hatched area in Figure 1-1, where politics, economics, and social welfare coincide.

Social welfare is a rather vague notion, while economics and

FIGURE 1–1
AREAS OF CONCERN IN SOCIAL WELFARE

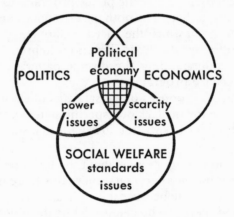

politics are somewhat more precise. Politics has to do with the authoritative allocation of values within a social system. Its driving force is the application of *power* in pursuit of the values to be adopted and thereafter to have sovereign force. Economics has to do with the way goods, resources, and services are utilized in a social system. The paramount concern of the economist is *scarcity*. Scarcity is the condition wherein desires exceed resources. As power is central to the study of politics, scarcity is central to the study of economics. This should not be taken to imply that the study of power is synonymous with the study of political science or that the study of scarcity is synonymous with the study of economics. There are significantly broader issues in both disciplines.

We could search in vain, however, for a similar central element in the study of social welfare. About as far as we might go would be an exemplar statement that most persons would agree that public assistance, social insurance, and public medical care for the poor are part of a society's social welfare system, while tariff regulations and the regulation of the interstate trucking industry are not. While politics and economics are fuzzy at their boundaries, social welfare is fuzzy at its core. Some scholars have simply singled out a group of public programs that have intensively employed social workers and called that the core of social welfare.[10] Others have singled out one or two kinds of programs which deal with income security and called them the core of the system.[11] Still others have selected certain goals and declared them to be the intent of the social welfare system and the criteria by which current programs are assessed.[12] Each approach has a manifest utility, and each reinforces the vagueness surrounding the issue of what social welfare is all about.

The use of social goals to establish the parameters of social welfare is both the most common and the most troubling practice. Often in discussion of law or public policies, people criticize specific programs on the grounds that they pursue the "wrong" goals or that in operation they inadvertently achieve the "wrong" goal. Those who criticize in this manner implicitly assume that they know what program goals are or ought to be. The most frequent error is to assume that stated goals in legislative preambles reflect the real goals of the law. Stated goals are in many cases symbolic. But it is often the case that goals are politically instrumental, and on occasion, blatantly false. The prime sponsors of a public housing law may intend to stimulate employment in the building trades or to preserve racial residential segregation. To evaluate the law in terms of its impact on the quality and price of low-income housing would thus miss the mark by far.

Looking at legislation in terms of its effects is equally troubling. A public assistance law may be more effective in maintaining a ready supply of low-wage workers than in improving the quality of life of low-income families. But we cannot assume that was the intent of the lawmakers; they may just have made an honest error. Even if we knew political actors' "real intentions," it would not help much, since laws and policies often have multiple goals, sometimes even contradictory goals. As a general rule, laws result from a compromise of contending interest groups. The identification of one interest group's goals is hardly a sufficient basis for separating social welfare policy from other forms of policy.

Any attempt to set the boundaries of social welfare policy thus must be deliberately done with a specific purpose in mind. The purpose here is to develop a critical awareness of the complex set of relationships which interact to produce a particular set of social welfare laws. The social worker in the field will surely observe instances where law and common sense appear at variance. Social workers need more than the capacity to identify bad laws; they also need to know something of how the laws have developed in that way.

THREE FEATURES OF SOCIAL POLICY LEGISLATION

This text defines social welfare in terms of observable legislative features. Our principal concern is with public programs that objectively do three things: (1) establish some minimal standard of social functioning, (2) identify a benefit schedule, and (3) identify a population group that is to be privileged with a public guarantee to the benefit. The legislation creates a specific program to enforce and deliver the standard or benefit to the eligible population. These three characteristics are the events of social welfare policy. They are discussed in the sections below.

Minimum Standard

We will not deal here with the normative problem of what the minimum standard ought to be,[13] or the equally important issue of how a minimum is selected. The concern here is with the concept of a minimum standard as one of the three central characteristics of a social welfare law, as defined in this text. One of the essential characteristics of a social welfare law is that it defines some minimal standard against which to measure the need of some group of people. This standard can be spelled out in great detail, or, as is the more usual case, it can be vaguely implied. In public assistance programs the standard is some income level which all qualified persons will be guaranteed. At times the state will only *offer* the standard; for example, various rehabilitation programs will be made available at no cost to users who meet eligibility requirements, but individual citizens or their guardians are free to reject the offer. At other times the standard is *imposed* on citizens, usually to protect others. An example is parenting practices enforced to protect children.

Empirically, the standard is the *base* against which a minimum level is measured to establish eligibility for a program. At its simplest level it establishes a socially defined minimum. The Wisconsin General Assistance statute states, for example, that "dependent persons are those without present available money or income to provide the necessary commodities as (they are) set forth by (city) statute."[14] All welfare laws do not establish precise minimum standards; rather, some are vaguely set goals for society. Most statutes fall between being hopelessly vague and inhumanly precise.

Vagueness in standards accomplishes many goals. Legislators

can point to high-sounding laws when running for reelection, while administrators are given some discretionary ground upon which to maneuver when dealing with the highly unique cases before them, and potential clients have a leverage to use in demanding that the public response be truly responsive to their unique needs. Yet vagueness in standards allows also for capricious behavior in the conduct of the program. The lines of eligibility and the benefits available vary from one situation to the next. The tension between the precision of a standard that guarantees that all persons similarly situated will be treated equally, and the general authorization which allows the line-level worker to react innovatively to a unique condition, is one of the fundamental issues in social welfare laws.

Establishing a minimum standard for policy execution purposes involves some very basic difficulties. First, it is necessary to specify the general delineation of circumstances existing in the real world which can be taken as the equivalent of an abstract notion like poverty, or deprivation, or child abuse. Then some simplified proxy of these circumstances must be found, so that it can be measured in new and unique conditions.

While in actual practice the usual condition is for the notions of benefit and standard to become merged, they are conceptually distinct. The minimum standard can be thought of as a universal guarantee for all persons within the protected group. Initially, at least, little thought is given to the dollar cost in the setting of a standard. The standard is a goal for the society, and the meeting of this goal will put a demand on society's resources. All mentally ill persons will be protected from themselves by a program of care, all children will be taught to read, all persons currently employed will have a public assurance that in the event of unemployment, their welfare payment will be $X\%$ (to a Y minimum) of previous wage earnings. These are all examples of setting the goal first and then calculating the cost. In the design of a program, considerations often go in the other direction. The first question is, how much does it cost to provide quality care to the mentally ill, or how expensive is an extensive reading program? Such issues involve the near-simultaneous treatment of standards, benefits, and costs.

Not only are standards and benefits conceptually distinct, but the political process which surrounds the articulation of a standard is not identical with that process when it comes to the specification of a benefit schedule. The fact that the two are merged into one program produces results that may be labeled as unfair. An examination of the legislative-administrative history of AFDC benefits suggests that a $447 benefit per month for a family of four would make political and economic sense. At the same time, an examination of the legislative-administrative history of unemployment benefits suggests that a benefit of $410 per month for a highly paid single worker also would make political and economic sense. But when the $447 benefit is compared to the $410 benefit, we wonder at the lack of sense in the system. The fractured political decision-making process discussed in Chapter 3 provides some insight into why our politicoeconomic system repeatedly produces welfare laws that are individually rational but collectively unreasonable.

Benefits

In a very general sense, benefits of social welfare programs can be thought of as existing on a continuum from minimal to restitutionary to developmental. At a minimal level the benefit is geared to some standard below which no eligible person will be allowed to fall. For instance, immediate disaster relief is structured so that all of the victims of the disaster will be given warm clothing, nourishing food, and a place to sleep. As the program becomes more generous, the level of benefit may be lifted to restore people to their previous level of functioning before the disaster struck. The most generous benefit schedules are those which are designed to aid individual recipients in developing to their highest capacity.

Benefit schedules are not selected from an unrestricted menu but are forced into programs by both economic and political factors. If the disaster is large and the resource base small, programs will of necessity be minimal. In some cases the benefit schedule is decreed by the level of technology available; for some severely retarded persons, for example, minimal creature comforts are all that can be provided. A lag in social welfare development occurs when a program is designed in one economic, political, and technological context but continues to operate in a rather drastically changed society. In welfare history, there is a permanent disequilibrium as programs change conditions and new conditions demand new programs. What a society can and ought to do for its poor, its mentally ill, its crippled, its law violators is subject to wide and often erratic swings of public opinion. The level of benefits which are actually provided and the level of benefits that ought to be provided thus become a point of political controversy.

The level of benefits provided is constrained by both resource limitation and value considerations. Clearly, in a finite economy, available resources influence decisions about the level of benefits. Yet value considerations impose constraints on how much a polity will tax itself to make those resources available. The interactive quality of resources and values is shown in this comment by Lawrence Friedman:

> Often the value choice comes first. It is decided that nobody ought to starve, that prisoners on trial for their lives must have access to a lawyer, that no one shall lack a smallpox vaccination by reason of poverty. These choices, of course, assume that the cost of fulfillment will not put a crushing burden on society. Sometimes that assumption turns out to be false. The Medicaid program gave to the states the right to set levels of benefits for the medically indigent. The states then made value choices; they decided what kinds of medical benefits everybody "ought" to have. When this turned out to call for billions of dollars, a certain amount of backtracking set in.[15]

Eligible Population

Welfare programs must have some way to define the class of beneficiaries. Universal programs have a nice rhetorical ring, but political considerations and cost efficiency require that all persons will *not* be helped equally. Few want to give the same aid to the voluntary dropout and the truly helpless. Offering standards of aid related to need calls for reasonably precise rules of eligibility. Welfare laws lay down the general rules for opening the door of aid to some while closing it to others. The Wisconsin AFDC statute established an eligible population with this language:

> ... a child under the age of 18, who has been deprived of parental support or care by reason of the death, continued absence from the home, or incapacity of a parent, and who is living with his father, mother, grandfather, grandmother,

brother, sister, stepfather, stepmother, stepbrother, stepsis-
ter, uncle, aunt, first cousins, nephews or nieces in a residence maintained by one or more such relatives as his or
their own home, or living in a residence maintained by one
or more of such relatives as his or their own home because
the parents of said child have been found unfit to have its
care and custody, or who is living in a foster home. . . .[16]

In addition, laws and administrative regulations define a process for testing eligibility. The procedural aspects of the program
describe the steps that must be taken by those who wish to make
a claim for the protection provided by the standard. The procedure defines responsibility for applicants; they must make application on a form provided by the department and provide
documentary evidence of some items of the information. The
procedure also sets responsibility for the state: "investigation of
the application shall be made and a written report of the results
shall be made within three working days."[17]
Since there can be, and usually is, a wide variation in actual
practice and statutory regulations, the procedural practices may
really determine who is, in fact, eligible. Some statutes define
various aspects of the eligibility process with care and precision,
while others are hopelessly vague. As a general rule, with notable
exceptions, the greater the political power of the potentially eligible population, the more precise the procedural rules and the
greater the likelihood that practice and statute will be in close
conformity.
All welfare laws must use some sort of procedure to test
beneficiaries. Even if a law were passed to give a specific credit to
all persons, rules would have to be made to prevent double credit-
ing. Sometimes a distinction is made between means testing and
eligibility by right. In practice the distinction is both artificial and
unclear. In theory, a rights program is one in which eligibility is
established by virtue of membership in a certain status group,
such as being a veteran. A means-tested program is one where
eligibility is established by proof of need, as is the case in most
public assistance programs. In a pure rights program, the only
relevant consideration is membership in the status group, while in
a pure means-tested program the only relevant consideration
would be need. In practice, most operative programs have components of a means-tested program and components of a rights
program.

Separating those in need by categories serves a political function. There is much discussion of the question of whether or not there is a culture of poverty,[18] but there is little doubt that the shape of poverty is enormously varied.[19] The black female-headed family living in the urban core is one type, and the aged couple whose pension rights have been eroded by inflation is another type. Political leaders often have reason to create and maintain a myth that these are two types of poverty and not two manifestations of a single problem of income inequality. One way to preserve the myth is to have programs of aid varied by standard, benefit, and eligibility procedures. If most blind are poor, if most aged pensioners are poor, if most disabled persons are poor, if most veterans can't afford college, it may be simpler and cheaper to award benefits on the basis of a group membership, even if some of the benefits leak out to those who, strictly speaking, do not need them.

Programs that rely most heavily on the means test tend to be those that are designed to benefit groups of inferior social position and limited political power. "These people need to be closely watched" is the prevailing justification for enormously high administrative costs. Persons on public welfare are "clients," while persons in the OASDI program are "beneficiaries." Public welfare recipients make excellent political scapegoats and, in times of financial stringency, the means test can be made to operate more harshly, more rapidly. Procedures, not laws, can be changed the fastest. Not lost on most observers is the fact that stringent (some would say annoying or tyrannical) procedures can deter even the potentially eligible from making application, thus "saving" money. For example, many university students eligible for food stamps do not apply for them because they find the process degrading. Onerous conditions of application raise the price, psychological or otherwise, of applying, thus ensuring that only those "truly in need" will go through the process. Daylong waits to see the intake worker serve political, economic, and psychological goals and are not mere accidental results of bad welfare planning.

Over the long term these circumstances lead to a kind of polarization of welfare programs, of which rights and means are only very rough proxies of the extremes. As a population of potentially eligible persons expands its political influence capability, it will demand that onerous conditions of eligibility be removed. Usually this takes the form of an entirely new program for a subset of the old program. Unemployment compensation, OASDI, and Medicare are examples of programs which are not strictly means-tested and which have been segregated out of a residual system of poor relief. The new programs contain no, or at least, less, stigma. They are administratively more precise, and their eligibility basis is broadened to include middle-class constituents. Often then the old programs, having lost much of their middle-class constituency, and along with it their political influence, become even more stigmatic and subject to administrative as opposed to legal controls.

CONCEPTUAL FORMS OF SOCIAL WELFARE

With a minimum standard, benefit schedule, and eligibility procedure stipulated, a welfare program results when specific enabling legislation and funding authorization are adopted. Two polar forms illustrate the essential features of U.S. welfare programs: the residual and the institutional.[20] The *residual approach* holds that social welfare institutions should come into play only when the normal structures for meeting basic needs have failed. Defects in the operation of the market system, the family, educational apparatus, the health delivery system, and so on may produce a need for a residual social welfare structure to meet needs that are not otherwise being met. The residual formulation is based on the premise that "artificial channels" of meeting an individual's needs are inherently inferior, and the social welfare system is, and ought to be, only an emergency network of aid. The *institutional approach* sees social welfare programs as a normal first-line function of a modern industrial society. This function has the unique characteristic of a broad integrative view of human need. It is not accident or failure that produces fissures in the fabric of an industrial society, but a simple fact of life. In this view, social welfare institutions provide the structures needed to promote individual well-being and fulfillment which are consonant with the resources of the community.[21]

The residual view sees social welfare programs as a stopgap device. Common human needs are to be met through a variety of interacting social institutions: The consumption needs are to be fulfilled through the public and private marketplace; care of children and procreational, sexual, and affectional needs are to be met through the family system; needs for communitywide decisions are to be met through the political system, and so on. Should a particular institution falter, or should there be some difficulty in getting two systems to work together, a social welfare program is created to care for the "accident." Closer examination reveals that this seminal distinction meets the test of neither inclusiveness nor exclusiveness. AFDC and OASDI both have residual and institutional features. Ideologically, a residual conception focuses attention on the failure of the individual in an essentially just society, while the institutional focuses attention on the failure of society to respond to individual needs.

The distinction between institutional and residual welfare programs has been one of the mainstays of 20th-century social work literature. Increasingly, however, it has been recognized that this distinction is at best ambiguous, at worst entirely contrived. As a consequence, recently social welfare programs have been subject to detailed descriptions.[22]

In describing social welfare programs, scholars have too often been guilty of normative pleading. They fail to distinguish between what they feel ought to exist and what does exist. In short, a major difficulty in forming a conceptualization of social welfare stems from confusion over what has happened in contrast to what many persons *wish* had occurred, or from a failure to distinguish between what was intended and what *really* occurred.

CONCLUSIONS

It is generally recognized that laws and public programs have multiple purposes. For a course of action to emerge as public policy it must typically satisfy a whole set of requirements. The requirements of one set of political actors may be only of minor concern to another set of political actors, yet the support of both sets of actors may be critical to the adoption of the policy.

Rather than try to classify legislative programs by some vague purpose, it is more useful to view them as a complex set of expenditures and services which have identifiable consequences. In this text, we identify as social welfare those programs which have three identifiable features. First, to qualify as a social welfare program, the legislation must explicitly establish some minimum standard that the government will guarantee. Second, social welfare programs establish a benefit schedule, stipulating the conditions under which this guarantee will apply. Third, they specify what portion of the population will be eligible for the guarantee. The legislation incorporating these three features establishes concrete programs to provide the guarantee to the eligible population.

Conceptually, social welfare programs can be perceived as existing as polar forms—the residual and the institutional. Programs in action, however, typically have elements of both forms.

NOTES

1. U.S. Office of Management and Budget, *The United States Budget in Brief* (Washington, D.C.: U.S. Government Printing Office, 1978).
2. See Jacques Barzun, *The House of the Intellect* (New York: Harper, 1959). This paragraph should not be taken to imply that the organization of knowledge within academia has been motivated by a desire to facilitate social problem solving. It does imply, however, that disciplinary specialization in some ways retards and in some ways facilitates a broad, comprehensive understanding of social problems. Any student who has participated in or observed an interdisciplinary discussion must have noted both the insight and the blindness that can be generated in the dissection of a social problem by an academic specialist.
3. Paul E. Weinberger, *Perspectives on Social Welfare* (New York: Macmillan Co., 1974).
4. Ibid. Many persons, trained in many ways, consider themselves to be social welfare professionals. Their professional identity may be that of planner, economist, public administrator, and so on, but they work in the arena of social welfare. *Social worker* is a more specific term, usually self-ascribed but sometimes limited to persons whose education qualifies them for membership in the National Association of Social Workers. Most, but surely not all, of these persons work in the social welfare arena.

    The topics covered in this text are of relevance to social welfare professionals whether or not they perceive themselves as social workers. We will not take up the knotty and perhaps insoluble problem of who is and who is not a social worker.
5. Martin Wolins, "The Societal Functions of Social Welfare," *New Perspectives*, vol. 1 (1967), pp. 1–18.
6. *NASW Encyclopedia of Social Work* (New York: National Association of Social Workers, 1971), p. 1446.
7. Walter Friedlander, *Introduction to Social Welfare* (Englewood Cliffs, N.J.: Prentice-Hall, 1955), p. 140.
8. John Turner, *Development and Participation* (New York: International Council of Social Welfare, 1974), p. 19.
9. Quoted in Alan C. Isaak, *Scope and Methods of Political Science* (Homewood, Ill.: Dorsey Press, 1975).
10. Walter A. Friedlander and Robert Z. Apte, *Introduction to Social Welfare* (Englewood Cliffs, N.J.: Prentice-Hall, 1974).
11. Eveline Burns, *Social Security and Public Policy* (New York: McGraw-Hill Book Co., 1956).
12. Roland Frederico, *The Social Welfare Institution* (Lexington, Mass.: D.C.

Heath & Co., 1976), and Richard Titmus, *Commitment to Welfare* (New York: Pantheon Books, 1968).

13. There is a large body of literature which deals with the problems inherent in setting a standard. One work which deals with standards in a variety of contexts is Samuel Beer and Richard Barrenger, *The State and the Poor* (Cambridge, Mass.: Winthrop Publishers, 1970).

14. *Wisconsin Statutes*, chap. 49.

15. Lawrence M. Friedman, *Social Welfare Legislation: An Introduction*, Institute for Research on Poverty Discussion Paper (Madison: University of Wisconsin, 1968), p. 47.

16. *Wisconsin Statutes*, para. 49:01.

17. Ibid.

18. Oscar Lewis, *The Children of Sanchez* (New York: Random House, 1961).

19. Bradley R. Schiller, *The Economics of Poverty* (Englewood Cliffs, N.J.: Prentice-Hall, 1976).

20. Harold Wilenski and Charles Lebeaux, *Industrial Society and Social Welfare* (New York: Russell Sage Foundation, 1958).

21. Ibid.

22. Frederico, *Social Welfare Institution*.

CHAPTER 2

POLICY ANALYSIS OF
SOCIAL WELFARE PROGRAMS

It is necessary to distinguish social welfare programs from other forms of domestic social policy, as we did in Chapter 1, if the scope of this inquiry is to have manageable limits. Yet it is often the case in social science that what begins as definition ends as classification. The sorting and classification of social welfare programs on the basis of their institutional or residual bias blurs the distinction between programs and heightens the distinction between analytic concepts. The definitional problems which emerge focus attention on the complexity of social welfare policy.

This text cannot provide an encyclopedic understanding of policy as a political process, as planning, and as administration. Such an understanding would greatly aid the practicing professional, who is often called to comment on the entire panorama of welfare laws, their real impact, and the alternatives available to the community. We can, however, provide an introduction to a select set of concepts which will enhance the ability to understand how policy develops and how changes occur.

This book is about public social welfare policy. Its principal focus is on why governments do what they do, and why they fail to do other things. The intent is to trace the link between a personal problem and a public response, or lack thereof. The book is also about the role of the professional in the identification, articulation, selection, and execution of public social welfare programs. This chapter identifies some of the analytic techniques used in the first three of these four functions.

There are many reasons to study social welfare policy. They range from simple curiosity about our social system to a sophisticated scientific inquiry. For example, in the scientific mode of inquiry, social welfare policies can be thought of as either the *dependent* or the *independent* variable.[1] In the former case the question asked is, What is it that produces a particular set of social policies? In the latter case the question is, What is the impact, both intended and unintended, of the adoption of particular social welfare programs? Social welfare policy might also be studied for purposes of political advocacy. An understanding of the origins and the consequences of current programs is important to anyone who seeks to alter current conditions. Perhaps most fundamentally, however, the social worker is concerned with public social welfare policy for professional reasons. This requires something *more* than the ordinary citizen's perusal of the evening paper and something *different* from the academic's specialized disciplinary inquiry. Professional "if . . . then" advice requires (1) a factual understanding of the conditions of the program, (2) a developed and tested paradigm which parsimoniously "explains" related events, and (3) a normative orientation that is capable of ordering, in some way, the relative desirability of various outcomes.

The professional social worker thus approaches the study of social policy with a different set of goals and a different set of skills than that of the economist or political scientist. Nevertheless, the first few chapters of this text will borrow heavily from economics and political science as aids to the understanding of social welfare policy development. While a comprehensive understanding of social welfare policy may not be within the scope of this work, we can identify a few of the links in the causal chain of events that produce social welfare programs.

The simplified diagram of Figure 2–1 shows that the number of linkages to be explored in order to understand the development of social welfare programs fully would be very large. If we were to be concerned only with the four illustrated factors, and with only two variables in each factor (an absurdly small number), there would be 48 principal linkages to be investigated! Clearly, speciali-

FIGURE 2–1
LINKAGES AMONG FACTORS INVOLVED IN THE SELECTION OF
SOCIAL WELFARE POLICIES

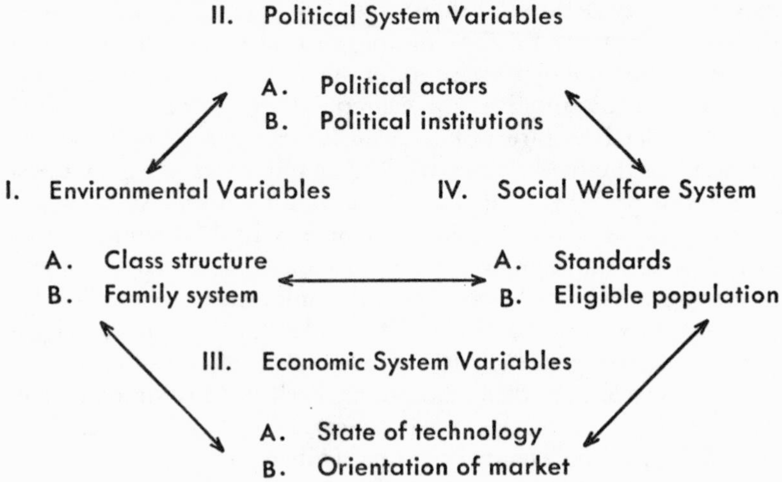

II.   Political System Variables

A.   Political actors
B.   Political institutions

I.   Environmental Variables   IV.   Social Welfare System

A.   Class structure   A.   Standards
B.   Family system   B.   Eligible population

III.   Economic System Variables

A.   State of technology
B.   Orientation of market

zation and selective orientations are required to provide even a hint of what is involved in a comprehensive awareness of social welfare policy development.

PERSPECTIVES ON SOCIAL WELFARE POLICY

Not only must a decision be reached as to which of the competing linkages demand the most attention, but there also is competition between markedly different frames of reference to guide the inquiry. There is on the one hand a *classical perspective*, which perceives the process of working out welfare arrangements in a society as one of many attempts to accommodate competing and contradictory demands on its presumably scarce resources. The analysis of public social welfare involves questions of available resources and the alternative uses to which they could be placed (the issues of scarcity, which will be discussed below). Since one pattern of allocation will please some and displease others, selecting among them involves the analysis of power (also discussed below). The classical perspective is the one that is used in this text.

There is an alternative, the *radical perspective*, which will not be discussed in detail here. The reader who is interested in exploring this perspective will find an important body of literature on it.[2] The critical feature of the radical approach is that welfare arrangements are seen not as an additional area of policy competition within a given economic system, but rather as an instrument which is used by those holding the power in the polity to preserve existing arrangements for decision making and economic (or, as the advocates of this approach might say, property) arrangements. The radical perspective is most consistently worked out with reference to traditional relief programs, but it can be extended to apply to social insurance, mental health, day care, and all other social welfare programs.

The radical approach argues that when there is a disruption in existing conditions due to a downturn in the economy, relief programs are expanded in order to reduce the tensions that the disruption generates. When the tension subsides and tempers are cooled, the welfare arrangements are contracted. This forces former recipients back into the labor market. In this way the state maintains, for the benefit of employers, a ready supply of cheap labor by expanding or contracting the supply of welfare programs available as conditions in the labor market dictate. The workers are, in effect, subsidized when the labor market does not need them. When blacks riot in the cities, urban renewal and economic opportunity programs are expanded, but when the threat of riot is diffused, these programs are withdrawn.

The radical perspective should be explored, but the classical perspective is essential to an understanding of social welfare policy. This text is confined to the classical view of policy choice as an expression of values in resource allocation. Even if the radical perspective were to become the accepted one in our society, the changes that would occur still would have to be implemented through a political process. The mere fact that welfare or public child care serves some extensive ideological purpose does not obviate a need for explaining how change occurs.

ORIENTATIONS WITHIN THE CLASSICAL PARADIGM

In the classical perspective, the analysis of public social welfare involves questions of available resources and the alternative uses to which they can be put. The choices, which are demanded by the condition of scarcity, are the stuff of the politics of social welfare. In studying welfare choice, the goal is to explain what did occur, or how choices were made. This goal can be approached from a variety of interrelated orientations.

One approach, the *empirical orientation,* is concerned with how welfare questions are perceived and interpreted. Empirical observations are potentially capable of verification—we want to know what did occur. Students sometimes think of empiricism as synonymous with science, particularly natural science, but science is broader than empiricism, and empiricism is not limited to laboratory investigation. We may wish, for example, to find out how welfare benefits are reduced when income from other sources increases. If we look at the statute books and administrative manuals we find two different answers, and if we ask clients to recall what happened to them we would get a third answer. In each case we would receive a truthful answer, but each is different. The empirical orientation demands attention to the precision with which questions are asked and the objectivity with which the answers are recorded.[3] It also demands attention to the quality of measurements used, so there is an opportunity for independent replication.

The *normative orientation* is often thought of as the domain of religion or philosophy, but it is also relevant to understanding social welfare choices. It concerns itself with the criteria through which judgments about the positive and negative aspects of programs are made. Normative propositions have to do with issues of "oughtness." They are not entirely subjective. Throwing people out of an airplane is not a "good way" of dealing with population pressure. The normative orientation demands that a systematic set of connections be developed between means and ends. Thus it blends into the positive orientation discussed below. But principally it requires a precise articulation of the values that we seek to maximize within any particular system.[4]

The *positive orientation* investigates the operation of the welfare system without regard for the desirability of the results. It is concerned with the logical interconnection of events and institutions in the development of welfare programs. Its purpose is to develop a set of conceptually interrelated propositions which provide a parsimonious explanation of empirically observable events. Positive propositions are thus tested empirically; we predict, for example, that if decision-making units are decentralized, such and such a result will occur. This can be tested by observing what does result in those conditions where the decision-making process has been decentralized. Empirically tested positive propositions are often used prescriptively. If we wish to produce such a result, then one of the options available is the decentralization of the decision-making process. The criterion of adequacy of such positive investigation is the accuracy and the usefulness of the hypothesis that it produces.

A purely empirical study, of which there are very few, can be done without an explicit theoretical frame of reference. A purely normative study, of which there are even fewer, can be done without regard to factual limitations. A positive investigation requires, at a minimum, a set of conceptually interrelated propositions; this is sometimes referred to as pure theory. Positive investigations typically go beyond this point and provide references to real-world conditions so that the abstract propositions might be objectively tested. Positive studies are principally concerned with the clarifications and the precision of concepts and definitions, their internal and external logic, and the interconnections between empirical statements, analytic concepts, and valued preferences.

ELEMENTS OF POLICY CHOICE

It would mean little for a society to select social goals which are unobtainable. As long as the economy functions as we know it, and as long as current technology exists as it does, a society cannot simultaneously provide a universal "right" to a job and a universal "right" to zero inflation. Perhaps, but not conceivably, we could guarantee one of these rights, but it is inconceivable that we could have both. The logic of our market system denies it. At another level, and again with current technology, we cannot have an absolute guarantee of the privacy of welfare recipients and an absolute guarantee of zero fraud in the distribution of welfare benefits. Of course, the selection of welfare programs would pose no problem if all of our values were identical. If we could disregard work effort impacts and fraud as problems, for example, selection would be enormously simplified. Two interrelated aspects of social choice must always be considered: the class of the possible, and the class of the desirable. Normative theory deals with the desirable, while positive theory deals with the logic of the possible.

In confronting the logic of the possible, there are two choices. First, the scholar can assume that people behave logically, observe their behavior, and then discover what goals must have existed to produce this behavior. In this procedure goals are inferred from (1) observation, and (2) an assumption of logic. This is the method of revealed preference which lies behind most empirical-descriptive inquiry. The second option available to the scholar is to assume a *goal* such as to win an election, or to adopt a particular program of aid. After the assumption of goals, behavior can be prescribed which is in accordance with the rules of logic and is goal directed. This is the method of posited preferences.

Which approach to use—the essentially empirical approach of revealed preferences or the more abstract approach of posited preferences—is determined largely by the question at hand. Most often in social work inquiry the researcher moves back and forth between the approaches. For illustration, the researcher begins an examination of the social worker in a welfare agency and posits that the individual's goals are the same as the officially specified goals articulated in statute. The researcher then finds some behavior well explained. Some behavior, however, is not explained. The researcher then turns to the worker's behavior and discovers goals that are quite different from, perhaps even antithetical to, the official goals.

The frequent shifting of approach can produce problems which become confused in the shifts. Suppose that by an exercise of positive theory behavior A is found consistent with a goal of aiding the poor, while behavior B is found consistent with the goal of controlling the poor. The agency's manual says aiding the poor—behavior A—is the agency's goal, but we observe behavior B in the operation of the agency. We are at a loss to say whether the workers really had a goal that is antithetical to the agency goals, or whether they simply behaved illogically. If we assert that controlling the poor is the *real* goal because it is what we observe, we deny the possibility of irrationality in the worker. If we assume that "an error" explains the lack of congruence of goals and performance, we deny the possibility that stated goals and intended goals are really different.

If in a construct connecting behavior A and goal A as well as behavior B and goal B (see Figure 2-2), the relationship in Quadrants I and IV gives us no difficulty, but the relationship in Quadrants II and III is mysterious: The goal produces the opposite behavior. All we can "know" is that one of these happens:

1. The goals are falsely stated and the behavior is rational.

FIGURE 2-2
RELATIONSHIP OF OFFICIAL GOALS AND SOCIAL WORKERS'
BEHAVIORS

	Goal A	Goal B
Behavior A	I	II
Behavior B	III	IV

2. The goals are honestly stated, but an error in logic produces irrational behavior.
3. The original construct which connects behavior A to goal A is faulty.
4. Faulty observations were made.

In practice, therefore, policy analysis reflects an understanding of (1) the special features of a concrete situation, (2) clear specification of the particular goals, and (3) a prescriptive analysis from some specialized domain (or discipline) of knowledge. While we cannot hope to touch on all of the relevant disciplinary knowledge required for expert policy analysis, we can consider in some detail the two central analytic concepts which are most frequently used to explain social welfare choice. These concepts are power and scarcity.

THE CONCEPT OF POWER

A polity is usually conceived of as a probably large but surely complex set of public and private decision-making systems. Within it, governments, interest groups, and individual actors interact to produce public policies. A *policy* is a representation of the values for which political actors bargain and compete. It is somewhat confusing that policy is also the term given to a state of affairs found within the polity and to the generic commodity produced by the policy process. The *policy process* is the term used to describe the patterns of interactions of actors and institutions as they pursue specific policy goals. *Policy goals* are manifest expressions of values which individual actors conceive of as the proper role of government under given conditions.

David Easton has argued that politics is concerned with the "authoritative allocation of values for a whole society."[5] The concern of this text is with the process whereby authoritative decisions about a polity's social welfare programs are made. We intend to shed some light on why governments provide benefits to some citizens and deny them to other citizens, and why governments suddenly commit massive resources to particular social purposes and then just as suddenly abandon those commitments.

Some writers view power as *the* central concept in the study of public choice. Harold Lasswell and Abraham Kaplan argue that "political science, as an empirical discipline, is the study of the shaping and sharing of power."[6] Despite power's important position in the study of politics, it remains an elusive concept. Machiavelli, whose name is synonymous with the study of power and whose writings mark the watershed from classical-normative political theory to modern empirical political theory, used a variety of terms—power, authority, influence, and rule—almost interchangeably. Many contemporary scholars have attempted precise typologies of these interrelated terms,[7] but there is no agreed-upon convention.

Power relationships are obviously involved in almost every aspect of human relations. This may make it impossible, or at least unproductive, to attempt to construct a theory of power which speaks to all of these relationships. Because of this difficulty, analysts of power have tended to confine their attention to subsets of power. Unfortunately, however, there is no agreement on the common characteristics of the various subsets.

Political power is the subset of power used in modern political science to refer to the capacity of some persons or groups to impose their preferences on all others within the collective. While power is clearly observable, it is not in any ordinary sense measurable. It is clear that the boundaries of the subset of political power are both ambiguous and imprecise. This ambiguity has plagued the empirical examination of power in modern social science. If a subordinate group (e.g., women or blacks) appeared to accept a social role for themselves in one time frame but appeared to reject this role in a later time frame, who is to say whether there has been a change in value orientations or a change in power relationships, or both?

In recent years more attention has been paid to power as a dependent variable. These studies have attempted to ascertain the sources of power within particular contexts, such as the city, the legislature, or the welfare board. From such investigations there has emerged an awareness that there are some common sources of power—knowledge, money, numbers, intensity of commitment, and so on—but each of these determinants of power has a different functional role in the varied contexts. Treating power as a dependent variable has helped to focus attention on the need for a precise, though operational, definition of power.

Somewhat arbitrarily, we specify that power involves (1) the interaction of preferences, (2) perceptions about the capacity of others to alter our preferences, (3) the intensity of our preferences and the mechanisms to alter them, and (4) changes in behavior.

Interacting Preferences

Power relationships exist when there is conflict. If there is no conflict over beliefs, actions, or rules there is no need for power. A matrix which illustrates this point for a society of two persons contemplating a change is shown in Figure 2-3. Both person A and person B can view the change as improving instead of either not affecting or impairing their well-being. This assessment includes A's regard for B, and vice versa.

FIGURE 2-3
BELIEFS ABOUT CHANGES AND THEIR CONSEQUENCES

B. Believes Change Would	A. Believes Change Would		
	Improve His Well-being	Not Alter His Well-being	Impair His Well-being
Improve His Well-being	1	2	3
Not Alter His Well-being	4	5	6
Impair His Well-being	7	8	9

If A and B are rational persons, change under conditions 1, 2, and 4 would occur without the exercise of power. Social welfare economists have provided a name for such choices: They are said to be *Pareto optimal.* The term comes from the work of the early 20th-century Italian economist and sociologist, Vilfredo Pareto.[8]

It refers to a choice that allows one to take an action that benefits at least one person without harming anyone else. After all Pareto-optimal choices have been made, a polity reaches a condition where it is impossible to take any action to increase the well-being of any person without simultaneously harming the well-being of some other person. This is referred to as a Pareto-optimum condition.[9] Changes under conditions 6, 8, and 9 are not Pareto-optimal and would not occur if the actors are rational and do not seek to hurt one another. Under conditions 3 and 7 there is a direct conflict of wills. The move is not Pareto optimum and would in the case of 3 be favored by B and opposed by A. Condition 7 would be the obverse. A power relationship thus exists in these two cases, and the expected outcome would be dependent on the relative power of A and B. Since a change can be detrimental only under a condition of scarcity, if there is a genuine conflict of interest between A and B, either the conditions of change must be altered, or power must be exerted.

Perceptions of Power as Involuntary Exchange

Power comes into play when changes (or exchanges) are perceived as being involuntary. For example, the "power" of the state is exerted to create ownership, or the "power" of the union is used to withhold work for anything but wages which are considered too high by management. The power emerges from the capacity to impose a change and is derived from a variety of sources: sovereign authority of the state, unequal wealth, physical capability to do bodily harm. When we feel oppressed we are oppressed. As we respond to the oppression we are acting in a political way to alter the conditions of coercion. Landowners are likely to think of unions as coercive instruments which violate voluntary exchange, and laborers may think of ownership as an unnatural and coercive element in exchange. Both will seek, or at least wish to alter, the prevailing relationship by use of their power.

Intensity of Preference

When there is a political conflict, the most powerful do not always win; success depends on skill and willingness to deploy the instruments of power. The result of a political conflict can be thought of as the product of power times intensity in interaction, with a countervailing power and a countervailing intensity. The larger product wins. Consider a group of welfare mothers aligned against the chairperson of the welfare board. The mothers have their sources of power: numbers, a degree of political sophistication, the support of certain community groups, perhaps a friendly reporter. The chairperson has personal political power: access to the mayor's office, continuing contact with the city and the welfare bureaucracy, support of some interest groups, and perhaps the support of a newspaper editor. If the issue is of deep concern to the mothers but not to the chairperson, they will be likely to "win"; if the reverse is the case, the chairperson will be likely to "win"; if both are deeply committed, the resources available and the skill with which they are deployed will dictate the outcome.

The sources of political power can be listed: money, time, knowledge, status, available allies, and so on. Groups with more of these attributes will be politically powerful (e.g., the American Medical Association). Groups with fewer of these attributes will have less power (e.g., the National Association of Social Workers), while groups with none of these will be without any influence (e.g., the anti-Vietnam War movement in the spring of 1963). The change in power of the anti-war movement shows that the power relationships are dynamic and heavily influenced by intensity of concern. The intensity of most participants on most issues is clearly zero. As a group of concerned citizens mount a political attack to change a policy or end a war, their first problem always is to get potential participants involved and committed sufficiently to invest political resources. The story of political conflict is really the story of the stage of the conflict and the ways in which actual and potential power resources are deployed. This will be illustrated later in the account of the failure of the income maintenance reform plan of 1972.

Changes in Behavior

The fourth characteristic of political power is that there is some behavioral response. For this to occur, certain necessary conditions must be met. First, the subordinate in the power relationship must know what is expected of him. Since power must be relational (i.e., exist in a relationship of conflict), the subordinate must comprehend the alternatives that are associated with a political command. He must know what compliance or noncompliance will mean.

Second, the reward or deprivation employed by the superordinate person must be similarly evaluated by the subordinate person for the political power to exist. Thus, threatening a starving man with loss of "dignity" may have no profound effect.

Finally, the subordinate person must really believe that the deprivation or reward can be delivered for a power relationship to exist. Power does not have to be actually used; it may be latent. It does not have to be real; it may be imagined. But the subordinate person or group in a political power relationship must at least believe in the efficacy of the threat or promise.

THE CONCEPT OF SCARCITY

As power is the central concept in the study of politics, scarcity is central to the study of economics. Scarcity is the condition which exists when wants exceed available resources. The productive capacity of any polity[10] is clearly limited. Land and its natural resources are limited by the spatial geophysical limits of the polity; labor is limited by the number, age, and work orientation of the population of the polity; capital is limited by the polity's past practice of saving and the degree of obsolescence induced by the current state of technology; and entrepreneurship is limited by the intellectual capacity of the population and its addiction to tradition and security. These limitations on productive capacity stand in juxtaposition to an apparently infinite set of desires. Of course, a society that is willing to lower its expectations can diminish, but hardly eliminate, the problem of scarcity.

Because of the condition of scarcity, the need for ground rules governing the operation of the economy is generally recognized. The form and content of these rules have been the grounds not only for fierce debate but also for wars and revolutions. In the capitalistic-democratic form of government there is a consensus that governments ought to perform an umpire function: enforcing contracts, sanctioning private property, outlawing theft, and regulating business in cases of politically significant externalities in production, consumption, or distribution.[11] There is also a demand that government should respond to scarcity in a positive fashion, a belief that government should redistribute the yield of public and private economic activity. The role of government in income redistribution is one of the principal public issues of social welfare; this debate is the subject of Part III. There is also a debate about how government should provide a special set of goods and services to certain classes of persons. This is another of the fundamental issues in the politics of welfare; the question is deferred until Part IV.

A highly central issue of social welfare is the optimal allocation of goods and services to be provided by the public and the private sectors. The term *social balance* has been used to describe a "satisfactory" relationship between goods and services supplied through the market and those provided publicly. The determination of a precise balance, most agree, is not possible because of theoretical and practical limits. The debate rages over the direction of the "error." The polar positions are epitomized by John Kenneth Galbraith and Milton Friedman.

Galbraith contends that there is a clear imbalance, with too large a share of the gross national product being consumed in the private sector. He admits that the precise point of a proper balance cannot be determined as of now. He believes, however, that the direction of the imbalance is unmistakably clear and uses an appealing rhetoric: "Alcohol, comic books, and mouth wash all bask under the superior reputation of the market. Schools, judges, and municipal swimming pools lie under the evil reputation of bad kings."[12]

It is Galbraith's argument that the imbalance is created through the efforts of modern advertising in behalf of market-provided goods. In a condition of truly free markets the consumer-voter can make a rational choice between public and private goods and the mix within each sector. But advertising and market controls create a dependence effect: that is, consumer wants are created by the productive process by which the goods are produced. Thus the consumer-voter cannot make a rational choice. The process is self-feeding to the private sector, while public-sector programs are increasingly starved.

Galbraith's critics argue that:

1. He is factually wrong in saying that the share of the gross national product going to private-sector programs has steadily increased.
2. The dependence effect works in both sectors of the economy; public relations programs do for the public sector what advertising does for the private sector.
3. Consumer-voters are more conscious of public benefits than

they are of public cost, and this creates a social imbalance in the direction of a too-large public sector.

Milton Friedman argues that it is absurd to conclude that the alternative to "bad" private spending is more public spending.[13] First, there is no meaningful way to define *bad*, and even if there were, better private spending would still be an alternative. Friedman suggests that rigid tests should be set for any public spending. He argues that when both the public and the private sectors can function with comparable impact on a social need, the nod should be given to the private sector because of the inevitable loss of freedom and incentives which *must* accompany public-sector allocation. Public production should be limited to the case of market failures only after all efforts to produce market success have been attempted.

Friedman's critics argue that:

1. There is no clear line to suggest market failure. Virtually all economic activities produce significant loss to persons who are not direct parties to the contract (e.g., pollution, or moral aversion to others' use of their freedom).
2. It is absurd to believe that "bad" public spending will be replaced by "good" private spending.
3. The private sector also creates loss of freedom by artificial constraints on access to resources.

THE SEARCH FOR A COMMON FRAME OF REFERENCE

If the debate over private-sector or public-sector provision of goods and services is to ever descend from ideological assertions played out on a battlefield of raw power conflicts, there is a need for some agreed-upon common frame of reference. Efforts have been made to provide this frame of reference in terms of economic concepts as they are made applicable to political choices.

Increasingly, policy analysts have been borrowing from microeconomics a set of concepts to be used in the clarification of public policy issues.[14] The concepts of *scarcity* and *exchange*, which are central to the analysis of microeconomic behavior, also are of use in the analysis of micropolitical behavior. We are interested in why certain policy goals and certain policy options are pursued, while others are neglected. In this section we explore a few notions that have a use in explaining the phenomenon of choice in public social welfare. We will consider first the utility approach and show its usefulness to politics, then examine indifference analysis and its potential in explaining policy choice. These concepts are introduced here but discussed in more detail in Chapter 4.

Utility Theory in Economics

Utility theory in economics is based on the idea that an individual gains units of satisfaction (utility) from the consumption of goods and services. Further, the rational individual will seek to organize his or her consumption in order to achieve the highest possible level of satisfaction (i.e., to maximize utility). There is a body of literature which deals with the issue of whether consumers actually seek to maximize utility or whether they have the more modest goals of simple satisfaction. In either case, the higher the level of satisfaction per unit of time, for a given cost, the more desirable a particular good. When alternative goods have a higher ratio of satisfaction to costs, the consumer seeks to alter his pattern of consumption. Utility maximization theory states that the individual consumer will continue to alter the pattern of consumption until, within a given budget limit, the highest attainable level of satisfaction (or utility) has been achieved.

Total utility is the total amount of satisfaction obtained from the various quantities of goods and services consumed. Any desirable good or service adds to total utility. The increment in utility that is derived from the consumption of one additional unit of the good or service is called the *marginal utility*. A *utility curve* is a graphic representation of the changes in utility as consumption of a specific good increases.

Figure 2–4 depicts the changes in utility as increasing quantities of a good are consumed. The slope of the utility curve reflects the notion of declining marginal utility; that is, as consumption increases, the additional increments in satisfaction become progressively smaller. At the apex of the curve, satisfaction from the particular good is at the point of satiation, and any additional consumption decreases total utility. Put another way, at that point the marginal utility has a negative value.

The marginal utility curve, depicted in Figure 2–5 illustrates the principle of diminishing marginal utility.

Satisfaction is enhanced until the point of satiation (consumption beyond that point has a negative value). It is the ratio of satisfaction (marginal utility) to marginal cost (the increment in

FIGURE 2–4
UTILITY CURVE: VARIATIONS IN TOTAL BENEFIT DERIVED FROM
VARIOUS QUANTITIES OF CONSUMPTION

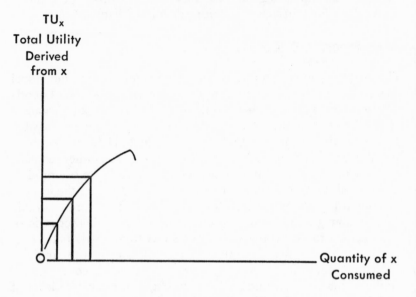

FIGURE 2–5
MARGINAL UTILITY CURVE: INCREMENTAL CHANGES IN UTILITY
DERIVED FROM ADDITIONAL CONSUMPTION OF A GOOD OR
SERVICE

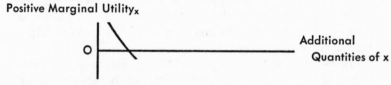

costs incurred by one additional unit of consumption) which dictates the pattern of consumption. A person seeking to maximize utility will alter his consumption so that all ratios are equal. Though I might enjoy one more concert and one more bottle of Scotch, for example, I would choose the one with the higher ratio and keep adjusting until each acquisition gives me identical satisfaction. Stated algebraically:

$$\frac{MU_x}{\text{Price}_x} = \frac{MU_y}{\text{Price}_y} = \cdots \frac{MU_n}{\text{Price}_n} \ . \tag{1}$$

At any given budget level, the marginal utility of x divided by the price of x is the marginal utility of x per unit of dollars, just as the marginal utility of y divided by the price of y is its marginal utility per unit of dollars. When the ratios of final consumption are identical, I cannot improve on my condition. There is, of course, a budget constraint—total spending must be equal to or less than total resources, so that the sum of the quantities selected times their unit price will equal available resources.[15] Algebraically, this is expressed as:

$$x \times P_x + y \times P_y + \ldots m \times P_n = \text{Budget constraint}, \tag{2}$$

where x is the quantity of x when $MU_x/\text{Price}_x = MU_y/\text{Price}_y$, and P_x is the average price at that quantity.

When the conditions expressed in Equations 1 and 2 are achieved, the individual has maximized utility. Of course, since price, satisfaction, and budget constraint are constantly in flux, the best one can do is to approximate this point.

Utility Theory in Politics

As the individual selects a market basket of goods and services in the marketplace, so, too, does she or he select a set of policies for government to pursue. Each policy has a positive or negative marginal utility to actors on the political scene. Each policy also has political resource costs. These are the cost to the individual of getting the policy adopted by government. The political maximizer would divide up the actual political resource pile so that the ratios of policy benefits at the margin to political costs at the margin are all equal, and the total supply of political credits would not be exceeded:

$$\frac{MU_a}{PR_a} = \frac{MU_b}{PR_b} \cdots \frac{MU_n}{PR_n} \ , \tag{3}$$

and

$$a \times PR_a + b \times PR_b + \ldots n \times PR_n = \text{Political constraint}. \tag{4}$$

As each individual allocates political resources for (or against) particular policies, these preferences are registered by the political system.

A perfectly functioning political system would simply sum political resources recorded in favor of a policy, and sum the resources opposed to that policy, and then give the nod to the winning side. To obtain from government a formal decree designating the second Sunday in May as Mothers' Day would require the expenditure of few political resources, for few would oppose it. To end the war in Vietnam required enormous political resources, for there were many willing to commit large political resources to the opposite policy objective. Since individuals have different political resource budgets to work with, their preferences are unequally recorded. In social welfare programs which tax bodies of citizens A through J to benefit citizens K through Z, there is almost certain to be intense political conflict. The manner in which this conflict is played out is reviewed in Chapter 3.

THE PROCESS OF SELECTION

The political process of selection is thus central to society's selecting or even approaching an optimum societal allocation. Kenneth Arrow and Jerome Rothenberg are two scholars who have dealt with the complications involved in social choices. Arrow set down a rigid set of requirements that must be met if there is to be a rational and comprehensive collective choice. Rothenberg points out that there is a knowable "value consensus" which exists in any ongoing society. The revelation of these values via anthropology, learning theory, political science, and sociological theory can supplement economic insights and give rational guidelines to what social choice ought to be.[16] There will continue to be a great deal of controversy over whether social scientists can say that one policy is better than another. What social scientists *can* do is to set forth with greater clarity the issues that are involved in public social welfare choices.

CONCLUSIONS

The critical problems of social welfare choice are not, of course, made simple by the appropriation of the concepts reviewed in this chapter. In the first instance, there is no precisely definable line that allows us to trade one desirable goal, such as better mental health services, with another, such as a cure for cancer. Nor can a wave of academic chalk prevent groups from deliberately imposing disutilities on one another. Various scholars have viewed the adoption of such concepts as genuinely insightful ways for ushering in Utopia, if politicians would only give way to technicians. Other scholars see these as in-vain attempts to measure the unmeasurable.

The economic and political concepts introduced in these chapters and the modes of analysis presented here are neither good for nothing nor good for everything. Admittedly much bad work will be done. The love of numbers and the mystery of mathematics will be used to bamboozle some, confuse others, and sometimes serve as a substitute for creative thinking. As the professional social worker becomes more proficient in understanding the processes through which policy is formulated, it should be easier to intervene in that process with greater effect; as the social worker enhances the understanding of the intended and unintended consequences of policy changes, programs can be more realistically ranked in terms of their relative desirability. As the goals of the social work professional are made more precise and less ambiguous, so will the social worker's potential contribution to a more desirable social welfare system be enhanced. In the years just ahead, as in the years just past, influences exogenous to the traditional concerns of the social worker will shape social welfare policy. The analysis and evaluation of current and proposed social welfare programs must be approached at two levels simultaneously: what is economically efficient, and what is politically feasible.

NOTES

1. Thomas R. Dye, *Politics, Economics and the Public: Policy Outcomes in the American States* (Chicago: Rand McNally & Co., 1966).
2. The radical perspective on social welfare policy has one central contention: that public welfare has throughout history had two main economic and political functions. The political function is the prevention and control of civil disorders. When, as a consequence of some exogenous factor, there is a disruption in the economy and resulting political unrest, the public welfare system is expanded to soothe the discontent. The economic function is to control the supply of labor. After the political crisis has passed, welfare programs are contracted, forcing low-wage workers back onto the labor market.

    This argument is made most precisely by Frances Piven and Richard Cloward in *Regulating the Poor* (New York: Random House, 1971). Jeffry H. Galper, in *The Politics of Social Service* (Englewood Cliffs, N.J.: Prentice-Hall, 1975), further expands the argument and suggests that the social worker's efforts to achieve a more equitable social system are frustrated by the political and economic "motives" of the capitalistic welfare system. Fundamental change is the only possible road if one wishes to truly improve the lot of those who are the victims of capitalism. Various authors—Joseph Feagin, *Subordinating the Poor* (Englewood Cliffs, N.J.: Prentice-Hall, 1977), David Gil, *Unravelling Social Policy* (Cambridge, Mass.: Schenkman Publishing Co., 1973), and Robert Knickmeyer, "A Marxist Approach to Social Work," *Social Work*, July 1972—have made various efforts to provide sociological, historical, and economic data in support of this position.

3. Alan C. Isaak, *Scope and Methods of Political Science*, rev. ed. (Homewood, Ill.: Dorsey Press, 1975).

4. William H. Riker and Peter C. Ordeshook, *An Introduction to Positive Political Theory* (Englewood Cliffs, N.J.: Prentice-Hall, 1973).

5. David Easton, "Political Systems," *World Politics*, vol. 9 (1956–57), p. 381.

6. Harold Lasswell and Abraham Kaplan, *Power and Society* (New Haven, Conn.: Yale University Press, 1950), p. xiv.

7. Peter Bachrach and Morton Baratz, *Power and Scarcity* (New York: Oxford University Press, 1970), pp. 17–39.

8. Vilfredo Pareto, *Manual d' Economie Politique* (Paris: Giard and Briere, 1909).

9. For a thorough discussion of the notion of Pareto-optimum conditions in the context of current thinking, see Francis Bator, "The Simple Analytics of Welfare Maximization," *American Economic Review*, March 1957. The student not versed in mathematical economics may find this reading difficult and is advised to consult Zechauser and Elmer Schaefer, "Public Policy and Normative Economic Theory," in R. Bauer and K. Gergen, *The Study of Policy Formation* (New York: Free Press, 1968), p. 51 ff.

10. Polity here refers to a specific political system within a geographic area. It may involve one or more governments.

11. John Kenneth Galbraith, *The Affluent Society* (Boston: Houghton Mifflin Co., 1958), p. 254.

12. Ibid.

13. Milton Friedman, *Capitalism and Freedom* (Chicago: University of Chicago Press, 1962).

14. There is a growing body of literature on this topic. It is suggested that the student wishing to pursue it read the principal books in the order they are listed below:

L. L. Wade and R. L. Curry, *A Logic of Public Policy* (Belmont, Calif.: Wadsworth Publishing Co., 1970).

Anthony Downs, *An Economic Theory of Democracy* (New York: Harper and Row Publishers, 1957).

J. M. Buchanan and Gordon Tullock, *The Calculus of Consent* (Ann Arbor: University of Michigan Press, 1962).

William Riker and Peter Ordeshook, *An Introduction to Positive Political Theory* (Englewood Cliffs, N.J.: Prentice-Hall, 1973).

L. L. Wade and R. L. Curry, *A Theory of Political Change* (Englewood Cliffs, N.J.: Prentice-Hall, 1968).

15. Actually, it will equal total resources since savings are a "good" in this sense. Dissavings can occur only when one has credit which is a resource.

16. Kenneth Arrow, *Social Choice and Individual Values* (New York: John Wiley & Sons, 1951), and J. Rothenberg, *The Measurement of Social Welfare* (Englewood Cliffs, N.J.: Prentice-Hall, 1961).

CHAPTER 3

MODELS OF
PUBLIC DECISION MAKING

Social welfare policy choices cannot be understood outside of the environment in which they are made.[1] As we have noted, social welfare policy choice involves simultaneously issues of power and issues of scarcity (see Figure 1–1 in Chapter 1). The scarcity issues, insofar as they can be separated from the power issues, are discussed in the next chapter. This chapter will focus on the power environment in which social welfare policymaking occurs and value judgments are made. Its purpose is to acquaint the student with some of the models which have been developed by political scientists to demonstrate how policy choice operates in the context of an unequal distribution of power. Political power, its meaning and its impact on policy, is the general topic.

The term *policy* is an elusive one. There is, as Hugh Heclo points out, no unambiguous factor that can be labeled policy.[2] To some, social welfare policy implies a set of goals surrounding the ends to be achieved by providing tangible and intangible benefits to various subsets of the population. To others, this policy refers to a highly specific set of procedures designed as a response to very vague ends, such as social security policy or AFDC policy. In this context policy is conceived of as legislatively enacted or administratively sanctioned procedures. Thus a welfare director might reply to a critic, "I don't know what happened in a specific case, but our policy is very clearly spelled out in. . . ." A third way the term *policy* is defined is in terms of observable consequences which are the result of vague goals and carelessly interacting procedures.

There are numerous other uses to which the term *policy* is put. For example, the term is used to describe three different aspects of policy:

1. *Goals,* or the ultimate values to be achieved.
2. *Procedures,* or the specific manner in which the political mechanisms decree that vaguely worded goals are to be achieved.
3. *Consequences,* or the highly specific results that can be more or less directly attributed to the implementation of vague procedures.

Whenever social scientists seek precision with regard to one aspect of policy, they introduce vagueness into other aspects. *Policy* could be used as an adjective within each of the contexts listed above: policy goals, policy procedures, policy consequences. When the single term *policy* is used in all three contexts, confusion is the inevitable result. A number of scholars have dealt with this definitional dilemma.[3] Their findings point to the importance of specifying the context whenever the term *policy* is used.

It is important also to develop a distinction between policy analysis and political analysis. Policy analysis is a basically intellectual search for a set of mechanisms that have a high probability of closing the gap between an existing state of affairs and some reasonably well-specified alternative state. It occurs in all aspects of life, from selecting the evening's entertainment to selecting a career.

A completed policy analysis leads to an *articulation* of a preference among alternative options. It does not necessarily lead to a public choice, for public choice is further influenced by the various preferences operating within the collective body. The man condemned to hang does not choose to hang, but a political analysis will help to explain why a collective might choose to hang him. All except one group in a society might agree with a policy analysis and express a preference for hanging (alternative A). The holdout might select some other punishment (alternative B). If the collective chooses B over A (or, for that matter, A over B), a *political* analysis is needed to explain the public choice.

In short, policy analysis leads to the articulation of a goal or a procedure, or to an explanation of what the real consequences are. Political analysis, the topic of this chapter, explains the choice. In social welfare, political analysis is used to explain why it is that a polity selects one set of welfare procedures over another or gives one goal a higher priority than another. Political analysis can explain why a state will suddenly require new buildings to be designed to allow access by the handicapped or why Congress fails to pass a welfare reform bill.

There are always two interconnected questions about social welfare choice. First we need to know, from a given value perspective, what choices *ought* to be made, that is, *the class of the desirable.* The identification of the desirable is the goal of policy analysis. Second, we need to know, for a given polity and for a given time, what choices *can* occur, that is, *the class of the possible.* The identification of the possible is the task of political analysis, which determines what power variables influence choice and how they must be altered to permit an alternative choice. As long as the study of social welfare policy is a practical inquiry, neither the class of the possible nor the class of the desirable can be ignored. If we seek only the desirable while neglecting the possible, something social workers are wont to do, we opt for utopian fantasy. Alternatively, if we ignore the desirable and focus only on the narrowly conceived possible, which social workers are also wont to do, we run the risk of passively accepting the results of political conflict without thought of how things might be made otherwise.

In this chapter, the focus of attention is on the realm of the possible. We begin this study with a look at the policy cycle.

THE POLICY CYCLE

Edward Banfield has indicated that decisions in the political system do not occur as a single choice, but rather as a series of decisions in a series of semidiscrete public events in the decision-making process.[4] The events in the process are:

1. Identification of Policy Goals
   a. *Initiation.* In the initial stage a problem is brought forward for public consideration. The initiation is most fre-

quently instigated by a citizen who feels unfairly treated by current policies.

b. *Placement on the political agenda.* In order to receive public attention, a problem must be invested with "publicness." This can be achieved by a problem which touches the lives of many persons and is susceptible to public action. What was not a public problem yesterday (e.g., employment discrimination of women) may become so today.

c. *Publication of the problem.* Publication influences citizens and groups so that when the problem is evaluated in the legislative and administrative phases, the likelihood of favorable action is enhanced.

2. Selection of a Procedure

a. *Application.* Expert analysis is applied to the central ideas so that the costs and benefits of the alternatives can be clearly shown.

b. *Negotiation of a plan.* Few public options are adopted without trades and compromises to make them more attractive to potential supporters or less objectionable to opponents.

3. Policy Consequence

a. *Administration of the plan.* The manner of administration is chosen to be most consonant with the diverse supporters of the policy innovation.

The stages in this process of combined choice are diagrammed in Figure 3–1.

This chapter provides the student of social welfare programs with a frame of reference for asking, in regard to a certain policy, what did happen and what could have happened. An observer of a public policy at best can see only a point in time or a phase in a continuing and dynamic process of policy development. A review of the attempts of political science at model building and theory construction can provide a more comprehensive understanding of the process.

THE STUDY OF PUBLIC CHOICE

The theory of public choice is a large, growing, and amorphous field of study which attempts to integrate concepts from political science, economics, organizational theory, and social psychology. The various parts of the field of study attempt to analyze its differ-

FIGURE 3-1 DIAGRAM OF A MODEL OF PUBLIC CHOICE

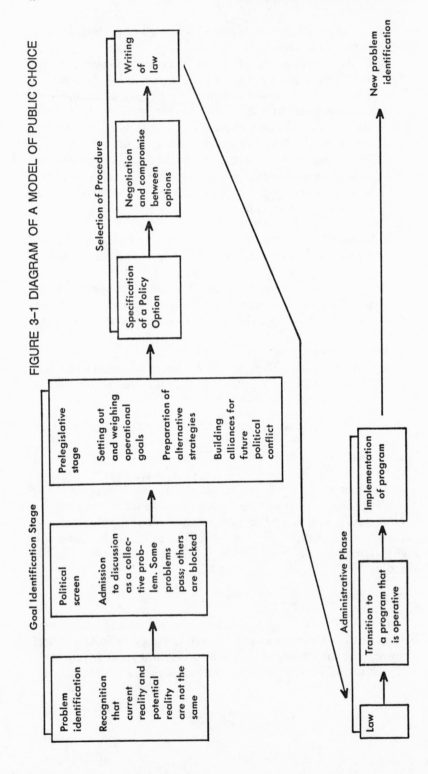

ent aspects. In an effort to facilitate understanding, political scientists have identified three major models which can provide insight into how public policy is formulated: the elitist, pluralist, and neoelitist models. These models are reviewed below.

The public choice literature reviewed in this chapter[5] is one of the areas of study with which the professional social worker should be familiar. In the sections below, a distinction is made between models and theories of public choice, and the utility of models is articulated. The principal models are explained, and their use in appraising policy change or lack of change is illustrated.

Models and Theories

The distinction between models and theories is not precise. Herbert Simon began a paper entitled "The Uses and Limitations of Models," for example, by refusing to make such a distinction, declaring, "In contemporary usage, the term 'model' is, I think, simply a synonym for 'theory.' "[6] May Brodbeck also noted the confusion in terminology: "What, exactly is a model and what purpose does it serve?. . . . I venture to suggest that ten model builders will give at least five different, or at least apparently different, answers to this question."[7]

Despite this similarity in usage, most social scientists see models and theories in different lights, each with a separate structural function to perform in the conduct of inquiry.[8] Theories of political choice such as those developed by Marx or de Montesquieu have attempted to order and predict development under a wide range of circumstances which are purported to reflect real-world conditions. Models, in contrast, are deliberately artificial constructs designed to yield insight into or to focus attention on a very specific segment of real-world conditions.[9]

Political theories generally are used primarily to explain political facts and thus, by logic, to suggest particular strategies of intervention. When theories are vested with normative characteristics, they blend into ideologies.[10] Models, as defined here, have a much more limited function. Models are structured so that the dimensions of reality are deliberately altered to improve insight into a particular political interaction. A model is neither true nor false—nor does it purport to be. It is only structured so that real-world conditions can be deliberately oversimplified to permit a beginning of understanding.[11] Anthony Downs notes that "The model is not an attempt to describe reality accurately . . . it treats a few variables as crucial and ignores others which actually have some influence.[12] Thus attention is focused on significant components of the process of choice which could easily be overlooked in a real-world situation.

The three models considered here focus attention on different components of choice. The elitist model focuses on the role of the few very powerful persons within a polity; the pluralist model focuses on the role of interest groups; and the neoelitist model directs attention to the institutional barriers that some citizens face when attempting to influence the direction of public choice.

Each of these models reflects, in varying degrees, the abstract notions and actual practice that must be comprehended in order to appraise a real-world policy. Taken individually, they could confuse our understanding of public policy because of their deliberate distortions. Collectively, they direct attention to the series of variables which generations of scholars have found important in three processes: (1) the simplification and clarification of our thinking about government and politics, (2) the communication of relevant knowledge about political forces, and (3) the development of an awareness of what forces and variables must be attended to if changes in society are to be produced.

For each model a set of postulates is given which states assertions the model makes without proof, either because they are self-evident or, for model-building purposes, they are assumed to be true and reflective of reality. From the postulates a set of theorems is evolved. These theorems are consequential statements or propositions that can be deduced from the set of postulates. Because they are assertions about real-world conditions, the theorems are capable of empirical verification or denial. The rejection of a theorem does not deny the model, however, since the model is structured only to facilitate understanding.[13]

If we postulate, for example, that (1) America's elite membership evolved slowly, with no serious breaks in ideas or values, and that (2) the Founding Fathers shared a fundamental consensus about the role of government in protecting private property over any competing claim to political liberty, we can deduce the theorem that today's elite believe that government has a greater responsibility to property than to liberty. Operational definitions about property, liberty, and governmental functioning allow a test of the theorem. Even if it fails we will have gained insight into the transmission of values through government by the elite over time.

The models reviewed here are more complex than this simple illustration; the point is that a model is structured not to reveal reality, but to facilitate insight into a highly complex process.

THE ELITIST MODEL: POLICY AS THE PREFERENCE OF THE FEW

The critical argument of the elitist model is that an elite group really governs America. "The people," their interest groups and political parties, are only actors on a stage, their lines being directed by an offstage elite. The central concept of the elitist model with regard to public welfare policy is that the public welfare policies evolve according to the perceived self-interest of those at the top. Both this proposition and its derived conclusion may in fact be blatantly false. Nevertheless, it is certainly true that a few powerful persons have a great deal to say about how welfare policies are developed and conducted. The elitist model is a useful device for understanding the interaction between the powerful and welfare policy.

Postulates of the Elitist Model

The principal postulate of elitism is that all societies are divided into two classes, a small class which actually governs (i.e., makes the choices for society), and the class of the many who are governed. The two classes are separated by agents, or minions, of the elite who are not strictly members of either one. Gaetano Mosca, a turn-of-the-century Italian political theorist, expressed this concept succinctly:

> In all societies—from societies that are very undeveloped and have largely attained the dawnings of civilization, down to the most advanced and powerful societies—two classes of people appear—a class that rules and a class that is ruled. The first class, always the less numerous, performs all of the political functions, monopolizes power, and enjoys the advantages that power brings, whereas the second, the more numerous class, is directed and controlled by the first, in a manner that is now more or less legal, now more or less arbitrary and violent.[14]

The second postulate of elitism is that the few who govern form a distinct social class, the members of which are interconnected by bonds of kinship, common ownership of property, and intermarriage.[15]

The third postulate is that the elite shares a basic consensus about the fundamental norms which are the underpinnings of the current politicoeconomic system. Further, they use the instruments of governments, its programs, and its policies to perpetuate these values. It is sometimes asserted that this ruling class also has a central set of selfish economic interests which it protects with public policies.[16] Whether values alone or values plus some selfish economic motivation are concerned, the postulate is that policies are structured to serve the perceived interest of the ruling class.

Since membership in the elite must be maintained across generations and adapted to exogenous changes, a fourth postulate states that some circulation of the elite is required. A semiopen elite class is required to assimilate potential leaders who might otherwise threaten the system as well as to accommodate newly emerging needs for expertise. Some nonelites, or minions of the elite, have to be admitted to the almost closed club of leaders. It is critical, however, that only those nonelites who have demonstrated their basic loyalty to the elite value system and its politicoeconomic structures be admitted.

Finally, elitism postulates that the masses are either passive, apathetic, or misled, so that they do not challenge the elite rule. It is not a case of the stronger dominating the weaker, but a matter of the rulers maintaining their control by an artful process of manipulation so that those at the bottom defer to those at the top and are even willing to defend their right to be ruled. Thomas Dye and Harmon Ziegler make this point well:

> Mass sentiments are manipulated by elites more often than elite values are influenced by the sentiments of the masses. For the most part, communication between elites and masses flows downward. Policy questions of government are seldom decided by the masses through elections or through the presentation of policy alternatives by political parties. For the most part, these "democratic" institutions—elections and parties—are important only for their symbolic value. They help tie the masses to the political system by giving them a role to play on election day and a political party with

which they can identify. Elitism contends that the masses have at best only an indirect influence over the decision-making behavior of elites.[17]

FIGURE 3-2
THE ELITIST MODEL

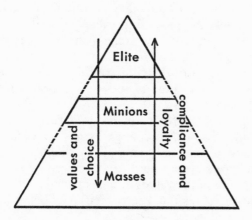

A diagram of the elitist model is given in Figure 3–2. In this model, a relatively small number of persons, self-selected by an intricate mechanism of property ownership, intermarriage, privileged education, and the gradual transmission of the machinery of mass control, actually possesses the only real capability of directing public choices. They always make the choices to preserve their privileged position and to inculcate in the masses the values that they believe the masses should hold. The masses, in order to gain access to the privileged class, and because they are given no opportunity to really know otherwise, secure their place in the social system by constantly demonstrating their loyalty and willingness to comply with the wishes of their governors. The masses may, in fact, be unaware that they are truly powerless. The elite, by their very membership in the elite circle, have truly demonstrated their allegiance to the dominant value system of the existing elite by adopting as their social role the task of preserving these critical values.

Theorems of the Elitist Model

If the postulates of the elite model are either self-evidently true or are assumed to be true for the sake of argument, then a set of

consequences should result. A few of the consequential statements, or the theorems, of an elitist model of social welfare policy
that could be developed are:

1. Public welfare policies—in fact, all public policies—would not
   reflect the demands of the masses for such basic rights as
   income security or equality of opportunity. Rather, they
   would reflect the prevailing values of the leadership, which
   may not be compatible with the wishes of those at the bottom
   of society.
2. Since the values of the elite are changed only gradually, the
   programs and outputs of the welfare system would change
   only gradually.
3. The top-level operators of the welfare system would alter
   policy in response to changed cues from leaders and not
   from new or changed demands by clients.
4. The welfare system would be structured so as to ensure the
   propagation of the values of the elite and to retard the development of values that are perceived as being hostile to the
   elite.

Many students of public welfare have asserted that they have
found such consequential statements to be valid. Notable among
these are Richard Cloward and Frances Fox Piven who argue that
welfare programs "regulate the poor":

> Relief arrangements are ancillary to economic arrange-
> ments. Their chief function is to regulate labor, and they do
> that in two general ways. First, when mass unemployment
> leads to outbreaks of turmoil, relief programs are ordinarily
> initiated or expanded to absorb and control enough of the
> unemployed to restore order; then, as turbulence subsides,
> the relief system contracts, expelling those who are needed
> to populate the labor market. Relief also performs a labor-
> regulating function in this shrunken state, however. Some of
> the aged, the disabled, the insane, and others who are of no
> use as workers are left on the relief rolls, and their treatment
> is so degrading and punitive as to instill in the laboring
> masses a fear of the fate that awaits them should they relax
> into beggary and pauperism. To demean and punish those
> who do not work is to exalt by contrast even the meanest
> labor at the meanest wages. These regulative functions of

relief, and their periodic expansion and contraction, are made necessary by several strains toward instability inherent in capitalist economies.[18]

This is not a confirmation of the elitist model, however, for the same results (if these *are* the results) could be due to other causes. When scholars seek to explain why certain policies are accepted and others rejected, they often conclude that the critical piece of evidence is the attitude of a thin stratum of persons at the top. V. O. Key has written on the topic as follows:

> The critical element for the health of the democratic order consists of the beliefs, standards, and competence of those who constitute the influentials, the political activists, in the order. That group, as has been made plain, refuses to define itself with great clarity in the American system; yet analysis after analysis points to its existence. If democracy tends toward indecision, decay, and disaster, the responsibility rests here, not with the mass of people.[19]

Generally speaking, researchers have found that variations in local welfare programs can be explained by the diversity of attitudes of community leaders, broadly defined. This does not prove that welfare choices are dominated by elite preferences. It may be that those charged with the making of official decisions are responding rationally to a complex set of events, and community leaders, who by definition are more articulate and presumably better informed than ordinary citizens, may be more likely to comprehend and express the views of officials. A model with a good track record of predicting results is, nonetheless, a valuable instrument for suggesting strategies of intervention to produce a different result. If one were convinced that an elitist model of choice in fact operates within the structure of welfare politics, then a strategy of change incorporating this insight would be adopted.

Application of the Elitist Model

Power in the elitist model is the capacity of a dominant group of persons to impose their will, economic preference, or value preference on all others within the polity. The elites are the people who occupy power roles in a polity; they are the ones who wield the authority to impose their preference. This authority allows them to guide the programs, policies, and collective activities of the polity. This authority may be legitimized by force, without recourse to legal processes, or it may be supported by both law and force.

Further evidence of elite domination can be gathered by documenting who the critical actors are, that is, the persons whose assent appears to be essential to a particular choice. If the same small group of assentors, with shared values, dominates one choice after the other, it appears that a presumptive case of elitism can be made. Even if minions appear to be the public actors, if the identifiable values of a small group always win out, the case is made for elite domination. There also is the possibility that the loser in any conflict may charge that, since his preferences were not ascribed to, he was victimized by an elite.

Elite domination can occur in a club, in a university, in a particular community, or in the whole of a polity. The Roman Catholic Church is theoretically the quintessential example of domination by an elite in the Curia of the College of Cardinals, with the Pope as their minion. University departments are sometimes thought of as being dominated by a handful of prestigious full professors.

The elite domination should not be confused with an oversimplified Marxian interpretation of domination of all relevant choices by the holders of great wealth. Such an assertion is easily refuted. Nelson Rockefeller certainly wanted to be president of the United States, but his four losses and ignominious dismissal as vice-president by a lawyer from Grand Rapids was hardly a sham to create the illusion that democracy really works. Rockefeller and his brothers, sons, and daughters do exercise enormously unequal influence. But, elitism is structured through an interlocking system of critical actors in policymaking positions. Elitist models must go beyond the simple policymaking pyramid in Figure 3–2 above. Important actors and critical links must be identified in directing our inquiry into explanations for policy choice outcomes.

Thomas Dye has postulated one such set of actors and links in Figure 3–3. A similar design for decisions about the conduct of social welfare programs which provide insight into choices at the federal, state, and particularly the local levels is shown in Figure 3–4.

Such interlocking decisional structures reveal how a dominant

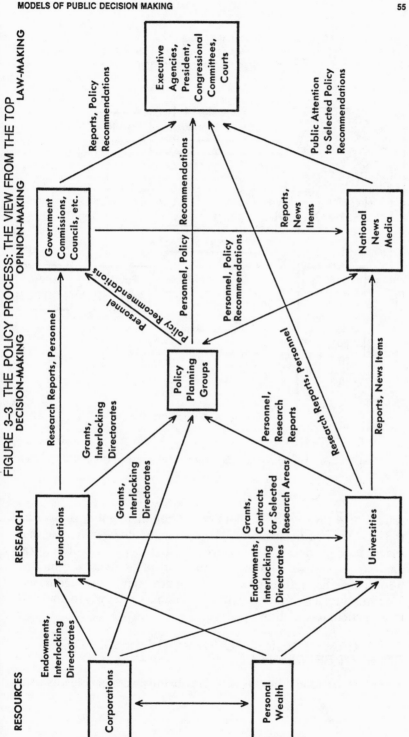

FIGURE 3-3 THE POLICY PROCESS: THE VIEW FROM THE TOP

FIGURE 3–4
THE SOCIAL WELFARE POLICY PROCESS:
PATTERNS OF INTERACTION

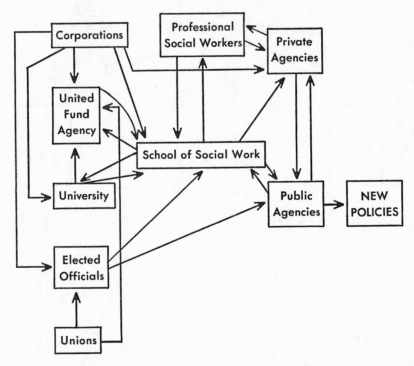

SOURCE: T.R. Dye, *Who's Running America?* (Englewood Cliffs, N. J.: Prentice Hall, 1976), p. 192.

set of corporate wealth holders might dominate policy choices by the local welfare department. The reader should bear in mind that the various models are being presented as facilitators of political analysis to explain choice, not to confirm or deny any model. Serious, perhaps disastrous, consequences can be avoided by examining alternate models before an action strategy is formulated in a particular situation.

THE PLURALIST MODEL: POLICY AS THE RESULT OF CONFLICT BETWEEN GROUPS

The pluralist model begins with the obviously defensible observation that when there is conflict over the selection of public options, various groups behave so as to optimize the likelihood that their preferred options will be selected. Then this model makes group conflict the central concept of politics. Politics is defined as the struggle among groups to direct choices for the society; each group advocates alternative desirable ends. Groups have different goals (based on their values), different preferences for procedures (based on their understanding of how particular procedures relate to their goals), and different capacities to impose their preferences on the community (based on their power). The determinants of political power are varied by political institutions and constitutional rules. In a constitutional democracy such as ours the relative power of groups is determined by their numbers, their wealth, their status, their education, their commitment to the goals of the group, and their skill in using these resources effectively.

The purpose of the political system is to manage this group conflict by: (1) establishing the rules of the game for the group struggles, (2) facilitating compromise between the contending groups so that the decision-making structure can maintain itself, and (3) using the sovereign authority of government to enforce the compromise so that faith in the decisional structure is maintained. Political behavior consists of those activities engaged in by groups to gain effective access to or control of the decisional structure.

Postulates of the Pluralist Model

The pluralist model focuses attention on group behavior. Its first postulate is that in the political process people function not as individuals but through interest groups. An interest group is broadly defined as any organized group of people with a shared value which they seek to have adopted as a public policy.

The second postulate of the pluralist group model is that all groups whose interests are at stake in a public choice have some access to government; that is, each relevant interest group has its "day in court." A critical belief of pluralism is that no single group dominates choice.

The third postulate of the pluralist model is that a political equilibrium is achieved by official decision makers who balance the claims of competing groups. Earl Latham describes public choice in terms of the group model as follows:

What may be called public policy is actually the equilibrium reached in the group struggle at any given moment, and it represents a balance which the contending factions or groups constantly strive to tip in their favor. . . . The legislature referees the group struggle, ratifies the victories of the successful coalition, and records the terms of the surrenders, compromises, and conquests in the form of statutes.[20]

FIGURE 3-5
THE LOCATION OF POLITICAL EQUILIBRIUM

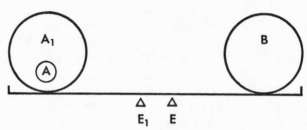

Figure 3-5 illustrates the equilibrium point between two interest groups, A and B. If the claims of group B are stronger than the claims of group A, then an equilibrium or choice is closer to B than to A. If A increases its power to A_1, a new equilibrium point, E_1, is established closer to the values of interest group A_1.

Policy is seen as the simple aggregation of a decision reached by a series of bargaining, negotiating, and compromising sessions. Political actors, congressmen, senators, even judges and presidents are appraised in terms of the constituent group with which they deal. Interest groups are evaluated in terms of their capacity to influence relevant political actors and the skill they use in the bargaining process.

The pluralist model defines claims on the polity in terms of an interest group's capacity to provide rewards to, or impose sanctions on, official decision makers. These rewards and sanctions may be bribes and threats, but more traditionally they are thought of as the capacity to reward officeholders (or candidates) with tenure in office. Voter loyalty, campaign contributions, precinct workers—these are the stuff through which an interest group exercises its claims. Each officeholder (or candidate) seeks to acquire these necessities by making the decisions on issues that will please the larger and more powerful interest groups. Since many

FIGURE 3–6
THE POLICY EXCHANGE

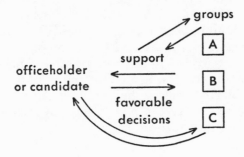

candidates seek office, the one who can satisfy the most blocks wins office; the others lose. There is thus a continuing exchange, the interest group providing support in return for favorable decisions by the officeholder or promises by candidates, as shown in Figure 3–6. The public official, or decision maker, seeks to implement no particular policy but supports those policies that are most likely to guarantee her or his tenure in office.

Theorems of the Pluralist Model

The theorems of the pluralist model are often stated in value terms. The first is that the national interest which emerges from a free system would be an optimum allocation. This is almost true by definition. Grant only constitutional safeguards to protect minority rights, and interest groups will coalesce and bargain with public officials in such a way that the group conflict will always define the national interest.

A second theorem is that the checking and balancing which would result from continued competition would also serve to maintain the equilibrium, or the national interest. Countervailing centers of power check the influence of a prevailing majority, and the maintenance of constant motion produces a consistent equilibrium through the political process.

A third theorem can be deduced from the pluralist model. It is that groups with larger amounts of political power would fare better than groups with fewer political resources. We would expect the aged, who tend to vote in higher proportions than most groups and who tend also to be better organized, more articulate, and more cohesive as a group, to be better treated than unmarried mothers, who do poorly on each of these dimensions. We would expect diseases which affect a large portion of the population without regard to class to be better researched in governmentally subsidized laboratories. In fact, we find all of these things to be true. The pluralist model thus enlarges the segment of public welfare policies which can be explained by the consideration of models in political analysis.[21]

Application of the Pluralist Model

Pluralist models assert that an understanding of social welfare policy choice is best achieved by observation of the conflict of groups, their varying access to diffuse power sources, and the skill with which these power resources are deployed. The account of the defeat of the Family Assistance Plan in Chapter 10 is illustrative of how power groups use, or fail to use, their instruments of power and how this distribution of power and its pattern of utilization structure the outcomes of political conflicts. Success or failure in conflict is attributable to the skill with which a winning coalition is put together.

Imagine a conflict between a taxpayer's alliance dedicated to preserving or obtaining a lower tax rate and a group of parents and professionals advocating a local mental health center for children. The task of the advocates is to structure their proposal in such a fashion that it neither arouses the opposition of the alliance or defeats them in open political conflict, if that conflict is unavoidable.

The professionals and parents have highly specific goals but comparatively few political resources. These resources must be carefully used and targeted to achieve the maximum results. Typically, information will be directed toward key decision makers in the form of memorandums, legislative committee testimony, and budget hearings, and perhaps a letter campaign to members of the relevant committees. The content of the proposal and the timing of its offering will be selected to avoid opposition from citizens and legislators who have the goal of cutting the budget and blocking new programs. The awareness of other citizens of the need for the mental health center, and hence their support, can be garnered by well-directed media campaigns.

Once each political resource has been used, it cannot be used again with quite the same impact. The tasks of the leaders of the political campaigns are to:

1. Structure the flow of information.
2. Evaluate the manner in which recommendations are placed before decision makers.
3. Augment the rational decision-making process with effective threat of political reprisal or promise of support in future campaigns.

Explaining a policy result from a pluralistic perspective requires an examination of (1) the sources of power in a polity, (2) the skill factors associated with the deployment of resources, (3) the incentives to compromise or engage in conflict, and (4) the structural and historical circumstances in which these occur. The problem of pluralism lies in the fact that in purporting to describe, it drifts toward an ideology which asserts that the critical goal of the political system is to assure near-equal access to power and the legitimate use of power. There are thus no inherent political goals, only process goals. Further, by focusing attention on public choice as a response to contending group pressures—bargaining, negotiating, compromising—the theory of pluralism tends to assume that there are many centers of power, none of which is sovereign, and then to demonstrate this in a study of conflicts between groups. This is not a problem with a pluralistic model which merely purports to demonstrate what to look for and where to look in studying group conflicts.

It is generally asserted that there is considerable dispersal of structural power on the state, federal, and local levels, and among the executive, legislative, and judicial branches. Further, in our social system, with overlapping ethnic, racial, sexual, economic, and regional interests, there is a constant shifting of the centers of power from one issue to the next and from one time frame to another. This constant demand for negotiations, according to Robert Dahl, will "perfect the precious art of dealing peacefully with their conflicts, and not merely to the benefit of one partisan, but to the mutual benefit of all the parties to the conflict."[22]

A final point to be made about pluralism is aptly phrased by Duane Lockard:

> So the contention that there is considerable dispersal of power in our politics makes more sense than the proposition that we are ruled by a conspiratorial elite. But it remains true that *the dispersal of power in combination with the great power that nearly all admit is clearly in the hands of the most powerful groups leads to some very harsh consequences for the have-nots in the United States.*[23]

THE NEOELITIST MODEL

The neoelitist model grew out of observations of nonpolitical phenomena or, perhaps more correctly, out of observation of political nonphenomena. The focus of attention is not on the politically active but on the politically quiescent. The basic question asked is of high relevance to social work practice: Why is it that some persons suffer apparent political abuse without visible response in the political system? The focus is on the politically powerless, who are as neglected in the political science literature as they are elsewhere.

While the full development of the neoelitist model took place in the 1960s, the germ of the idea is clearly identified in E. E. Schattschneider's *Semi-Sovereign People,* first published in 1940.[24]

Postulates of the Neoelitist Model

The central postulates of the neoelitist model are these:

1. The pluralist postulate that all of the relevant actors and interest groups will have their day in court is accepted, but this model further states that their power to speak in court can be so limited that they are not heard.
2. Some groups and interests are systematically excluded from participation in the political arena because of the threats they pose to established patterns of political brokerage which are currently operating inside the arena. Groups which challenge the system are subject to reprisal.
3. Other groups also are excluded from the political arena, not by design but because they fear reprisal if they act. In fact, however, the powerful group does not intend reprisal.

4. It is difficult to distinguish empirically between these conditions.

The neoelitist model accepts the propositions of the pluralist model that there are groups with power (A, B, and C in Figure 3–6 above). Its focus, however, is on the political prospects and political behavior of other groups which cannot compete because they lack the attributes of power essential to pluralistic political conflict. The critical first postulate of the neoelitist model is that groups with power effectively conspire to keep powerless groups out of the political game. For example, large landowners, the petty bourgeoisie, and small landowners work together to keep the landless from having a political voice. In the elitist model the few control the choice for the many. In the neoelitist model, the majority conspire to keep the few from having any influence in public choices. The neoelitist's first postulate is that this conspiracy takes place *effectively* but not necessarily *deliberately*.

The second postulate of the neoelitist model is that the conspiracy to deny a voice in government is achieved by the creation of barriers to the political arena. These can be barriers of values ("We can treat communists differently"); barriers of information ("The news media system will not print stories that will incite people"); or barriers of institutions ("We will use paper ballots and have few voting booths so that it will take a long time to vote").

Theorems of the Neoelitist Model

A theorem which is central to the neoelitist model is called the nondecision. A nondecision is not a nonevent but is the product of a decision that is instrumental in preventing an issue that is perceived as being threatening to the current brokerage system from reaching the agenda of the decision-making arena. Nondecisions can take a variety of forms. Some of these are:

1. Establishing a bias that some issues are simply not within the purview of government. These conflicts are to be settled, if at all, outside of government.
2. Symbolic denial of legitimacy of actors in the political sphere. A case in point is the outside-agitator theme often invoked in local civil rights arguments in the 1950s and early 1960s.
3. The government's improper classification of information as

secret. The classification allegedly may be made in the interest of "national security" but actually be part of a scheme to
support a particular issue position.
4. Threats—real, implied, or imagined—against new interest
groups pressing their claims in the public arena.

These are only a few of the forms that a nondecision can take.
Often the mere anticipation of such action will stop a potential
interest group from pressing its cause in anticipation of reprisal
from the established order.

A second theorem of the neoelitist model is that excluded
groups would not be able to press their claims in traditional ways
or within the current system. Thus, policy changes to accommodate the interest group would not take place, and the group would
be forced to take parapolitical actions such as revolutions, insur-
rections, and threats to the civil order in order to open up the
system. If these are not possible, then the decisions of the polity
would continue to exclude the preferences of the excluded group
or groups from their deliberation.

The operation of the neoelitist model is illustrated in Figure
3–7. Groups in society have differing amounts of power, depending on their claims or access to money, status in society, membership, and other attributes which are translatable into power. All
groups face barriers to entry into the political arena, but some,
like A, B, and C, can overcome those barriers. Others, like D, have
insufficient power to overcome the barriers and are thus effectively excluded from the political arena.

Application of the Neoelitist Model

Prison riots are an example of the consequences attendant on
operation of the neoelitist model. Prisoners, particularly those in
a traditional authoritarian prison, have no formal role in their own
governance. Not only that, but formal and often elaborately rigid
rules of communication and decision making are established to
maintain this minimal involvement. The prisoner social system
must therefore be structured to counter the formal decision-making system. One of the critical tasks of the prisoner social or
political system is to find and employ nonsanctioned avenues to
oppose the authority of officials who formulate prison rules.[25]

Figure 3–8 illustrates the prisoner protest model. Assume that
the prisoners (A) select a prison leader (B) and expect him to

FIGURE 3–7
THE NEOELITIST MODEL

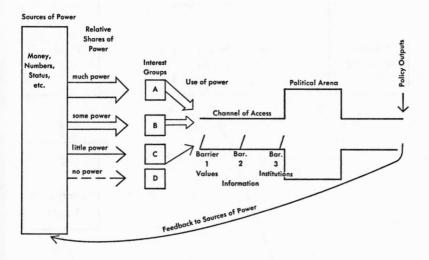

bargain on their behalf with the warden (C). The warden is responsible, however, to the head of the state correctional system (C_1), and indirectly to citizens' interest groups concerned with prison life (D). Therefore, B must find ways to communicate with D and often must rely on the ordinary printed and electronic news media (E) to do so. To gain the attention of the warden, the prisoner leader might have to provoke a newsworthy incident (a riot, perhaps) to attract media attention. The media report the riot and in so doing publicize the list of changes the prisoners want instituted. The interest groups, who do possess political bargaining power, then press the case with the correctional system and hence with the warden. This is why so-called prison riots are often carefully controlled by the prisoners and "end" after contact with the communications media is achieved.[26]

FIGURE 3–8
THE PRISONER PROTEST MODEL

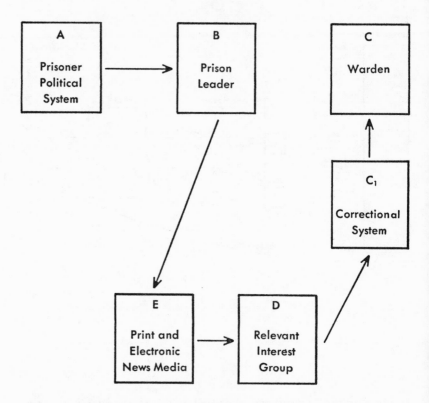

The circumlocutory communication process diagrammed in
Figure 3–8 illustrates the multiple opportunities for miscommuni-
cation and for distortions of the political bargaining system which
are possible with the neoelitist model.

CONCLUSIONS

None of the three models discussed in this chapter uniquely reveals the full dimensions of the multiple paths that lead to the
formation of public welfare policies. In fact, used separately, each
would distort our understanding of the policy process. The distortion is deliberate so as to magnify and thus reveal the importance
of elites, parties, interest groups, and institutional barriers to
decision making. Each gives a conflicting rationale of why things

work as they do. As a model, each provides a unique and helpful way to examine the questions of why particular choices are made. Yet no one model offers answers to all of them. The models are simplified interpretations of reality. Professional social workers who apply, therefore, must consider what the situation would be like *if* a certain model described reality. By comparing this scenario with the observed condition, they can see the importance of each of the principal components in the complex process of policy formation.

Collectively, the models illustrate an identifiable set of institutions and actors who can transfer problems into policy and then back into problems. The value of the models lies not in the answers they give but in the precision with which they pose such questions as:

1. How and where do the elite dominate policy choice?
2. What role do interest groups play in the formulation of welfare policy?
3. How do political parties respond to and act as brokers for expressed desires for change in welfare policy?
4. What is the significance of institutional, informational and value barriers to the process of public choice?
5. Where and how might the professional affect the content and direction of policy choice?

Each model, of course, suggests only one way to perceive the public policy process. *Reification* of the models is the term given to attempts to convert these abstract formulations into descriptions of reality. The three models make some very different assumptions, in fact, conflicting assumptions. One does not have to accept these assumptions to use the insight that the models provide, however.

Full understanding of the decisional process of government is distorted by attempts to measure the comparative role of elites, parties, and interest groups or the structures which facilitate the exclusion of certain groups from the process of public choice. Each plays a role, but the roles are not competitive, in an explanatory sense. In an explanatory sense they are complementary—each model is a potential link in a chain; none of the links is expendable, and none can be truthfully described as being inferior to any of the others. Each policy story will have its unique set of best links.

NOTES

1. The impact on policy choices of structural and institutional forces in the environment is highly complex. A good place to read more on this topic is Chapter 2 of James E. Anderson's *Public Policy Making* (New York: Frederick A. Praeger, 1975), and Charles O. Jones, *An Introduction to the Study of Public Policy*, 2nd ed. Duxbury (North Scituate, Mass.: 1977).
2. H. Hugh Heclo, "Review Article: Policy Analysis, *British Journal of Political Science*, vol. 2 (1972), p. 84 ff.
3. Heinz Eulau and Kenneth Prewitt, *Labyrinths of Democracy* (Indianapolis: Bobbs-Merrill Co., 1973). An extended discussion of the definition of policy is found in *International Encyclopedia of Social Science* (New York: Macmillan Co., 1968). This is a primary source for clarification of most of the concepts used in this text.
4. Edward Banfield and Martin Grodzins, *Government and Housing* (New York: McGraw-Hill Book Co., 1958).
5. A useful bibliography of the current literature is found in J. L. Walker, "A Critique of the Elitist Theory of Democracy," *American Political Science Review*, vol. 60 (June 1966), p. 286. An early, useful seminal review of the literature is Ray Wolfinger, "Reputation and Reality in the Study of Community Power," *American Social Review*, vol. 25 (1960), pp. 636–44. Also see Hubert Kaufman and Charles Jones, "The Mystery of Power," *Public Administration Review*, vol. 14 (1954), pp. 205–12.
6. As reprinted in L. D. White, *The State of the Social Sciences* (Chicago: University of Chicago Press, 1956).
7. May Brodbeck, "Models, Meanings, and Theories," in L. Gross (ed.), *Symposium on Sociological Theory* (Evanston: Row & Peterson, 1959), p. 374.
8. For an extended discussion of this see Abraham Kaplan, *The Conduct of Inquiry* (San Francisco: Chandler Publishing Co., 1964), chap. 8.
9. Robert Bash et al., "Models, Mathematical," in *International Encyclopedia of Social Science* (New York: Macmillan Co., 1968), p. 385.
10. For a full discussion, see Karl Mannheim, *Ideology and Utopia* (New York: Harcourt Brace, 1959).
11. E. J. Meehan, *The Theory and Method of Political Analysis* (Homewood, Ill.: Dorsey Press, 1965), chap. 5.
12. Anthony Downs, *An Economic Theory of Democracy* (New York: Harper, 1957), p. 3.
13. Meehan, *Theory and Method of Political Analysis*.
14. Gaetano Mosca, *The Ruling Class*, trans. by Hannah D. Kahn (New York: McGraw-Hill, 1939), p. 50.
15. Thomas Dye and Harmon Ziegler, *The Irony of Democracy* (Boston: Duxbury Press, 1972).
16. Richard A. Cloward and Frances Fox Piven, *Regulating the Poor* (New York: Random House, 1971).
17. Dye and Ziegler, *Irony of Democracy*.
18. Cloward and Piven, *Regulating the Poor*, as quoted in Williamson, Boren, and Evans, *Social Problems: The Contemporary Debates* (Toronto: Little, Brown, & Co., 1974), p. 483.

19. V. O. Key, *Public Opinion and American Democracy* (New York: Alfred A. Knopf, 1961), p. 558.
20. Earl Latham, "The Group Basis of Politics," in Heinz Eulau, Samuel J. Eldersveld, and Morris Janowitz (eds.), *Political Behavior* (New York: Free Press, 1956), p. 239.
21. In American political literature, group theory can be said to have had its origins in James Madison's Federalist Paper No. 10, which, far from making a self-correcting set of assumptions about the behavior of groups in politics, argued for constitutional safeguards against the abuse of government by majority interest groups. The germ of the pluralist argument is found in Madison's dissertation on minority interest groups, which he thought would naturally be controlled by a desire to be part of the majority. In order to do this, they would compromise on some issues in order to win on others. This process of achieving bargaining power would make minority interest groups an aid rather than a threat to democratic government. Modern-day pluralists accept Madison's argument for minority interest groups.

The danger of minority interest groups was persuasively specified by John C. Calhoun in his *A Disquisition on Government*, published in 1853 (1953 ed., edited by C. Gordon Post, Bobbs-Merrill Co., Indianapolis). One important aspect of Calhoun's argument was that the individual participates in government only through the group, and groups not in the majority should be provided constitutional safeguards to protect the individual from government. Contemporary scholars have emphasized the first but not the second part of his argument. Arthur Bently, in *The Process of Government* (Chicago: University of Chicago Press, 1908), David Truman, in *The Governmental Process* (2nd ed., New York: Alfred A. Knopf, Inc., 1971), and various books by Robert Dahl, particularly his *Who Governs?* (New Haven, Conn.: Yale University Press, 1961), are traditionally cited as the modern exponents of pluralism.
22. Robert Dahl, *Pluralist Democracy in the United States* (Chicago: Rand McNally & Co., 1967), p. 24.
23. Duane Lockard, *The Perverted Priorities of American Politics* (New York: Macmillan Co., 1971), p. 18.
24. E. E. Schattschneider, *The Semi-Sovereign People* (New York: 1960), p. 71. Bachrach and Baratz, in a 1962 *American Political Science Review* paper, made the most precise articulation of the model.
25. Richard McCleary, *Policy Change and Prison Management*, East Lansing: Institute for Community Development, Michigan State University, n. d.
26. Michael Lipsky, "Protest as a Political Resource," *American Political Science Review*, vol. 62 (December 1968), p. 1144 ff. Lipsky has labeled his version of the neoelitist model a *Protest* model.

CHAPTER 4

THE ECONOMICS OF
SOCIAL WELFARE

Any attempt to discuss the economics of social welfare is influenced by some very basic difficulties. It is clear that the U.S. polity has decided that certain activities are best performed by government, while others are best left to the private sector. Many activities, by a long historical tradition, are provided by various levels of government, enforced by the sovereign authority, and paid for by taxation. Others are equally firmly rooted in the private sector. The legitimacy of the division between public- and private-sector activities is a staple issue of political economics.[1]

Without digressing into that important debate, we can state that there is a large, relatively stable, and broadly uncontroversial governmental "sector" for this and every other polity. The controversial border between the public and private sector is not, however, fixed; it is set by economic reasoning, historical tradition, and current political conflicts. The American polity has produced a condition where it is expected that "ordinary goods," those consumed privately without undue impact on others, should be produced and distributed privately, while those goods and services that by their nature are consumed collectively (e.g., national defense) must be publicly provided. This chapter will focus attention on public responsibility for social welfare activities which in the past score of years have dramatically increased. This growth needs to be placed in a historical and theoretical perspective.[2]

EFFICIENT ALLOCATION AND EQUITABLE DISTRIBUTION

At any given point a society has a fixed stock of personnel, natural resources, capital goods, and technology. Decisions need to be made as to how these resources will be allocated to satisfy the competing private and social desires of the society. *Allocation* has to do with the ways in which valuable resources are parceled out to satisfy human wants. A given pattern of allocation has a *distributive effect*. *Distribution* has to do with the pattern of assigning use of the goods and services produced among the many households that comprise the polity. Any pattern of distribution has an *allocative effect*. Thus, the system of allocation and the system of distribution are inseparably linked to one another, as shown in Figure 4-1.

FIGURE 4–1
THE FLOW OF SERVICES AND GOODS AND THEIR
COMPENSATION

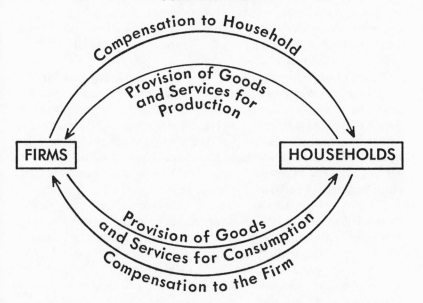

An efficient economy, as suggested in Chapter 2, will allocate resources in such a fashion that no alternative allocation could increase the well-being of any one citizen without harming some other citizen. In a more narrow sense, *efficiency* refers to the maximum production of valued goods and resources for a given input, without regard to which particular citizens receive the benefits. If society can find a way to increase the output of some valued goods, with no decrease in the output of other valued goods, it has scored an increase in efficiency. This increase in efficiency can (but will not necessarily) have an impact on the pattern of distribution.

A fundamental economic truism is that there is no free lunch, every use of resources must somehow be paid for. This means that resources used in one way cannot be used in some other way. More work means less leisure; more cake today means less cake tomorrow; building a better defense system may cost us in terms of the quality of our educational system or some other socially desirable entity. The trick is to find the best balance between work and leisure, cake today and tomorrow, education and defense. The exchange or allocation system is supposed to work to help find the "best balance." But here there is a problem; if a society, in the pursuit of efficiency, values the product of citizen A over that of citizen B, inequalities will result. A "gifted" rock singer can be paid in one evening concert what it would take a social worker a year or more to earn.

When market forces produce a particular pattern of distribution, two issues emerge: one of basic fairness, or equity, and the other of efficiency. A socioeconomic pattern often develops in which it is at least *believed* that greater efficiency can be purchased at the price of greater inequality. Such is not always the case, of course. Measures to increase the earning power of the poor, in fact, can have the ultimate effect of making both rich and poor not only better off but also more equal.

If a class of persons is excluded from educational and job opportunities because of economic, racial, or sexual discrimination, not only they but society as well are losers. Antidiscrimination efforts can promote both equality and efficiency, but in other cases a particular program to aid the poor will have demonstrably adverse efficiency-incentive effects. The programs may make the poor better off, but they may do so at the expense of those who are not so poor. This is a case where efficiency has to be sacrificed for equality. There are some who argue that such is the case with a progressive income tax.

A third class of program has positive impact on efficiency but negative consequences for equality goals.[3]

FIGURE 4–2
POSSIBLE POLICY IMPACTS

Efficiency Effect

Equality Effect	Positive	Neutral	Negative
Positive	A	B	E
Neutral	C	no effect	X
Negative	D	Y	Z

When a condition arises where the goals of equality and efficiency are in conflict, either a choice must be made, or a compromise must be reached. Some social critics have no trouble when faced with such a choice; they would always give the nod to equality goals.[4] John Rawls's position seems to be that "All social values are to be distributed equally unless an unequal distribution is to the advantage of the least advantaged."[5] Other social critics also consider unequal distribution a problem, except that they would almost always give the nod to efficiency.[6] Most critics argue that the choice between the goals of equity and efficiency has to be made in ʼcontextual situations. The real trouble is that we value both equality and efficiency, and neither takes absolute priority over the other.[7] To complete the typology, some social programs might have adverse effects on both efficiency and equality. No social critics could be found to applaud such a choice, though defects in the political system often allow such a social choice to be made.

Figure 4-2 summarizes the consequences with regard to efficiency and equality of a contemplated program. Most would argue that programs A, B, and C should be accepted, while X, Y, and Z ought to be rejected. Political and ideological conflict should be expected to surround D and E. The evaluation of social welfare programs involves both a technical judgment as to the most probable location in the matrix and a political judgment regarding selection among programs. The greatest difficulty is in selecting between approaches D and E. The critical problem is to find, identify, and adopt policies which are likely to yield the results achieved by programs A, B, and C. The social welfare system comes into play to facilitate this search. But this system also plays a role in specifying the conditions under which a society should actually sacrifice a higher level of efficiency in order to promote an acceptable level of equality (case D). The public economic system comes into play because in some situations (to be discussed below), the principles of efficiency demand that the simple trading between households and firms be supplemented by some public mechanisms. Some but by no means all of the public programs so selected will be in pursuit of the social welfare objectives described in Chapter 1.

The social welfare system may also come into play because the pattern of efficient allocation might produce an unacceptable pattern of distribution. Thus a program of income redistribution, or in-kind distribution to promote equality, is required. In this chapter we will discuss first the justifications of social welfare programs under conditions of increased efficiency. We then will discuss technical problems in judging social welfare programs. The final section of this chapter will examine some actual patterns of spending for social welfare programs. The discussion of redistributive social welfare programs is deferred to a later section of this chapter.

SOCIAL EFFICIENCY AS A GOAL OF SOCIAL WELFARE PROGRAMS

Citizens expect of government a justification of spending that is related to a notion of social efficiency. As individual utility (discussed in Chapter 2), is concerned with the attempts of each individual to allocate his private budget among competing desires to achieve the highest possible level of lifetime satisfaction, social utility or efficiency is concerned with efforts to provide for the total well-being of all citizens. When public actions can be taken to improve the life quality and opportunity of any citizen without a larger cost to other citizens, that action is justified as being socially efficient. Similarly, the failure to take such actions can be decried as being socially inefficient. The relevant issue is what the total benefits and total costs are. Efficiency principles are silent as to who pays and who benefits. The latter is a distributive question to be judged on equity, not efficiency, grounds.

The task of this section is to articulate the efficiency principles which underlie the public provision of noncash welfare programs. Cash transfer programs will be discussed in the next two chapters.

Noncash Social Welfare Programs

Noncash programs of social welfare come in a variety of forms, three of which have a higher visibility than others. These are (1) opportunity programs, (2) service programs, and (3) in-kind transfer programs.

Opportunity Programs. Public opportunity programs are those that set up, by law, a system of rewards and punishments designed to establish a systematic set of incentives and sanctions, so that particular groups are most likely to benefit from the operation of the politicoeconomic system. Social welfare programs are concerned with the creation, distribution, and alteration of a polity's opportunity structure. Because of past practice, white male Protestants of prime age have a better vista of opportunities than do others. Social welfare programs address the problems produced by this advantage.

Equality of opportunity is one of the critical social norms of American society. Yet everywhere there is perverse evidence of inequality. Affirmative action programs which demand that institutions receiving public funds conclusively demonstrate their efforts to employ minority persons are one form of equal opportunity program. Prohibition against particular practices of discrimination, once considered legal, are another form of efforts to expand equal opportunities. The provision of special programs to groups which have been the victims of discrimination is a third way that states may promote equality of opportunity.[8]

A critical political issue is how to improve the advantage structure of one set of citizens without decreasing the advantage structure of a second set. Under conditions of scarcity the advantages must somehow be shared—all citizens cannot be "privileged." The removal of privilege is a very difficult task.

The Supreme Court was faced directly with this question in the Bakke case. The Court was asked if specific minorities who were previously the victims of discrimination could be placed on a special agenda for a privilege such as admission to medical school. In a curious 4–1–4 decision the court said racial minorities could *not* be given special privilege in admission, but admission procedures could consider race in establishing the structure of the entering class. The Court ought not to be judged too harshly for equivocating on a critical social dilemma, however. The mechanism of redressing past injustices is, after all, one of the most tortuous questions of our time.

Social Service Programs. A social service program is a somewhat more specific form of social welfare program. It is the provision of a service which will contribute to improved social functioning. Just what is meant by "improved" social functioning is, understandably, a subject of much political dispute. Social services tend to be structured to augment social behavior about which there is a high degree of consensus, such as child welfare, family stability, jobholding, prevention of juvenile delinquency. Political argument over the expansion of social service programs often involves disputes over whether a program will contribute to a desirable end; for example, Will psychological counseling help persons to locate, apply for, and retain jobs? One question which should be asked is, Could the same result be achieved with a less costly intervention? There also are disputes about whether the end is itself desirable. "Moral" considerations often cloud the discussion; for example, Should public funds be used to provide abortions? The structure, range of operation, and manner of delivery of social services will be dealt with in some detail in Chapter 1 of Part 4.

In-Kind Programs. In-kind programs refer to the vast array of goods (as opposed to services) that are provided to social welfare clients outside of the traditional market arrangements. These include the varieties of housing aid programs, the food stamp program, and the provision of medical care. The fact that a client is helped to purchase, or is provided with, a specific good by the welfare system is deeply troubling to some persons. Why a welfare recipient should be given a food voucher or a food stamp rather than cash to buy food, or why an aged person should have medical insurance provided rather than the cash to purchase medical insurance is troubling to some liberals, who do not like the interference with the individual's choice, and to some conservatives, who do not like the interference with traditional market forces.

In-kind programs are, however, the fastest growing social welfare programs in the United States. Medicare-Medicaid, established in 1964, and the present food stamp program, which was not inaugurated until 1969, together now cost over $25 billion.[9]

Efficiency Principles

Social welfare programs inevitably exist because of political circumstances. It might be demonstrated that a particular service program would greatly improve the quality of life of a particular group of citizens. But unless that group of citizens or their advocates can convince an effective majority of their fellow citizens of the wisdom of the projects, they will not be undertaken.

However, social welfare programs are not created in an economic vacuum. Otto Eckstein has described three conditions which are cited to justify the creation of public programs from a social efficiency perspective.[10] These conditions are based on the principles of collective goods, divergency between private and social benefits, and extraordinary risk.

Collective Goods. The products of some social welfare programs are collectively rather than individually consumed. Such programs cannot be efficiently sold on the open market, since those who refuse to pay cannot be excluded from the benefits of the product. Persons who consume such goods without paying any share of the cost are often called *free riders.*

National defense is the traditional non–social welfare example. Once national security is provided to a nation-state, its "benefits" are automatically extended to all nationals within the boundaries of the state. All receive the same protection, whether or not they are willing to pay for it, and there is no way of segregating the market into those who are willing to pay and those who choose to be free riders. In such a situation the rational and wholly self-interested consumer will not pay voluntarily, since he or she can achieve the benefit without paying. But it is also rational to cast a vote to provide for defense and to impose a tax to finance it. In short, the consumer will be willing to vote to compel himself to pay in order to impose the compulsion on others. Ordinary private goods are free from this difficulty, because if someone refuses to pay, the seller simply refuses to allow that person to receive the benefit; if you don't buy a ticket, the ballet manager will see to it that you don't see the ballet.

This critical distinction has been called the *exclusion principle*. If a good inherently violates the exclusion principle, then it is called a *collective good*. Exclusivity or nonexclusivity does not exist on an either/or basis. In some cases exclusivity is simply impossible (e.g., national defense); in others exclusivity can be enforced, but it is expensive to do so. The decision to compel payment for a service is an essentially political choice. The exclusion principle does not demand the provision of any particular public service. It does state that some goods, like national defense, will not be purchased by a rational person, but that person will vote to tax self and others to provide a particular good.

For collective goods in social welfare programs, the benefits are spread over a large population of citizens, only some of whom are in direct contact with the program. A recreation program for delinquency-prone children is an example. Presumably the program benefits the children in the program plus an unspecified number of others who are thereby protected from vandalism. The direct beneficiaries are impossible to single out. Thus the support for such a collective benefit is highly diffuse. Few would pay directly, but all could be hurt if the program is not undertaken.

Divergency between Private and Social Benefits. Some goods, when they are consumed by one individual, have a secondary impact on other persons. Inherently such goods enter the utilities of more than one person. In such cases individual consumers may not be willing to pay all of the costs incurred in the production of that good, since none of them will reap all of the benefits from its consumption. The price they are willing to pay thus does not reflect the true value to the economy as a whole. The divergence is called an *externality*, and it may be either positive in the case of benefit or negative in the case of a cost. The distortion in price from unrecompensed benefits or costs could yield a significant dislocation in the utilization of resources. A moment's reflection will convince the reader that virtually all consumptive and capital goods have some externality, or social cost or benefit, which represents the divergence between cost of production and the price the consumer is willing to pay.

In a complex society the well-being of each individual is influenced not only by her or his own consumption but by the consumption of others. Social welfare programs are frequently structured to take this into account by providing a large array of services and programs at little or no cost to the direct consumer.

A society which values monogamy, such as ours, will provide marriage counseling services below costs of operation. A society which believes in the work ethic will seek ways to encourage work, even though it might be costly to do so. Prison rehabilitation also has spillover effects beyond the immediate consumer. These and many others are illustrations of social welfare expenditures being incurred because of social benefits that go beyond the benefit of individual consumers of the service.

Extraordinary Risks. While much of the mythology of private enterprise is based on the notion of risk taking, some risks are large—so large that only a collectivity is sufficient to absorb failure should it occur. In some cases the return on capital is so long deferred that only a collective is willing to extend credit. Other risks are not adaptable to market procedures. In each case government assumption of the risk, either through direct provision or some side payment, is required if the good in question is to be produced at all.

A few examples of risks *extraordinaire* for which public intervention is a viable substitute should make this point clear. The front-end capital required for the development of an entire river basin is so large—running into the billions of dollars—that private enterprise simply will not invest in it. But such ventures (e.g., the Tennessee Valley Authority) have shown that from society's perspective, their benefits exceed their cost. Thus a rational person would refuse to invest his own funds voluntarily but would tax himself to take the risk, if the risk can be collectively shared. Another example would be a redwood reforestation project which would require over a century for a positive return to capital. Only the state has a sufficiently long time horizon to justify capital investments, but the failure of society to make such investments would be considered a major disservice to future generations. Finally, consider investment in medical research. Unlike technological advances, medical research is not amenable to market adjustments. We might be willing to pay a higher price for instamatic color television to cover the deferred cost of television research, for example, and we would not worry that the benefits of instamatic color are not available to all. We would be less willing to allow a pharmaceutical company to charge a high price because of past investments for a miracle drug that is certain to save lives. Pharmacy companies know this and will therefore confine their research to lower cost programs and more trivial projects such as buffered aspirin. The company knows it can charge a higher price for buffered aspirin, even though some people will have to make do with the plain variety. The basic research into life-saving drugs which, once discovered, will be made universally available will have to be done by government, if it is to be done at all.

The principles of collective consumption, divergence between social and individual benefits, and extraordinary risk apply in common to public social welfare programs which are designed to produce a socially efficient result that would not occur in an un-regulated free market system. They can be thought of as socially corrective programs of the opportunity, service, or in-kind trans-fer type. The assertion is that such programs promote social effi-ciency and thus, theoretically at least, can be tested and evaluated on efficiency grounds. We ask whether the social benefit of these programs outweighs the social cost, without regard to which citi-zens benefit and which citizens pay.

TECHNICAL JUDGMENTS OF SOCIAL EFFICIENCY

In each case of social efficiency, technical judgments are theoreti-cally possible. Where equity considerations do not apply, most would agree that the social benefits to be derived from a social program ought to exceed the real social costs. Deciding whether such is the case is an undertaking of enormous technical difficulty, though not impossible. When we find that a program has a posi-tive social benefit, it has to be compared with other programs that also have positive social benefits. Yet, as William Gorham testi-fied:

> Let me hasten to point out that we have not attempted any grandiose cost-benefit analysis designed to reveal whether the total benefits from an additional million dollars spent on health programs would be higher or lower than that from an additional million spent on education or welfare. If I was ever naive enough to think this sort of analysis possible, I no longer am. The benefits of health, education, and welfare programs are diverse and often intangible. They affect dif-ferent age groups and different regions of the population over different periods of time. No amount of analysis is going to tell us whether the nation benefits more from send-

ing a slum child to preschool, providing medical care to an old man, or enabling a disabled housewife to resume her normal activities. The "grand decisions"—how much wealth, how much education, how much welfare, and which groups in the population shall benefit—are questions of value judgments and politics. The analyst cannot make much contribution to their resolution.[11]

What *can* be done are analytic studies of specific policy goals, with a precisely articulated value base. Programs that have highly similar goals and reasonably similar resource requirements can be usefully compared by the application of a standard comparison system. Within a given value system, the notion is clear; social benefit should exceed social cost at a maximum level. This maximum benefit is achieved at the point where marginal benefits are precisely equal to marginal cost. Marginal benefit is defined as the increment in valued social output secured by one additional unit of the good in question. Marginal cost is the increment in social cost incurred by one additional unit being made available.

Table 4–1 illustrates this point, assuming we can know with precision the total and marginal costs and benefits of varying numbers of mental health clinics. As long as marginal benefit is greater than marginal cost, social value is increasing. At the point of equality, social value is static, but when marginal cost exceeds marginal benefit, social value declines (see Figure 4–3). Expansion beyond the fourth clinic is costly to society; stopping before the fourth clinic is costly to society in the sense that we forego greater benefits than costs. Building the fourth clinic precisely equates marginal cost with marginal benefits.[12]

There are obvious complications in the application of this principle. Public budget limitations may make it necessary to stop far short of the point where marginal benefits are equal to marginal cost. Political pressures can work in the other way as well, causing programs to expand beyond their optimal level. Nonetheless, the concept is useful for gaining insight into how society *might* secure the greatest possible level of well-being: the point where the public budget is exhausted and in every public program marginal cost and marginal benefit ratios are exactly equal. This is the point at which society has achieved its maximum value without any regard for which citizens benefit.

It is difficult to disagree with the above reasoning, for it merely

FIGURE 4-3
BENEFITS AND COSTS OF PROGRAM EXPANSION

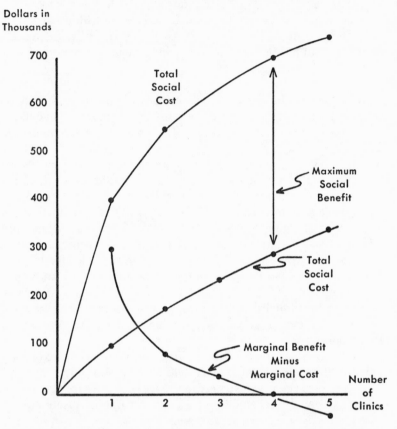

asserts that when equity considerations do not apply, and when social cost and benefits are precisely known, public budgets should be constantly shifted so that the maximum attainable level of social value is achieved. See the Appendix at the end of the chapter for a discussion of some of the technical problems involved.

During the past score of years there has been a significant increase in the application of economic criteria to governmental expenditures for social welfare programs. Operating under a variety of names—cost/benefit analysis, planning-programming-budgeting, cost-effective analysis, input-output analysis—a number of similar yet distinct types of economic studies have been

TABLE 4-1
COST/BENEFIT COMPARISON OF VARIOUS NUMBERS OF MENTAL HEALTH CLINICS

Number of Clinics	Total Cost	Marginal Cost	Total Benefits	Marginal Benefits	Marginal Benefit Minus Marginal Cost	Total Benefit Minus Total Cost
0	0		0			0
		$100,000		$400,000	$300,000	
1	$100,000		$400,000			$300,000
		75,000		150,000	75,000	
2	175,000		550,000			375,000
		65,000		100,000	35,000	
3	240,000		650,000			410,000
		50,000		50,000	0	
4	290,000		700,000			410,000
		45,000		40,000	−5,000	
5	335,000		740,000			405,000

instituted to "rationalize" public choice within an economic framework. The ostensible purpose of such analysis was stated, in the executive order establishing PPBS, as:

1. To identify our national goals with precision and on a continuing basis.
2. To choose among those goals the ones that are most urgent.
3. To search for alternative means of reaching those goals most effectively at the least cost.
4. To inform ourselves not merely about next year's costs, but on the second, third, and subsequent years' costs of our programs.
5. To measure the performance of our programs to ensure a dollar's worth of service for each dollar spent.[13]

Each technique of economic analysis has its own set of conceptual pitfalls. As a group, these techniques provide a framework for the reduction, but not the elimination, of value judgments.

ECONOMICS OF DISTRIBUTIVE CHOICE

In the discussion of efficiency in social welfare programs, the assumption has been that the polity is indifferent to who benefits and who loses, being concerned only with net social gains. Social welfare programs of this type are promoted in order to avoid the inefficiencies that would result if citizens did not work together collectively. For these programs, there is at least a theoretical, but not necessarily practical, "best answer." A much more difficult problem emerges when the polity seeks to pursue a public interest. This requires a ranking of social orders that are equally efficient, but in one order A is better off than B, while in the second, the reverse is the case. Here the polity becomes concerned with the relative well-being of its citizens—it begins to make interpersonal judgments. Social welfare programs designed to promote fairness, justice, equity, or the like cannot be judged by the technical criteria which are applied to efficiency judgments.

Most readers of this text probably believe that the most efficient welfare system is not necessarily the best welfare system. Fairness, justice, and stability are factors of equal importance. To examine these aspects of the economics of social welfare requires an alternative perspective, that of *distributive justice*. This section of the chapter serves as a very brief introduction to the leading concepts of distributive justice: one based on a criterion of merit, and another based on a notion of need, that is, justice or fairness. The two concepts exist in dynamic tension with one another.[14] This summary does not do justice to either position, but it does indicate their central place in the politicoeconomic setting of social welfare.

The case for distributive justice based on merit is based on arguments first attributed to Aristotle and since rephrased in thousands of ways. Aristotle, in Chapter IX of Book 3 of *Politics*, enunciated a moral theory of distributive justice based on "proportionate equality":

> As A and B have given to the state, in the way of personal merit and personal contribution to its well-being, so A and B should receive from the state, in the way of office and honor. If the personal merit and personal contribution of both are equal, they will receive equal amounts: if they are unequal, they will receive unequal amounts: but in either case the basis of proportionate equality will be observed, and the proportion between the thing A receives and A's personal merit will be the same as that between the thing B receives and his personal merit.[15]

Aristotle recognized that what constitutes merit would vary from one community to the next. Thus, "different formulas for distributive justice frequently contradict one another."[16]

The principal alternative theme was given classic expression by L. Blanc and later quoted by Karl Marx: "Let each produce according to aptitude and his force, let each consume according to his need."[17] Need, however, is difficult to define; strict equality is not. Neither distribution on the basis of need nor distribution on the basis of merit is the functional equivalent of distribution on the basis of equity (or equality). There are at least three competing principles of distribution and many variants of each: (1) merit, or contribution to production; (2) equality; and (3) equity. These concepts of distribution are neither exhaustive nor mutually exclusive.

Distribution on the basis of productivity would reward each according to his "contribution," but how do we calculate the share of the banker, the designer, the administrator, the tool and die maker, or the assembly-line worker in the value of the automobile being produced? How do we factor in the contribution of the policeman, the teacher, the sanitation worker? Wage and productivity are not synonymous terms. Merit distribution, whatever its philosophic benefit, is impossible to calculate. Our distribution system is based not on distribution relative to merit or productivity but on wages and return to privately held property. This has very little to do with productivity.

Distributing rewards equally is easier—society can give all persons an identical share. But a share of what, and when? The accounting problem encountered in utopian experiments is evidence that equality in distribution is difficult to accomplish, even when perceived as being politically desirable.[18]

Distribution on the basis of equity or fairness is obviously conceptually soft. Do the aged deserve more than the young, the productive more than the unproductive, the beautiful more than the ugly? Each mode of distribution requires hard definitions.

As a matter of practical political reality, the discussion of public welfare economics tends to have little reference to any such theories of distributive justice. Pragmatic political choices generally are made in specific contexts that appear to violate both efficiency and equity.

SOCIAL WELFARE EXPENDITURES

Having established some generalized guidelines for appraising public welfare choices, we can proceed to consider more concretely the pragmatic efforts of governments to deal with conflicts over social goals. Almost all of society's goals can be achieved in a variety of ways. We may pursue them in the private sector or the public sector, or in some combination of both. We can provide maximum efficiency and then deal with the consequences of inequality, or we can focus on equity and deal with the problems of inefficiency which may result. The analysis of the substantive problems of choice must depend, at least in part, on an understanding of what choices the polity has made in the most recent past.

While there is no pristine account of welfare expenditures anywhere, a good source of information is the social welfare expenditure series produced by the Social Security Administration. This series is based on a somewhat precise definition of social welfare programs which includes programs that provide cash and/or in-kind payments to individuals and families for their direct benefit (i.e., public assistance, social insurance, Medicare, Medicaid, and public housing), and also includes various deferred compensation payments to government employees.

Obtaining accurate estimates of the specific purpose, or even the magnitude, of social welfare expenditures is difficult. In the first place, social welfare is not a precise concept. Thus decisions about which expenditures to include and which to exclude must be arbitrary. For example, an interior park budgeted in the Capital and Operating Cost account of the Public Housing Authority is considered a social welfare expense, while a park across the street charged to the city's Parks and Recreation Department is not. Social insurance programs which supplement the retirement incomes of wealthy persons are included in social welfare; the cost of a legislatively mandated pension security plan is not. Accounting conveniences often dictate the decision to include or exclude a particular expenditure. Intergovernmental transfers complicate the estimates; some of the money spent by state and local governments often comes to them from federal sources, and both units of government count the same dollars as a "social welfare expense." Estimates over time become misleading if corrections for inflation are not made. Tax expenditures are not counted,[19] and those dollars that are lost as government revenue do not show up in the expenditure column. The purpose of even those expenditures that are counted is not always clear. Cash transfer payments are often made in lieu of direct provision of a health or welfare service, but just as often, direct health and welfare services are provided in lieu of cash transfer payments. Classification of welfare expenditures by institutional arrangement (i.e., what agency spends the money) are useful to provide insight for students into how governments provide funds to meet social welfare goals, but, for the reasons enumerated above, such expenditure estimates must be treated as approximations.

With these caveats in mind, it is possible to take a short-term and long-term look at the trends in social welfare expenditures under public auspices. The relative magnitude and the composition of the public social welfare structure shifted significantly in the third quarter of this century. After allowing for both inflation and population growth, total social welfare expenditures increased by 314 percent, far outstripping expenditures growth in all other public programs. Since 1960, human resource expenditures have increased by 694 percent in current dollars, while national defense has grown by *only* 208 percent. Other government expenditures have gone up by 509 percent.[20]

TABLE 4–2
SOCIAL EXPENDITURES AS A FUNCTION OF GOVERNMENTAL EXPENDITURES FOR ALL PURPOSES
(Constant 1975 dollars, in millions)

	1929	1950	1960	1965	1970	1973	1975*
GNP	$310.76	$549.90	$824.63	$1,030.82	$1,281.61	$1,477.93	$1,424.30
Public expenditures as percent of GNP	10.7%	23.6%	27.7%	27.8%	31.9%	31.6%	34.4%
Public budget	$33.21	$130.05	$228.16	$285.28	$408.27	$466.36	$489.42
Social welfare expenditures (SWE) as percent of public budget	36.3%	37.6%	38.0%	42.4%	47.8%	55.3%	58.4%
Public SWE budget	$12.1	$48.90	$86.70	$120.97	$195.15	$257.90	$285.82
Federal share of public SWE	20.4%	44.8%	47.7%	48.9%	53.1%	57.2%	57.9%
State and local welfare as percent of all S&L expenditures	38.2%	60.1%	58.3%	61.7%	62.3%	64.2%	64.4%

* preliminary estimate.
SWE = Social work expenditures.
S&L = State and local.
SOURCE: Various tables, Social Security Bulletin.

Table 4–2 presents a mosaic picture of the political economy of social welfare. This table reveals a number of important facts about the pattern of social welfare expenditures, including the following:

1. The economy is growing in real terms; except for the 1973–75 recession period, there has been an expanding GNP.
2. The public sector is expanding more rapidly than the private sector—a larger proportion of the allocative decisions is now reached collectively, outside of traditional market forces.

3. Social welfare expenditures are growing relative to other expenditures. Even during the years of the Vietnam buildup, social welfare programs grew faster than defense expenditures.
4. The federal share of social welfare expenditures has increased markedly.
5. Local governments experienced a dramatic increase in the proportion of their budget being directed to welfare in the period 1930–50 and have been experiencing a slow but steady increase since then.

From 1929 to 1950 the public social welfare budget held a nearly constant share of a greatly expanded public budget. From 1950 to 1960 social welfare programs generally exceeded economic growth by receiving a slightly larger share of the moderate increase in public expenditures. From 1960 to 1965 the budget share going to welfare increased, while the public-sector growth was held in check. In the last decade there has been (1) an expanding economy, except for the past few years, (2) an increased share of public-sector activity, and (3) an increased proportion of public dollars being directed to social welfare ends. Combined, these forces have contributed to an enormous expansion of social welfare programs.

This expansion in social welfare expenditures has been reflected in a proliferation of programs and activities and a rapid increase in the spending of some programs already in place. After 1965 the tempo of social welfare expenditures rose, rapidly averaging a growth of 16.9 percent a year, after correction for inflation. In no year in the last decade was the real growth in social welfare expenditures less than 11 percent.

The allocation of dollars being spent in 1965 and 1975 is instructive. The changing composition is revealed in Table 4-3 and Figure 4-4. The preponderate growth area in the social welfare sector was social insurance, OASDI in particular. Alone it accounted for 44 percent of the real growth in actual expenditures. All public welfare programs received much political attention during the decade; this reflected a change in share from 5.2 percent in 1965 to 12.1 percent in 1975. The federal social service programs inaugurated in the 1960s reflected a growth from zero dollars in 1965 to $712 million in 1970 and $2.5 billion in 1975 and a projected $2.9 billion for 1979. Despite this growth, these pro-

TABLE 4-3
CHANGES IN SPENDING FOR SELECTED SOCIAL WELFARE
PROGRAMS, 1965–1975 (constant dollars)*

	1965 (In millions, 1975 value)	%	1975 (In millions, 1975 value)	%	Percent Increase 1965–75
Social insurance					
OASDI	$26,725.6	50.2%	$78,456.3	45.7%	193.5%
Medicare	—	—	14,781.4	8.6	N.a.
Unemployment	4,721.1	8.9	14,396.5	8.4	204.9
Worker's compensation	2,980.2	5.6	6,437.5	3.8	116.0
Public aid					
Categorical aids†	4,135.9	7.8	11,120.1	6.5	168.8%
Vendor medical payments	872.6	1.6	12,968.0	7.6	1,386.1
Social services (PA)	—	—	2,522.5	0.2	N.a.
SSI	—	—	4,641.9	2.7	N.a.
Food stamps	56.0	0.1	4,677.4	2.7	8,252.5
Other‡	586.5	1.1	3,211.9	1.9	477.6
Housing	500.2	0.9	2,954.0	1.7	490.5
Other social services§ ...	3,248.0	6.1	7,877.5	4.6	142.5
Veteran's services (except education)	9,418.4	17.7	12,240.2	7.2	30.0
Total	$53,244.5	100.0%	$171,642.8	100.0%	222.4%
Percent of GNP		5.2%		12.1%	

*Deflector, 1975=1.00; 1965=0.636.
†Represents categorical programs under the Social Security Act plus General Assistance.
‡Federal Work Relief, Emergency Aid, and other special programs.
§Social service programs under the Social Security Act, plus some child welfare programs.
N.a.=Not available

grams comprised less than 1 percent of the total social welfare dollars.

CONCLUSIONS

A rapidly changing society places stress on a social welfare system. As old norms and values are made anachronistic by newly emerging economic relationships, the social welfare system must be restructured to respond to the new conditions. As we shall see in the chapters to follow, the social welfare system has had difficulty in achieving this adjustment.

This chapter has shown how the social welfare system is pressed to achieve the twin goals of economic efficiency and democratic equality. The rationality of efficiency was explained, and the necessity of a public response based on the principles of collective consumption, a divergence of social and private cost or benefit,

FIGURE 4–4
CHANGES IN SIZE AND COMPOSITIONS OF WELFARE BUDGET,
1965–1975
(1975 Dollars)

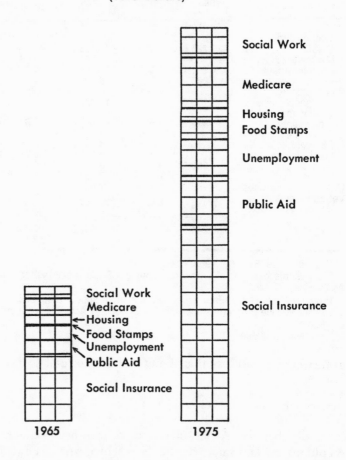

and extraordinary risk conditions which prevail in a market-domi-
nated economy was pointed out. The social welfare pattern of
response has been with opportunity programs, social service programs, in-kind transfers, or cash transfers. (Cash transfer programs are deferred for discussion to the next two chapters.) In this
chapter, one focus was on the technical evaluation of how well
expenditures achieve social efficiency and of how social welfare
expenditures have grown.

The growth of the social welfare system was described as emanating from three combined streams: (1) an expanding economy, (2) an expanding share of the economy being vested in the public sector, and (3) a larger share of the public sector fitting into the traditional concern of social welfare. The implication of this rapid growth for the social welfare system is the topic of the next chapter.

APPENDIX: MEASURING COSTS OF SOCIAL PROGRAMS

Public programs are typically undertaken because it is asserted that the expenditure will add to the total social well-being. But because the benefit is diffuse rather than specific, it is difficult, and sometimes impossible, to measure benefits. Saving lives by safer highways is valuable, but how valuable? One mechanism for estimating such products' value is the use of a "shadow price." The price of similar services is observed; the value of a highway, for example, is *minimally* the value of traveling time, estimated at the wage rate of the traveler,.and the value of the energy saved over the next best mode of transportation. This may be hard to measure, but it is at least conceptually precise. The purpose of the analysis is to make the choice somewhat *more* rational, albeit not perfectly so. If the analyst makes clear how benefits are estimated, the decision maker has a better basis upon which to select from among alternatives. No one wishes to choose between saving babies and saving aged persons. By articulating social benefits as precisely as possible, however, we make the choice perhaps not easy and rational, but at least *less* difficult and *more* rational.

Measuring Costs

In its purest sense the public cost of any social program is the total value or benefit of the next best alternative use of the same set of resources. Since all possible alternatives, and the values thereof, cannot be known, the best available practice is to use as a proxy for social costs the market value of the resources that will be used up in the project. Thus, in estimating the costs, the procedure typically used is to sum all the expenditures for salaries, rents, materials, and so on. Such a procedure typically underestimates the real social costs involved. If a training program is going to use the agency auditorium but no rent is to be paid, the cost is artificially made lower than the real market value of the resources used.

A social worker considering the use of social cost and benefit procedures should consult the literature on the techniques available for the most precise estimation of social costs, and the problems associated with them.

The Plan of Analysis

After the expected benefits and costs of a contemplated social welfare program have been expressed in dollar terms, there is a standard *numeraire* for comparison of programs with similar, or different, policy objectives. It is not possible to simply total up costs and benefits, because projects have different magnitudes and different time horizons. We will look at the problem of time first and then examine the formal mathematical models used in cases where programs are of different magnitudes.

The Discount Factor. A program that produces an immediate benefit is, all things being equal, more valuable than a program with a long-deferred benefit. Future benefits need to be discounted to reflect this fact. Because of inflation, uncertainty, and the fact that dollars spent today could otherwise earn interest, we have to get more than $100 a year from now to make a $100 expenditure now worthwhile.

The present value of a future benefit is equal to the future benefit divided by a *discount factor*. The size of the *discount rate* is determined by our beliefs about certainty, inflation, and the interest rate our money could earn. The discount factor is determined by how long we have to wait for the benefit. If the discount rate is set at 10 percent, then to calculate the value of a $100 benefit one year deferred, we have to divide by $(1 + d)$, or 1.10, or multiply by $(1 \div 1.10)$. If the benefit is to be deferred for two years, we must raise the expression to the second power, for three years to the third power, and so on. Clearly, as the discount rate is increased, as well as the length of time the benefit is deferred, the value of the present benefit falls exponentially (see Table 4A–1).

Mathematical Models. Once the benefits and the costs have been adjusted for time lags between investment and return, the construction of complex mathematical models aids in making a choice between projects. One way of comparing projects is to compare the magnitude of the present value of net benefits. For each year, the benefit less its cost is discounted for the discount factor for that year. The sum of all such values is the present value of the project (see Table 4A–2).

TABLE 4A-1
PRESENT VALUE OF $1

Years Until Benefit Is Achieved	Expression	Discount Factor Multiplication (d = 0.10)	Present Value of $1 Invested
0	—	1.00	1.00
1	$1/1 + d$	0.90	0.90
2	$1/(1 + d)^2$	0.82	0.82
5	$1/(1 + d)^5$	0.62	0.62
10	$1/(1 + d)^{10}$	0.39	0.39
20	$1/(1 + d)^{20}$	0.15	0.15

TABLE 4A-2
PRESENT VALUE OF PROJECTS A AND B OVER A FIVE-YEAR SPAN
(millions of dollars)

	Project A					Project B				
Year	Cost	Benefit	Net	Discount Factor (d = 0.10)	Present Value	Cost	Benefit	Net	Discount Factor (d = 0.10)	Present Value
1	$5.0	$0.0	−5.0	0.90	4.50	$1.0	$1.6	+0.6	0.90	+0.54
2	3.0	1.0	−2.0	0.82	−1.65	2.0	4.0	+2.0	0.82	+1.65
3	2.0	4.0	+2.0	0.75	+1.50	1.0	1.2	+0.2	0.75	+0.15
4	1.0	6.0	+5.0	0.68	+3.41	1.0	1.0	0	0.68	0
5	0.5	7.0	+6.5	0.62	+4.03	1.0	0.5	0.5	0.62	0.31
	$11.5	$18.0			Σ$2.79	$6.0	$8.3			Σ$2.03

$$\text{Present value} = \sum_{t-0}^{t \cdot n} \frac{Bt \quad Ct}{(1 + d)^t}$$

Knowing the present value of a project gives us an important piece of information. It is clear that, with equity considerations deferred, all projects with negative present value should be rejected. We also know that if the programs have similar resource requirements, we should select the program with the largest present value. Most plans will not fit so nicely in the example, however.

Table 4A-2 shows that project A produces a positive net value of $2.79 million but requires a total of $11.5 million in costs over the five years. Project B has a positive net value of only $2.03 million, but it also has a resource requirement of only $6 million. The first project has a resource requirement nearly twice that of the second.

Surely our insight into choice would be better if we looked at the benefit/cost ratios (see Table 4A-3). The increment in knowledge of the benefit/cost ratio is as follows. If project B could be doubled, with no change in the ratios, its present value in five years

TABLE 4A–3
BENEFIT/COST RATIO OF PROJECTS A AND B OVER A FIVE-YEAR
SPAN (in millions of dollars)

	Project A		Project B	
Year	Discounted Benefit	Discounted Cost	Discounted Benefit	Discounted Cost
1	0	4.5	1.44	.90
2	0.82	2.46	3.28	1.64
3	3.00	1.50	.90	.75
4	4.08	0.68	.68	.68
5	4.32	0.31	.31	.62
	Σ12.22	Σ9.45	Σ6.61	Σ4.59
	Benefit/Cost Ratio = 1.293		Benefit/Cost Ratio = 1.44	

$$\text{Benefit/Cost Ratio} = \frac{\displaystyle\sum_{t=0}^{t=5} \frac{B_t}{(1+d)^t}}{\displaystyle\sum_{t=0}^{t=5} \frac{C_t}{(1+d)^t}}$$

would be $4.06 million (double the $2.03 million shown in Table
4A–2). This is much better than project A. All other things being
equal, we would select the program with the highest benefit/cost
ratio and reject all programs with a benefit/cost ratio of less than
1.

NOTES

1. Peter O. Steiner, "The Public Sector and the Public Interest," in R. H.
   Haveman and J. Margolis (eds.), *Public Expenditures and Policy Analysis*
   (Chicago: Markham Publishing Co., 1970).
2. The field of economics has a subfield called welfare economics, as
   noted in Chapter 2. This is not to be confused with the economics of
   social welfare programming, which is the topic of this chapter. Welfare
   economics is the study of the normative or basic value principles which
   are at the base of policy considerations, broadly conceived. It is not
   concerned solely with welfare programs as described in this text but has
   a much broader and more theoretical concern with the optimal allocation of inputs among industries and sectors and the optimal distribution of commodities and services among consumers. The student with
   a background in economics is referred to the seminal work in this area:
   I. M. D. Little, *A Critique of Welfare Economics* (London: Oxford Press,
   1958). The student without such a background is referred to chapter 15
   of Edwin Mansfield, *Microeconomics* (New York: W. W. Norton & Co.,
   1970).

3. Arthur M. Okun, *Equality and Efficiency: The Big Trade-off* (Washington, D.C.: Brookings Institution, 1975).
4. John Rawls, *A Theory of Justice* (Cambridge, Mass.: Harvard University Press, 1971).
5. Ibid., p. 62.
6. Milton Friedman, *Capitalism and Freedom* (Chicago: University of Chicago Press, 1962).
7. Okun, *Equality and Efficiency.*
8. As an exemplar of this social work approach see M. G. Foster, "Eliminating Sex Discrimination in the Law," *Social Casework,* vol. 58, no. 2 (1977), pp. 67–76.
9. J. L. Palmer and J. J. Minarik, "Promoting Access to Goods and Services," in Henry Owen et al. (eds.), *Setting National Priorities: The Next Ten Years* (Washington, D.C.: Brookings Institution, 1976), p. 514 ff.
10. Otto Eckstein, *Public Finance* (Englewood Cliffs, N.J.: Prentice-Hall, 1967), chap. 1.
11. Aaron Wildavsky, "Rescuing Policy Analysis from PPBS," in Haveman and Margolis, *Public Expenditures and Policy Analysis,* p. 470.
12. In the example, the construction of the fourth clinic neither adds to nor subtracts from the total social benefit, but this is a defect of an oversimplified illustration.
13. L. B. Johnson, Executive Order establishing PPBS, August 25, 1965.
14. Okun, *Equality and Efficiency.*
15. Ernest Barker, *The Politics of Aristotle* (New York: Oxford University Press, 1958), Appendix 25.
16. Ibid.
17. Karl Marx, *Critique of the Gotha Program* (Moscow: Foreign Languages Publishing House, 1947).
18. Okun, *Equality and Efficiency,* chap. 3.
19. *Tax expenditure* is the term given to the phenomenon which occurs when the government delays or forgives a tax that would otherwise be collected if the taxpayer performs certain functions, such as paying interest on a mortgage. The resulting loss of income to government is a tax expenditure.
20. *The United States Budget in Brief* (Washington, D.C.: U.S. Government Printing Office, 1978).

PART II

THE POLITICS AND
ECONOMICS OF POVERTY

CHAPTER 5

POVERTY AND
SOCIAL WELFARE

The political process which culminates in policy change is often obscure and always complicated. In Part I we identified a conceptual framework to provide insight into the political and economic environment of social welfare policy. Now, in Part II, we will illustrate, by example, the way the concepts in this framework are explicitly and implicitly employed in the evaluation of problems encountered in social welfare practice.

This part is concerned with a major social problem, that of poverty. Its overarching goal is to isolate the problem of poverty as a politicoeconomic policy opportunity. It is curious to think of poverty as an opportunity; normally, it is anything but. Nevertheless, the problem dramatically reveals the political and economic forces which interact to produce, or fail to produce, public policy responses to cases of individual want in an abundant society.

THE MEANING AND MEASUREMENT OF POVERTY

The public policy debate over poverty begins with a conflict over its definition. Both the direction of the debate and the evaluation of the programs proposed and rejected as a consequence are critically affected by the terms accepted in a definition of poverty.

An economic perspective on poverty has dominated this debate in the second half of the 20th century. The economic perspective rather uncritically accepts the notion that the well-being of a family is principally related to its ability to consume goods and services. The consumptive ability, in its turn, is related to the flow of income and goods and services to the family as well as the wealth upon which that family can draw. Insufficiency of consumptive ability is the central element in this poverty definition. The insufficiency must obviously be related to some standard of sufficient ability to consume, and it is generally accepted that dollars of income is the best single indicator of this capacity. Economic definitions of poverty thus turn on income and a *poverty threshold.*

The economic perspective has been narrowed quickly to an examination of how income should be counted and what the proper poverty threshold is.[1] Figure 5–1 illustrates the income notion of poverty. It also illustrates that income, as conceived of for a definition of poverty, is only a distant cousin of income as the term is used in ordinary language. Figure 5–1 sketches the flow of income for a family. Establishing instruments to measure the flow of income in on the left side of the diagram and establishing the standards of need, or the flow of income out, on the right side of the diagram are the tricky problems in this definition of poverty. If the poverty threshold is designed with only narrow consumptive needs in mind, or if income is defined by considering only a few of its many streams, the dimensions of poverty within a society will be poorly specified. Errors in the definition can either overstate or understate the magnitude of poverty.

In the income notion of poverty, which is the theme of this chapter, we refer to an insufficiency of goods and services as measured by dollars received or spent by a family unit over a specified time span. The term used to describe this condition is *income poverty.* The implicit assumptions of such a reference are that:

1. An individual's real welfare is accurately measured by his or her opportunity to consume goods and services.
2. Consumption opportunities are accurately measured by receipts or expenditures.
3. The family unit rather than the individual or some larger collective is the appropriate unit of analysis.

FIGURE 5-1 THE INCOME NOTION OF POVERTY: FLOW OF INCOME FOR A FAMILY

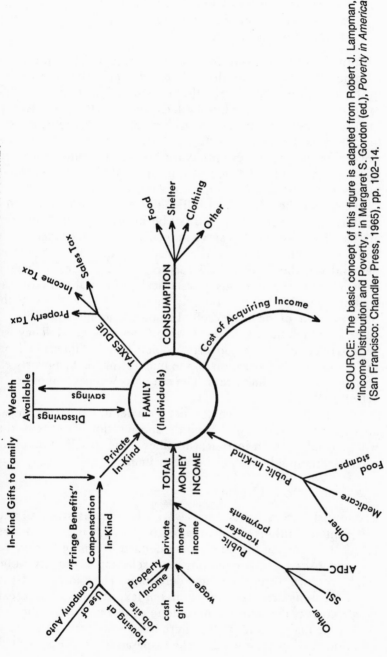

SOURCE: The basic concept of this figure is adapted from Robert J. Lampman, "Income Distribution and Poverty," in Margaret S. Gordon (ed.), *Poverty in America* (San Francisco: Chandler Press, 1965), pp. 102–14.

4. Poverty is a dynamic rather than a static concept and has meaning only over some established time frame rather than at some instant in time.

Even if all of these assumptions were accepted, much that we commonly associate with the term *poverty* would still be excluded in this definition. There are other considerations of lifestyle, life expectations, and sociocultural values implicit in the term.[2] Nevertheless, the term *income poverty*, with all of its limitations, is used because it is the least subjective of the available notions. Income poverty is, at best, a mere proxy for poverty, but other considerations lie beyond the scope of this analysis. Government documents also rely on the income measure.[3]

In light of the conceptual difficulties which are inherent in a definition of poverty, it should not be surprising that definitions are frequently selected to serve immediate political or ideological ends. If we simply disregard an income source for, or income demand on, the family, the structure of the political debate is restructured. There is thus a great deal of political maneuvering around the definition of poverty that has little to do with the phenomenon of poverty itself. Incumbent administrations will search for definitions that will make them look good. They will seek to overestimate the poverty problem that they inherited from the previous administration and to underestimate the poverty extant as reelection time nears. The out party will have an opposite set of goals.

In a technical sense, the conflict over definition occurs in two specific contexts. One of these is the specification of the items that will be used to count income; the other is the specification of the poverty threshold or official poverty line.

The Specification of Income

Economists, accountants, social workers, and housewives all have different definitions of income, each of which is more or less relevant to the use for which it is intended. Defining income for the purposes of understanding and selecting a poverty policy might require an entirely new definition. The same word with many meanings creates confusion, but text writers cannot create single correct definitions where none exist. Even within the area of income maintenance policy there will be different demands on definitions of income to meet the disparate needs of policymak-

ers, policy administrators, and policy analysts. The critical problems in any definition of income, however, include the decision of
what to count as income, and what the proxy to be used is when
counting it. The principal disputes involve the treatment of various aspects of income: taxes taken out of income at the source,
public in-kind income programs, gifts and services in the private
sector, fringe benefits, other in-kind compensation, private
wealth, the cost of securing income, and expected future income.
There are arguments for and against the inclusion of each of these
income streams and the methods to be used in figuring them.[4]

The Social Security Administration is one agency which has
struggled with the issue of defining income for the purpose of
policy analysis. These administrators would prefer a conceptually
clean and comprehensive measure. Unfortunately, enormous data
problems prevent treating national income statistics as clearly as
they would like. The analysts at the Social Security Administration
therefore have hit upon a definition of *income* which:

1. Uses the family as the unit of analysis.
2. Selects one year as the time frame.
3. Counts cash income from all sources, public and private,
   except capital gains or losses.
4. Excludes in-kind income from both private and public
   sources.
5. Counts cash income before taxes are deducted.[5]

Poverty Thresholds

Setting the standard by which income, however estimated, is
judged sufficient or insufficient is not one whit less difficult. At the
core of the dispute of poverty thresholds there is the conflict
between relative and absolute conceptions of poverty. The problem is compounded by the fact that the dollar, the usual unit of
measure in poverty thresholds, fluctuates over time.[6] Figure 5–2
illustrates family income distribution for two time points, 1964
and 1976. The shape of the curves has not significantly changed,
reflecting a stability in the distribution of income. The curves have
merely shifted to the right, reflecting both inflation and economic
growth.

Some theoreticians would define poverty in terms of the dollar
value of minimal market-basket needs of families at the bottom of
the income scale. If such poverty thresholds are not shifted up-

FIGURE 5-2

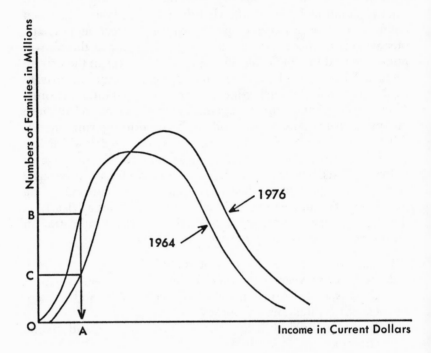

SOURCE: U.S. Department of Commerce, Bureau of the Census, *Current Population Reports,* Series P-60 (Washington, D.C.: U.S. Government Printing Office).

ward to account for inflation, inflation alone would bring about the reduction of poverty (from *OB* families to *OC* families, in Figure 5–2). It has therefore been suggested that the poverty line should be periodically raised to account for the increased cost of the minimum market basket. Others say that this is not enough; the poverty line should be set initially in some specific relation to the apex of the income distribution curve. The poverty line is thus automatically adjusted to economic growth and inflation. The critical problem with the second approach is that unless there is a shift in the distribution of income, the percentage of the population at the poverty level remains relatively constant. Thus, those who want to show progress against poverty point to the number of families below some previously established income point, adjusted for purchasing power. These theoreticians have an *absolute* definition of poverty. Others seeking to show how programs have failed will find that the number of persons some specified distance from the apex has not changed over time. These persons hold a *relative* view of poverty. Figure 5–3 shows how the size of the poverty population is influenced by the selection of either an absolute or a relative definition of poverty.

Relative Definitions of a Poverty Line. Relative poverty refers to a

FIGURE 5–3
DIVERGENCE OF ABSOLUTE AND RELATIVE DEFINITIONS OF POVERTY OVER TIME

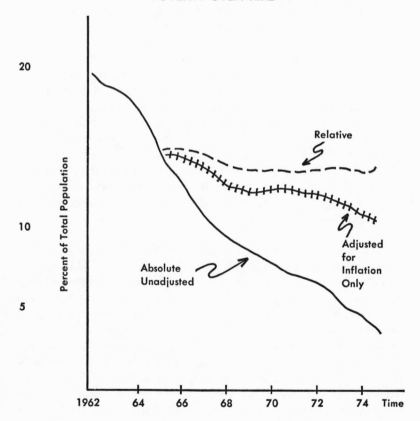

position, relative to others, along the distribution scale; in this definition there will always be a bottom third, or fifth, or tenth. Relative definitions of poverty which speak in terms of the elimination of some bottom share are clearly impossible in any society which permits income inequality. To talk about eliminating the bottom third of an array is semantic nonsense. It is not semantic nonsense, however, to talk about the demographic characteristics of the family units which populate the bottom third, or about policies which would make the demographic characteristics of the lower third more random. It should be clear that such policies are not policies of relative poverty elimination, but policies for the creation of *equality of opportunity*.

A somewhat more realistic definition of relative poverty has been provided by Victor Fuchs, who sought to define poverty as one-half of the polity's median income:

> By the standards that have prevailed over most of history, and still prevail over large areas of the world, there are very few poor in the United States today. Nevertheless, there are millions of American families who, both in their own eyes and in those of others, are poor. As our nation prospers, our judgment as to what constitutes poverty will inevitably change. When we talk about poverty in America, we are talking about families and individuals who have much less income than most of us. When we talk about reducing or eliminating poverty, we are really talking about changing the distribution of income.[7]

Such a definition is a potentially realistic policy goal even in a society with income inequality. A Fuchs point, as the concept has come to be known, has several advantages over a simpler relative definition. First, the percent of households with income below the Fuchs point tells us something about the distribution of income. Second, it informs us how well the poor live relative to the rest of the population. Perhaps its greatest advantage is that it is capable of being a point of measuring the degree to which a polity is providing a socially relevant minimum. The particular *location* of a Fuchs point, at one-half, or one-third, or one-quarter of the median, is subjective. The concept of a Fuchs point itself is not subjective. It informs us about the magnitude of the population which lags behind the rest of society.

Absolute Definitions of a Poverty Line.   Relative definitions inform us about the consumptive opportunities of poor persons relative to their fellow citizens. This view needs to be supplemented by some objective base: *How much* food, housing, clothing, and so on can be purchased? This traditionally involves the specification of some concept of *minimum need.*

This approach to poverty-line setting requires some estimation of the price of essential goods and services, as well as a delineation of the items to be included in the minimum market basket. The first crude delineations of the poverty line were achieved in this fashion. Officials in the Department of Agriculture calculated the cost of minimally adequate diets under a variety of conditions (e.g., rural or urban resident, age and family make-up). Previous household surveys had identified the fact that low-income families spend one-third of their budget on food. In 1965, therefore, Mollie Orshonski of the Department of Health, Education, and Welfare simply multiplied the USDA food budget by 3 in order to designate income lines for poverty.[8] In the years since, the approximation of an income poverty line has become more sophisticated.[9]

Comparison of Absolute and Relative Definitions.   There is no inherent superiority in either relative or absolute definitions of poverty. Nor is there a rigid distinction between them. The goods and services included in a minimum market basket vary by the wealth of a society, and also the manner in which essential goods are made available for consumption. If only a few in society could afford comfortable and stylish clothes, clothing would probably not be included in the market basket. In a society with many millionaires, a man with only a few hundred thousand dollars may feel poor. In a society with free medical care for all, the costs of Medicare need not be included in the market basket. Thus, absolute definitions have relative components.

Behind each approach, however, there are truly different concerns about the health of the political economy. Absolute approaches highlight a concern with the well-being of the poorest citizen, while relative approaches highlight a different problem— that of basic inequality. An absolute approach creates an artificial distinction between the problems of want for those at the bottom of the economic order and the problems of inequality. It makes an assertion that a political system can eliminate "want" while preserving inequality. This is more than a definitional statement; it is also an ideological one. The relative approach, in contrast, fosters the impression that all poverty is relative; it demands that the centerpiece of attention be not want, but inequality. This, too, is far more than an exercise in definition. It is the articulation of an ideology. Thus poverty can and must be viewed in both absolute and relative terms.

TABLE 5–1
SHIFTING DISTRIBUTION OF INCOME (constant 1975 dollars)

Income Below Designated Level	Percent of Households Below Designated Level			
	1955	1965	1970	1975
$3,000	12.6%	7.4%	5.3%	4.5%
$5,000	22.9	15.6	12.0	12.0
$7,000	35.7	24.7	19.5	20.3
$10,000	58.3	39.8	32.5	33.1
$12,000	13.1	50.8	42.1	42.0
$15,000	84.3	66.8	56.9	55.4
$25,000	97.2	91.8	87.4	85.7
Median Income	$8,881	$11,867	$13,676	$13,719
Fuchs Point	4,440	$5,933	$6,838	$6,859
Percent below Fuchs Point	19.0%	20.0%	19.2%	20.3%

SOURCE: U.S. Department of Commerce, Bureau of the Census, *Current Population Reports: Consumer Income*, Series P–60 (Washington, D.C.: U.S. Government Printing Office, 1976).

With a focus on income poverty, it is useful to begin the search for a policy-relevant definition by examining the distribution of income among families over time. The distribution of income for U.S. families for the years 1955 through 1975 is given at intervals in Table 5–1. To facilitate comparisons, the dollars are all adjusted to the 1975 price index. Individuals living alone are excluded, so that the main picture can be focused. Among the observations that can be made about the table are these:

1. Real incomes have steadily increased.
2. The relative pattern of income distribution has not been significantly altered in this half of the 20th century.
3. The absolute numbers and the percentages of families below some arbitrary minimum consumption level have dropped dramatically.

Intent of the Definition. The distinction between relative and absolute income definitions of poverty does not exhaust the prob-

lems associated with the definition of poverty thresholds. Mythology clouds our understanding; we observe, for example, the
self-sufficient backwoodsman and see in our mind's eye not a poor
person but Rousseau's noble savage. Ideology affects our judgments particularly as our perceptions of what is and what could be
become confused. It is generally agreed that a definition has to be
constructed with a specific intent in mind. We must constantly
recall the limitations imposed by the necessary assumptions involved in the articulation of a definition.

The Social Security Administration made such a choice when it
selected as a measure of the official poverty line a pretax, post-
transfer, income definition in which a family unit is the unit of
analysis, a year is the time frame, and a market basket adjusted by
cost of living is the threshold. The framers of that definition freely
admit that the choice was made principally because of the availability of data, rather than the conceptual purity of the definition.[10]

Official Poverty Lines

The current market-basket calculation involves a complex, simul-
taneous treatment of 124 family types and more than 500 budget
items. No matter how refined the budget standard, however, inherent in all are disputable judgments made by data analysts. The
current poverty line is structured by an interagency task force
involving representatives from labor, commerce, agriculture,
Housing and Urban Development, and HEW. The dollar lines in
use in 1975 are given in Table 5-2.

Official poverty lines have a significant number of uses, once
their beguiling appearance of objectivity is put into perspective.
Because these lines are given official status, scholars can agree to
use them, despite conceptual and perhaps personal reservations.
Because of their precision, they can be used as an instrument in
a large set of sophisticated statistical tests of progress against
poverty. They are reliable, even if of questionable validity, as estimates of who is poor and under what circumstances. They provide
a common talking point, at least.

There are, to be sure, numerous conceptual and empirical
inadequacies with official poverty lines. To name but four:

1. The measure used fails to deal with how far below the official
poverty line a household is located; a $1 and a $4,000 dollar deficiency both rank a person as poor. To compensate, scholars also

TABLE 5-2
WEIGHTED AVERAGE THRESHOLDS—POVERTY CUTOFFS IN 1975 BY SIZE OF FAMILY AND SEX OF HEAD, BY FARM OR NONFARM RESIDENCE

Size of family unit	Total	Nonfarm Residence			Farm Residence		
		Total	Male head*	Female head*	Total	Male head*	Female head*
1 person (unrelated individual)	$2,717	$2,724	$2,851	$2,635	$2,305	$2,396	$2,224
14 to 64 years	2,791	2,797	2,902	2,685	2,396	2,466	2,282
65 years and over.....	2,572	2,581	2,608	2,574	2,196	2,216	2,187
2 persons	3,485	3,506	3,515	3,460	2,955	2,963	2,834
Head 14 to 64 years	3,599	3,617	3,636	3,530	3,079	3,086	2,933
Head 65 years and over	3,232	3,257	3,260	3,237	2,772	2,772	2,770
3 persons	4,269	4,293	4,317	4,175	3,643	3,652	3,480
4 persons	5,469	5,500	5,502	5,473	4,695	4,697	4,616
5 persons	6,463	6,499	6,504	6,434	5,552	5,552	5,595
6 persons	7,272	7,316	7,322	7,270	6,224	6,230	6,105
7 persons or more	8,939	9,022	9,056	8,818	7,639	7,639	7,647

*For one person (i.e., unrelated individual), sex of the individual.
SOURCE: U.S. Department of Commerce, Bureau of the Census, *Current Population Reports: Consumer Income*, Series P-60 (Washington, D.C.: U.S. Government Printing Office, 1976).

identify a *poverty gap:* the total number of dollars required to bring the total income of every poor family up to the poverty line.

2. The measure used fails to deal with income over a period longer than, or shorter than, one year. Thus, high-income persons experiencing low incomes temporarily are included—for example, the student, or the businessman experiencing short-term losses. Conversely, persons falling into long-term poverty from a high base income are not included as being poor until they have been below the poverty line for one calendar year. Individuals who experience serious income deficiency for only part of a year are excluded from this measure of poverty. Good estimations of the magnitude of "erroneous" inclusion or exclusion have not yet been developed.

3. The measure fails to deal with the problem of wealth—it is an income measure of poverty, not an expenditure measure of poverty. The use of savings and the availability of borrowing are not calculated in this income measure of poverty, despite their obvious importance in estimating capacity to consume.

4. The measure used does not account for in-kind compensation (e.g., housing, autos) or public in-kind welfare payments such as food stamps. Such inclusions could dramatically alter the magnitude of poverty.[11]

THE DEMOGRAPHY OF POVERTY

With an operational definition of income and poverty thresholds established, an examination of the poverty population can begin with counting the persons (or families) with incomes below the appropriate poverty threshold. Describing the poverty population is a bit like describing an ever-changing snowscape. Poverty policy analysts have an interest in the magnitude of poverty and its trend over time. Also significant are its composition and incidence by various subgroups within the polity. *Composition of the poverty population* refers to the percentage of the poor who possess an important common characteristic: age, sex, race, family status. *Incidence of poverty* refers to the percentage of all persons sharing a particular characteristic who are poor. If P = Total population of poor persons, X = All persons within the polity who are over 65, and X_P = Number of aged poor, then $X_P \div P$ yields the composition, while $X_P \div X$ yields the incidence.

Though these terms are commonly confused, they provide the

policy student with very different kinds of information. The composition of poverty is a result of the contribution of each group
to the poverty population; this contribution is the result of the
incidence of poverty within that group and the size of the group
relative to the entire population. Thus the incidence of poverty
among married white males is low (06.4 percent), but its composition relative to the total population is high (17 percent). Conversely, the incidence of poverty among unmarried aged persons who
are black is quite high (61 percent), but the composition is low
(less than 0.02 percent). These results occur because of the relative size of the two groups in society at large. In this section on
the demographics of poverty we will look at some long-term and
short-term trends in poverty, the shifting composition and incidence of poverty in the short term, and the current incidence and
composition of poverty among some policy-relevant groups.

Trends in Posttransfer Poverty

Table 5–3 enumerates persons counted as being poor by the official poverty count. These persons are those in families whose
money income, after the receipt of public payments such as OAS-
DI, AFDC, and SSI, but after the payment of taxes, is less than the
"official threshold" line during the calendar year observed. For
the decade 1965–75, the *magnitude* of official poverty declined by
14 million persons, and the *incidence* of poverty dropped by 3.3
points. The magnitude of relative poverty, as defined by the Fuchs
point, actually increased, due to population growth, while the
share of the poverty population below the Fuchs point declined
only imperceptibly, by one-half point.

TABLE 5–3
OVERALL TREND IN POVERTY REDUCTION, 1965–1976, SELECTED
YEARS, BY OFFICIAL LINES AND BY FUCHS POINT

	Official Poverty Line		Fuchs Point	
Year	No. of Persons	Incidence	No. of Persons	Incidence
1965	39,000,000	15.6	29,900,000	15.6
1968	25,055,000	12.8	28,657,000	14.6
1970	25,516,000	12.6	30,443,000	15.1
1975	25,877,000	12.3	N.A.	N.A.

N.A. = Not available.
SOURCE: Calculated by author from U.S. Census, P–60 Series.

The progress against poverty has not been even among all demographic groups. Tables 5–4 and 5–5 reflect the fact that the greatest strides have been among the aged and the blacks, particularly in the South. The incidence of poverty among the aged has dropped from 28.5 to 15.3, while among southern blacks it has dropped from 50.1 to 36.6.

Composition and Incidence of Poverty

In the past decade, the incidence of absolute poverty has declined by 16.7 percent. This decline has been coupled with important shifts in the composition of poverty, as well as in the incidence among various demographic groups. In Table 5–6, composition percentages are given first, followed by incidence figures in parentheses. The incidence of poverty declined slightly for female-headed families, from 39.8 to 37.5, while the composition of poverty of female-headed families increased by nearly 10 percentage points. This shift is due, of course, to the rapidly rising number of female-headed families in the population at large.

Obtaining an accurate understanding of the shifting poverty problems from demographic descriptions is as difficult as discerning the plot of a motion picture from an examination of a few selected stills. Clearly, the selection of the stills is crucial to one's understanding of the plot. Robert Plotnick and Felicity Skidmore have described the poverty population and its changes over time. They have calculated the probability of being poor, given a particular demographic group (Table 5–7). With important qualifications, this can be taken to mean that the reduction in absolute poverty has not been accompanied by any important shift in the overall patterns of economic distribution which produce poverty.[12]

The Myth of Permanent Poverty

Another important survey, recently completed, has contributed to our understanding of the dynamics of poverty. James Morgan and colleagues at the University of Michigan followed the economic fortunes of 5,000 American families for a decade.[13] The group was selected to be statistically representative of the nation. Morgan and his colleagues have largely destroyed the myth that poverty is a permanent, intractable condition. Only 1 person in 5 who was poor in 1975 had also been poor in each of the previous nine

TABLE 5-4
PERSONS BELOW THE POVERTY LEVEL, BY AGE, 1966–1974*

Year	Number (millions)						Poverty rate (percent)					
	All Persons	Under 14 Years	14 to 21 Years	22 to 44 Years	45 to 64 Years	65 Years and Over	All Persons	Under 14 Years	14 to 21 Years	22 to 44 Years	45 to 64 Years	65 Years and Over
1966......	28.5	10.0	3.8	5.3	4.3	5.1	14.7	17.9	14.3	9.8	11.0	28.5
1967......	27.8	9.4	3.9	4.9	4.2	5.4	14.2	16.9	14.2	9.1	10.4	29.5
1968......	25.4	8.7	3.7	4.6	3.8	4.6	12.8	15.8	13.1	8.2	9.4	25.0
1969......	24.3	8.0	3.5	4.3	3.7	4.8	12.1	14.7	12.2	7.7	8.9	25.3
1970......	25.5	8.5	3.7	4.8	3.8	4.7	12.6	15.7	12.6	8.3	9.0	24.5
1971†.....	25.6	8.4	4.0	5.1	3.8	4.3	12.5	15.9	13.2	8.5	9.1	21.6
1972......	24.5	8.1	4.0	5.0	3.7	3.7	11.9	15.7	12.8	8.2	8.6	18.6
1973......	23.0	7.5	3.9	4.7	3.5	3.4	11.1	15.0	12.2	7.6	8.1	16.3
1974......	23.4	7.9	4.0	4.9	3.4	3.1	11.2	16.0	12.3	7.7	7.9	14.6
1975......	25.9	8.6	4.6	5.7	3.7	3.3	12.3	17.8	14.1	8.8	8.6	15.3

*Excludes inmates of institutions and members of Armed Forces residing in barracks.
†Beginning with March 1972 Current Population Survey, data based on 1970 census population controls.
SOURCE: U.S. Department of Commerce, Bureau of the Census, *Current Population Reports*, Series P–60, nos. 95, 98, and 102 (Washington, D.C.: U.S. Government Printing Office, 1976).

TABLE 5-5
PERSONS BELOW THE POVERTY LEVEL, BY REGION AND RACE OF FAMILY HEAD, 1967–1974*

Year	Number of persons (millions)						Poverty rate (percent)					
	North and West			South			North and West			South		
	All Races	White	Black and Other Races	All Races	White	Black and Other Races	All Races	White	Black and Other Races	All Races	White	Black and Other Races
1967...	14.8	11.7	2.8	13.0	7.2	5.7	10.8	9.4	27.3	22.1	15.3	50.1
1968...	13.3	10.7	2.3	12.1	6.7	5.3	9.5	8.5	21.8	20.4	14.0	46.7
1969...	13.1	10.5	2.3	11.2	6.2	4.9	9.5	8.3	22.2	18.3	12.6	41.0
1970...	14.0	11.4	2.4	11.5	6.1	5.3	10.0	8.9	22.8	18.5	12.4	42.7
1971†...	14.4	11.5	2.6	11.2	6.3	4.8	10.2	9.0	24.2	17.5	12.2	40.0
1972...	13.5	10.2	2.9	10.9	6.0	4.8	9.6	8.0	26.2	16.9	11.5	39.8
1973...	12.9	9.7	2.9	10.1	5.4	4.5	9.1	7.6	26.0	15.3	10.3	36.3
1974...	13.1	9.9	2.8	10.3	5.9	4.4	9.2	7.7	25.2	15.4	10.8	34.9
1975...	14.8	11.5	2.8	11.1	6.2	4.7	10.4	9.0	25.2	16.2	11.4	36.6

*Excludes inmates of institutions and members of Armed Forces residing in barracks.

†Beginning with the March 1972 *Current Population Survey*, data based on 1970 census population controls.

SOURCE: U.S. Department of Commerce, Bureau of Census, *Current Population Reports*, Series P–60, nos. 86, 98, and 102 (Washington, D.C.: U.S. Government Printing Office, 1976).

TABLE 5–6
COMPOSITION AND INCIDENCE OF ABSOLUTE POVERTY, 1966
AND 1975, BY DEMOGRAPHIC STATUS

	1966	1975
Families	83.51% (13.1)	80.34% (10.9)
Male head	59.45% (10.3)	46.15% (07.1)
Female head	24.06% (39.8)	34.19% (37.5)
Unrelated	16.49% (38.3)	19.66% (25.1)
Males	4.60% (29.3)	6.44% (19.9)
Females	11.89% (43.5)	13.22% (28.9)
White	67.66% (11.3)	68.67% (9.7)
Nonwhite	32.33% (39.8)	31.33% (29.3)
Children in family	42.60% (17.1)	42.05% (16.8)
Other family	40.91% (N.A.)	38.29% (N.A.)
65 years or older	17.94% (28.5)	12.82% (15.3)
N =	28,510,000 (14.7)	25,877,000 (12.3)

SOURCE: U.S. Department of Commerce, Bureau of the Census, *Current Population Reports* (Series P–60, Nos. 86, 98, 102).
N.A. = Not available.

years. This means that a scant 0.03 percent of the population can be considered permanently poor by official poverty lines.

On the other hand, 1 American in every 3 fell below the poverty line once in the decade. The structure of poverty is influenced by shifts in marital and family status and changes in work experience. The largest single factor appears to be a shift in family composition. One-third of all divorced persons not remarried within a year fall into poverty.

Three Streams of Current Poverty

An examination of the demographic features of the poverty population in any one year will reveal conditions that are highly similar to those in the year following. This is so despite the fact that there is considerable turnover of the individuals at poverty levels. This is because there are, in fact, three streams of poverty.

The first, and by a large margin the smallest (about 22 percent of all poor, and 0.03 percent of the total population), are those who are experiencing more or less permanent poverty. The persistent poor are estranged from the labor market, also on a more or less permanent basis. They are most likely to be members of families headed by a person who is old, or black, or female, or disabled,

TABLE 5-7

PREDICTED PROBABILITY OF BEING POOR FOR REPRESENTATIVE
GROUPS (ABSOLUTE POVERTY DEFINITION)

		1965	1972
1.	Black, female head with children[a]	.77	.70
2.	Southern, poorly educated black family[b]	.64	.55
3.	Black, urban elderly woman[c]	.55	.40
4.	White, urban elderly woman[d]	.37	.25
5.	Young, well-educated white male[e]	.38	.30
6.	Young, black male[f]	.36	.29
7.	Middle-age female head[g]	.29	.25
8.	Black, male head[h]	.13	.11
9.	Poorly educated, white male head[i]	.14	.11
10.	Elderly couple I—metropolitan white[j]	.06	.04
11.	Elderly couple II—nonmetropolitan black[k]	.65	.51
12.	Middle-age nonmetropolitan family[l]	.08	.07
13.	Well-educated young family[m]	.03	.02
14.	Single, middle-age man[n]	.10	.09
15.	Single, middle-age woman[o]	.14	.12

[a]black, female, family, age 14–29, 9–12 years school, non-South, in SMSA
[b]black, male, family, age 14–29, 0–8 years school, South, not in SMSA
[c]black, female, individual, age 65+, 9–12 years school, non-South, in SMSA
[d]white, female, individual, age 65+, 9–12 years school, non-South, in SMSA
[e]white, male, individual, age 14–29, 13+ years school, non-South, not in SMSA
[f]black, male, individual, age 14–29, 9–12 years school, non-South, in SMSA
[g]white, female, family, age 30–64, 9–12 years school, non-South, not in SMSA
[h]black, male, family, age 30–64, 9–12 years school, South, in SMSA
[i]white, male, family, age 30–64, 0–8 years school, South, in SMSA
[j]white, male, family, age 65+, 9–12 years school, non-South, in SMSA
[k]black, male, family, age 65+, 0–8 years school, South, not in SMSA
[l]white, male, family, age 30–64, 9–12 years school, South, not in SMSA
[m]white, male, family, age 14–29, 13+ years school, South, in SMSA
[n]white, male, individual, age 30–64, 13+ years school, non-South in SMSA
[o]white, female, individual, age 30–64, 13+ years school, non-South in SMSA
SOURCE: Robert Plotnick and Felicity Skidmore, *Progress against Poverty,
1964–1974* (New York: Academic Press, 1975), p.103.

or poorly educated. Most frequently the persistent poor possess
two or more of these demographic characteristics.

A second stream of the poor (for which there are no good
estimates of the magnitude) is composed of those who are counted poor because of the limitations of the poverty definition. Examples are:

1. Students, whose wage and cash transfer income is quite low,
   but whose real consumption of society's goods and services
   might be very high. They are deferring direct consumption
   or receiving compensation in kind rather than in cash.
2. Persons in business or independent professions just getting

started or experiencing a period of downturn in their enterprise. These persons' actual consumption might be high, but
it is because they are using savings or borrowing against
future earnings.
3. Still others whose real economic income is not adequately
   assessed by a cash and transfer income include retired persons living on savings, or living in religious communities, or
   those who directly produce their own consumption goods
   and services.

Estimating the magnitude of this poverty stream is one of the real
unmet needs in poverty research.

Case Poverty

The third (and presumably the largest) stream includes the class
of persons who individually might move in and out of poverty, but
as a class swell the numbers of poor to their present proportions.
The proximate cause of their poverty is unique in each case, but
there are some clear describable factors producing this poverty
which are relevant for public policy.

The longer we think about poverty, the more certain is the
conclusion that it is not solely an economic problem of too few
jobs or a social organization problem of discrimination in opportunities, though both are surely involved. Out of the debate on the
demography and etiology of poverty, only a few consensus propositions emerge:

1. It is a problem of multiple causation, and its solution will
   require multiple paths of action.
2. Poverty cannot be dealt with in anything less than holistic
   terms; strategies to reduce the probability of poverty among
   one class of persons run the risk of increasing the likelihood
   of poverty of some other class of persons.
3. A profile of poverty demands characterization of economic,
   social, psychological, and political elements. Concentration
   on one element uniquely distorts our perception of other
   elements.

One of the most difficult aspects of the problem to be faced, yet
clearly the most important, is the simple fact that poverty involves
specific individuals and families. For all of its ethereal qualities, it
is a concrete problem, not an abstract one. General theories and

complex typologies are critical for the evaluation or selection of poverty policy. But the generalized framework is at times inappropriate and even dangerous. A person who is poor has a very specific problem. Her or his unique poverty is in most instances a complex condition involving immutable characteristics: age, general education, intelligence, sex, and so on. A person's poverty is also structured by characteristics subject to change, such as skills, health, and motivation, and by both immutable and changeable community characteristics. At a general level there exists an important debate about the relative reliance on policies which impact on individual and community characteristics, which are subject to change.

There is a further concern: Strategies to reduce and eliminate poverty must ultimately be adjusted to the needs of the individual household which experiences poverty. It is useful for understanding, though probably impossible in practice, to draw some distinctions in forms of intervention. First, policies pursued by government are segregated into those that have the reduction of poverty as a specific goal and those that have other intents. Antipoverty strategies are further segregated into those that focus on change within the individual or the immediate environment and those that focus on community change. And individually oriented strategies are separated into those that attempt to lead and shape agency practice in terms of the individual and those that attempt to aid the poor to adapt to current conditions in such a way that the threat of poverty is reduced.

Case poverty strategy requires precise application of diagnostic skills in judging the proximate course of poverty and the application of available community resources. From the time of the friendly visitor to that of the contemporary social worker, the profession has carved out its particular role with various means:

1. Programs structured to aid poor families to cope with acute problems of economic functioning. This is a response to the varied, unique, emerging circumstances that produce poverty.
2. Programs structured to aid poor families to gain access to and to utilize services generally available to the community at large, but not readily available to persons experiencing poverty.
3. Programs structured to provide resolution of, or response

to, economic behavior problems that retard the family's capacity to achieve economic independence.[14]

CONCLUSIONS

This chapter has defined poverty in order to describe it, and described it in order to evaluate causal arguments. As James Sundquist pointed out, "That the word itself (poverty) embodies various definitions, each leading logically into its own line of attack, only became apparent as the War on Poverty developed."[15] Definitions of poverty require an examination of both relative and absolute notions of the phenomenon—both are legitimate, but neither is solely legitimate. An exclusive focus on income poverty suggests that a necessary component of comprehensive antipoverty programs must include jobs for those poor who are able to work and who are expected to work, and poverty-free income maintenance programs for those poor outside of the labor market: the aged, the disabled, and the single parents of very young children. Such a dual approach of jobs and income maintenance programs is at the center of the Carter welfare reforms discussed in Chapter 10. Another problem is one of equality of opportunity, or rather the lack of it. This suggests that antidiscrimination laws must be the frontal force of an assault on poverty. A perspective on case poverty leads to a cry for a comprehensive social service strategy; this is also a theme to be taken up below.

Despite the complexities in the analysis of the phenomenon of poverty, one thing is clear. As a polity, we clearly possess the *resources* to abolish absolute poverty. There are those who clearly suggest that we have done so,[16] when the "proper" uses of income and in-kind income flows are included in the definition. Having the resources to eradicate poverty does not mean an automatic commitment to this goal, for it is still necessary to identify a politically possible and economically efficient solution.

NOTES

1. Attempts at reasonably precise definitions of poverty can be traced back many years; see Seebohm B. Rowntree, *Poverty: A Study of Town Life* (London, 1901). Much of the current views on a specific poverty threshold springs from Mollie Orshonsky, "Counting the Poor: Another Look at the Poverty Profile," *Social Security Bulletin*, January 1965, pp. 3–29. Orshonsky in turn acknowledges a debt to Marsha Froeder, "Technical

Note: Estimating Equivalent Incomes or Budget Costs by Family Type," *Monthly Labor Review*, November 1960, pp. 1197–2000, and Milton Friedman, "A Method of Comparing Incomes of Families," *Studies in Income*, vol. 15 (New York: National Bureau of Economic Research, 1952). To bring the technical and ideological aspects of the debate forward, the student should consult *The Concept of Poverty* (Washington, D.C.: U.S. Chamber of Commerce, 1965); H. Watts, "The Iso-Prop Index: An Approach to the Determination of Differential Poverty Income Thresholds," *Journal of Human Resources*, vol. 2 (1967), pp. 3–18; and Bradley Schiller, *The Economics of Poverty and Discrimination* (Englewood Cliffs, N.J.: Prentice-Hall, 1967), chap. 1. Current information on establishing poverty income thresholds can be obtained from Robert Plotnick and Felicity Skidmore, *Progress against Poverty, 1964–1974* (New York: Academic Press, 1975), and the series of reports on methodology found in U.S. Department of Commerce, Bureau of the Census, *Current Population Reports: Consumer Income*, Series P–60 (Washington, D.C.: U.S. Government Printing Office, 1976), p. 60.

2. Chaim I. Waxman, *The Stigma of Poverty* (New York: Pergamon Press, 1977), chap. 1, "The Cultural Perspective."

3. S. M. Miller and Pamela Roby, *The Future of Inequality* (New York: Basic Books, 1970). Miller and Roby discuss both the advantage and disadvantage of the purely consumptive opportunity measure of poverty.

4. See William A. Klein, "The Definition of Income under a Negative Income Tax," Discussion Paper 111–72, Institute for Research on Poverty, Madison, Wisconsin, 1972.

5. Michael M. Weinstein and Eugene Smolensky, "Poverty," forthcoming.

6. John E. Tropman and Alan Gordon, "The Welfare Threat: AFDC Coverage and Closeness in the American States," *Social Forces*, vol. 57 (December 1978), pp. 697–712.

7. Victor Fuchs, "Redefining Poverty and the Redistribution of Income," *The Public Interest* (Summer 1967), p. 97.

8. Orshonsky, "Counting the Poor."

9. U.S. Department of Commerce, Bureau of the Census, "Revisions in Poverty Statistics," *Current Population Reports: Special Studies* (Washington, D.C.: U.S. Government Printing Office, 1976), p. 23.

10. Orshonsky, "Counting the Poor."

11. Tim Smeeding, "Measuring the Economic Welfare of Low-Income Households, and the Anti-Poverty Effectiveness of Cash and Non-cash Transfer Programs," unpublished doctoral dissertation, University of Wisconsin, 1975. See also Martin Anderson, Welfare:"The Political Economy of Welfare Reform in the United States"(Palo Alto, Calif., Hoover Institution Press, 1978).

12. Plotnick and Skidmore, *Progress Against Poverty*, p. 231.

13. James N. Morgan et al., *Five Thousand American Families—Patterns of Economic Progress: Analyses of the Panel Study of Income Dynamics*, 5 vols. (Ann Arbor: Institute for Social Research, University of Michigan Press 1974–1977).

14. Joseph Heffernan, "Impact of a Negative Income Tax on Awareness of Social Services," *Social Work Research and Abstracts,* vol. 13 (Summer 1977), p. 817 ff.
15. James Sundquist, *On Fighting Poverty* (New York: Basic Books, 1969), p. 8.
16. Martin Anderson, *Welfare: The Political Economy of Welfare Reform in the United States.*

CHAPTER 6

CURRENT INCOME SECURITY:

PROGRAMS AND ISSUES

The maintenance of income security for citizens is one of the most fundamental of all governmental roles. Not only does government provide overt income security programs, such as social insurance, public assistance, and means-tested in-kind aids, but there are also numerous indirect income security programs. In a general sense, all that governments do or fail to do has a fundamental impact on income security.

The individual family's consumption opportunities can be aided as much by a tax which is deferred or avoided as they can by a cash benefit from government. There is a term, *tax expenditure*, which describes public revenue foregone by virtue of tax exemptions, deductions, or deferrals, or preferential tax treatment. In fiscal 1975 the special exemption for the aged, blind, and disabled "cost" the federal government $11.7 billion dollars in revenue not obtained. This is 10.5 percent of the direct cash payments.[1] Other federal tax procedures are manifestly designed to promote income security; examples are the federal employment tax credit and retirement income tax deferral.

Governmental programs, such as those for manpower training and development, public employment, and publicly subsidized private employment have income security goals that are every bit as direct as cash and in-kind payments. A significant portion of the mandatory legislation on minimum wage, fair employment practices and pension fund regulations has a manifest income security objective.

Income security objectives thus can be obtained by (1) tax expenditures, (2) general government activity, (3) mandatory legislation regarding the operation of the labor market, (4) publicly provided and publicly subsidized jobs, or (5) cash and in-kind benefits. The fifth category, which includes the most overt income security programs, will be the principal topic considered in this chapter, which reviews the various elements in the structure of the American income security systems.

In the United States, however, there is no system of income security in the sense of a number of interacting and mutually reinforcing programs, acting in concert to achieve a single overall goal. Rather, there is a set of programs which are sometimes contradictory, or at least counterfunctional to one another. Each individual program has a history and a political constituency to which it responds.[2] Hugh Heclo notes that government income security programs "appear confused and tangled to the man in the street because they are confused and tangled, not because devious middlemen have subverted clear and overarching purposes."[3] As we recount in detail in Part III, there is nothing to resemble a political consensus on the goals of an income security system.

While there is no positive goal consensus, there is a strongly held value that individuals should provide for themselves and their families by working in the regular economy. It is also generally agreed that they should save part of their income or otherwise insure themselves against any sudden disruption in their flow of income from work and privately held property. It is recognized, however, that circumstances may arise which will prevent a family from earning its own way. If there is an organizing principle behind our income security system, it is that it is structured around the reason for the disruption in the flow of ordinary income. The certainty of help, the generosity of help, the stigmatic characteristics of income assistance are all fundamentally influenced by the circumstances that place a family in need.

The four principal public components of the income security system are (1) social insurance, (2) public assistance, (3) manpower, and (4) in-kind aid programs. Programs in each of these

categories have reasonably distinct political histories and somewhat less distinct current political environments. But the programs themselves are neither distinct nor rationally integrated,
and this poses a problem for the recipients of public support.

In this chapter we will review the magnitude and growth of the
income security system in relation to the rest of the economy.
Then the essential features of the components of each of the four
elements in the income security system will be discussed.

EXPANSION OF THE INCOME SECURITY SYSTEM

In terms of scale and impact on the remainder of the economy, by
far the most important social welfare development is the income
security system.[4] Perhaps the single most startling aspect of the
income security system has been its rapid expansion in the late
1960s and into the late 1970s.[5] This expansion appears to have
been an acceleration rather than a redirection of long-term trends
(see Table 6–1).

TABLE 6–1
GROWTH OF INSURANCE AND ASSISTANCE PROGRAMS, 1950–1977.

Year	GNP	Personal Income	Wage Income	Social Insurance Benefits	Public Aid Benefits	Property Income
1950	$286.2	$226.1	$147.0	$7.0	$2.3	$72.7
1955	399.3	308.8	211.7	13.1	2.5	86.7
1960	506.0	399.7	271.9	23.9	3.3	109.9
1965	688.1	537.0	362.0	34.2	4.1	150.0
1970	982.4	801.3	546.5	65.4	9.5	207.9
1975	1,528.8	1,253.4	805.7	143.7	20.9	333.5
1977 (est.)	1,869.0	1,517.3	986.5	169.3	21.9	407.6

SOURCE: Table M–39, *Social Security Bulletin,* October 1977, p. 65.

Over the quarter century 1950–75, the greatest growth was in
the social insurance programs, which developed more than three
times faster than the cash assistance programs did (see Table
6–2). Placing the in-kind and manpower programs in historic perspective is more difficult, since they were essentially creatures of
the 1960s.

In the decade 1965–75, public aid expenditures rose more rapidly than the gross national product (GNP), while social insurance
grew more rapidly than the GNP but less rapidly than public aid
(see Table 6–3). In the two years 1975–77 GNP increased more

TABLE 6–2
INCOME SECURITY EXPENDITURES, 1975, AND PERCENTAGE
INCREASE 1970 OVER 1950

	1975 Millions of dollars	1975 Expenditures in 1970 Dollars (per capita) / 1950 Expenditures in 1950 Dollars (per capita) (constant dollars)
Social Insurance		
OASDHI	$66,923	
Unemployment compensation	17,996	1763%
Workers' compensation	4,492	
Veterans' compensation	7,668	172%
Public Assistance		
AFDC	10,495	
SSI	5,180	552%
General Assistance	1,138	
	Fiscal year 1974	
In - Kind Aid		
Food	4,500	∞
Medicaid	10,681 ⎫	
Medicare	5,833 ⎬	➤ 571%
Housing	4,000	∞
Total	$139,506 (actual)	$12,172 (actual)
Percentage share of GNP	9% (1975)	4% (1950)
Manpower programs (1974)	$4,666	∞

SOURCE: Various tables, *Social Security Bulletin,* October 1977.

rapidly than either insurance or public aid expenditures. Spotting
trends in welfare expenditures is, however, far more complex than
looking at simple numbers. The weight of professional evidence
seems to indicate that social insurance expenditures will continue
to rise relative to the economy, while the great expansion in public
aid expenditures seems to have run its course.[6]

TABLE 6–3
RECENT GROWTH RATES IN INSURANCE AND ASSISTANCE
PROGRAMS IN COMPARISON TO GNP (percentage increase)

Time Span	GNP	Social Insurance	Public Aid
1950–65	140%	389%	78%
1965–75	122	320	410
1975–77	23	18	5

SOURCE: Calculated from the *United States Budget in Brief,* various years.

THE STRUCTURE OF CURRENT PROGRAMS

Social Insurance

The *public income security program set* refers to the mix of programs established by law to provide cash benefits to individuals to make up a loss or a deficiency in earnings or property income which prevents a family from participating in an "ordinary" pattern of earnings and consumption.

One component of this set is social insurance programs, a 19th-century invention in which the primary function is the replacement of a portion of the income flow disrupted by a highly specific factor such as death, retirement, disability, unemployment, or industrial accident. Benefit formulas are more or less connected to previous wage history or past contributions to an insurance trust fund. These benefits are generally perceived to be an earned right, and the recipient does not have to demonstrate need. Of the three major social insurance programs operating in this country—old age and survivors' insurance, unemployment insurance, and workers' compensation—the first is a federal program, the second a federal-state venture, and the third principally a state function.

Another component, public assistance programs, are the remaining vestige of the archaic poor laws. They have as their primary function the provision of a minimum level of benefits for citizens in need as a result of a wide variety of circumstances. Benefits are calculated in response to community standards, available resources, and beliefs held about what minimal needs are. The programs are funded out of general revenues, often with more than one level of government sharing fiscal and administrative responsibility. There is little belief in a right to assistance. Eligibility is premised on the proof of need and the willingness of the recipient to comply with often highly specific eligibility rules: being available for work, complying with a search for support from absent fathers, and so on. The programs are often highly stigmatic for the recipient. Their administration is an intergovernmental bureaucratic labyrinth. Of the major assistance programs—Supplemental Security Income, Aid to Families with Dependent Children, and General Assistance—the first is operated by the federal government, the second is a conjoint federal-state operation, and the third is operated by states, counties, or, in some cases, townships.

The third component of the public income security set is manpower training and publicly provided or subsidized job programs. These bear a more indirect relationship to income security programs. There has been a long history of direct relief versus work relief (see Chapter 8). There are millions of Americans with undesirable jobs or no jobs at all, and thus with little income security. There are millions more who hold jobs with skill and wage levels that are far below their capacity. Historically, beyond work relief and general monetary and fiscal stimulation, U.S. governments have been reluctant to do very much. The Employment Act of 1946 established the goal of maximum employment,[7] but the machinery created has been more concerned with inflation levels than unemployment. Since the mid-sixties, however, and particularly since the mid-seventies, there has been more discussion about public responsibility for unemployment and underemployment.

The fourth component, in-kind aid to those in need, has had a checkered political history. On one side there has been a desire to provide aid in kind, rather than cash, to ensure a particular consumption for those who are aided. The fear that the welfare poor will waste public money gives rise to a host of aids in kind. Also, there is a particular desire to use in-kind aid in housing and medical care because of market problems in the housing and medical industries. The composition, structure, and intention of the $30 billion in-kind aid system can most charitably be labeled a political quagmire.

COMPONENTS, STRUCTURE, AND ISSUES OF SOCIAL INSURANCE

All of the major social insurance programs in the United States are employment related. The purpose of this strategy of insurance income security is to provide a flow of income to the worker (or the worker's family) when wage income is disrupted by virtue of death, disability, retirement, unemployment, or work-related injury. Over the years other social goals (health insurance, minimum benefits for the aged and unemployed) have been appended to the social insurance system. These amendments have placed serious operating strains on the system as a vehicle for public insurance. As demands on assistance programs are assumed by the public insurance programs, and as general income equality issues such as tax policies enter into the social insurance debate, it is becoming increasingly unrealistic to speak of social insurance as a separate income security system.

Old Age, Survivors, and Disability Health Insurance: Social Security

Old Age, Survivors, and Disability Health Insurance (OASDHI) is popularly known as social security. Actually, the Social Security Act is the name of the omnibus legislation which created the federal income security system in 1935.[8] The act remains the centerpiece of the public income security system, and OASDHI is the centerpiece of that legislation.

Originally conceived of as an old-age retirement program, the program has since been progressively broadened. Survivors insurance was added in 1939, a disability insurance program in 1956, and health insurance in 1964. Also in 1964 the Council of Economic Advisors recommended legislation, later enacted by Congress, which used the social insurance program to guarantee minimum income to "selected" classes of persons. Since 1964 "revisions" of OASDHI have become a staple before Congress. It is one of the few issues regularly on the congressional agenda which stimulates constituent, as opposed to interest-group, attention. With 32.7 million households dependent on OASDHI for all or part of their current cash income, and with the OASDHI tax being the largest single tax paid by most Americans, it is not surprising that veteran legislators regularly report that whenever OASDHI issues are before Congress, their offices are inundated with inquiries and requests. Unlike interest group-paid lobbyists, who buttonhole congressmen early in the legislative stage (while legislation is incubating in committee), constituents tend to hold off until the bill is on the floor of Congress. This presents problems for the efficient processing of constituent pressure, expert analysis, consideration, and passage. The problem of massive, largely uncoordinated constituent pressure has been commented on by Edward Cowan:

> Although intended to be only a part of retirement income, social security has come to be a principal or sole source of old-age sustenance for millions of elderly persons. It is probable that no other federal issue except the personal income tax touches as many voters or is as closely watched by them.

For elected politicians, whose thoughts are rarely far from the next election, that makes social security a politically dangerous issue. No wonder that Carl Vernon Patton writes ... that "politics will continue to be the largest single influence on policy." The social security crisis, then, is an amalgam of fiscal or actuarial problems and equity issues about taking and giving, all overlaid with acute political sensitivity.[9]

OASDHI is also more heavily laden with ideological overtones than most issues before Congress. At the core of much of the controversy lies the failure to distinguish in OASDHI between a program of public insurance created because of market failure to provide one (see Chapter 4) and a public insurance program created because individual consumers would not care for their own future needs.[10] An additional issue is the degree to which OASDHI should be modified to accomplish social assistance objectives. All of these forces converge to generate two fairly stable, and reasonably evenly matched, contending groups responding to the issues of OASDHI, a group on the Right and one on the Left. The Right asks that (1) OASDHI be funded out of trust funds and not be dependent on general revenues, (2) parity between employee and employer tax payments be retained at a parity of 1:1, (3) benefit schedules be linked to previous tax payments, and (4) a public health insurance program, if there is to be one, should follow "insurance" principles. The Left responds that the so-called insurance principles are but a fog to cover a desire to fund welfare objectives in a regressive tax structure. This group contends that benefits should be structured to current circumstances rather than past contribution to the trust fund, and the so-called trust-fund principle is an accountant's myth. In addition, the health insurance system, if there is one, should be freely designed and not constrained by income insurance security issues.

The Issue of the Social Security Trust Fund. OASDHI is much in the news at the present time, in part because of the fact that the stability of the coalitions of the Left and the Right is breaking down. At the core of the political stability problem is the issue of the resilience of the trust fund. It must be recognized at the outset that the trust fund is essentially a political, not an economic, instrument. It is not like a personal or corporate trust account which will run dry if not properly managed. The use of a segregated tax structure to accomplish social welfare objectives has much to be

FIGURE 6-1
OLD AGE, SURVIVORS, AND DISABILITY INSURANCE PROGRAM,
PROJECTED BENEFICIARIES PER 100 COVERED WORKERS,
1976–2050

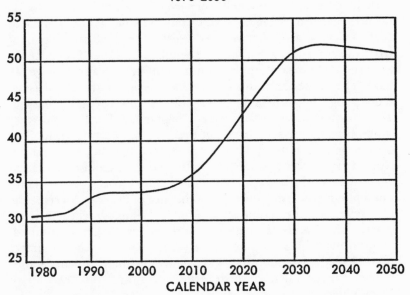

CALENDAR YEAR

PRINCIPAL ASSUMPTIONS:
   Mortality rates were assumed to decline overall by about 15 percent from 1976 to 2050.
   Fertility rates were assumed to continue decreasing to *1.75 children per woman in 1977 and then slowly increase to an ultimate rate of 1.90 children per woman in 2005.*
   Female labor force participation rates were projected to increase to an ultimate level 22 percent greater than the 1975 level. The unemployment rate for the total labor force was assumed to be *5 percent after 1981.*
   Disability incidence rates were projected to continue increasing to a level 33 percent higher than the 1975 level.
   Under these assumptions the population would grow from its level of 223 milion in mid-1975 to 274 million by the year 2015, remaining slightly above that level through the year 2050.
   SOURCE: Edward Cowan, "Background and History: The Crisis in Public Finance and Social Security," in M. J. Boskin (ed.), *The Crisis in Social Security* (San Francisco: Institute for Contemporary Studies, 1977).

said in its favor or disfavor, but both have little to do with the ability of government to finance welfare objectives.

   There are, nonetheless, reasons to be concerned about trust-fund operations. First, the assumptions about the age structure of the population, valid when the legislation was first adopted, are no longer valid. Figure 6–1 shows that the ratio of beneficiaries to covered workers will rise from .31 in 1976 to .51 in 2030.[11] Second, we have simultaneously adopted tax reforms and broadened social security coverage and benefits in such a fashion that the OASDHI tax is the largest single tax paid by most low-income workers, and these workers also receive the lowest amount of cash payment from the program when they are eligible. Continued reliance on a segregated tax does imply continued reliance on a regressive tax base. The presence of this tax makes redesign of the social assistance programs difficult because of the prohibitively high marginal tax rates which result (see Chapter 7). Finally, two very time-immediate issues have put pressure on the trust fund. The trust fund is countercyclical. Taxes exceed benefits during a period of rising wages and lower unemployment, and benefits exceed taxes during periods of falling prices and rising unemployment. Largely as a consequence of the energy crisis, the mid-seventies were a time of both rising unemployment and rising prices. The OASDHI trust funds suffered, as did almost all fiscal institutions. The other immediate pressure was a technical defect in the 1972 legislation which gave newly retiring recipients a double benefit for inflation which resulted in a short-run drain on an already declining trust fund.

Table 6–4 demonstrates some of these pressures on the OASDI trust fund. It also shows that on balance the accounts are far more stable than the political rhetoric would imply.

TABLE 6–4
OASDI TRUST FUND STATUS 1940–1975 (IN MILLIONS OF DOLLARS)

	Net Income	Net Expenditures	Assets
1940	$550	$29	$1,745
1945	1,432	265	6,613
1950	2,362	783	12,893
1955	5,525	4,436	21,141
1960	10,359	10,869	20,828
1965	16,443	15,660	19,698
1970	31,745	29,024	32,616
1975	58,757	64,294	39,947

SOURCE: Table M–5, Social Security Bulletin, October 1976.

Current Tax and Benefit Structures. OASDI and OASDHI payments are made from separate trust funds. These funds are created by tax payment to the fund by wage earners and their employers, plus the interest which is earned by the existing trust. The funds are depleted by payments to individuals and to the vendors of the medical care for recipients. The future viability of a trust fund is determined not by its current bank statements but by actuarial estimations of future demands in relation to future inputs. Rising real benefits, a changing age structure of the population, and inflation all have contributed to short- and long-term pressure on these trust funds.

A number of suggestions have been considered by Congress to ease the pressure on the trust funds. Most seriously debated was an idea to allow for general revenue reimbursement of the trust fund during periods of high unemployment. This was rejected. Instead Congress decided to raise both the tax rate and the base upon which the tax was charged. In 1977 the wage earner paid a tax of 5.85 percent on earnings up to $16,500. The employer paid a similar tax. Nine-tenths of 1 percent of wage tax funded the health insurance trust, and the remainder funded the OASDI trust. Recent legislation changed the formal name of the trust from Old Age, Disability, Survivors Insurance Trust to the Retirement, Survivors, Disability Insurance trust. Table 6–5 shows the changes in rates for both employee and employer contributions to the RSDI and health insurance programs.

The general effect of these changes has been to make the trust fund less vulnerable and to reduce the inherent regressivity of a payroll tax. Congress intended that the increase on lower earners would be slight; a family with a single earner and a $10,000 wage would pay only $20 a year more; the same family earning $16,500 would pay $33 more; and a family earning $17,700 or more would pay $106 more. However, it was the future projection that created the political stir; a family with $30,000 a year in earnings from one worker would be paying $1,030 in social security taxes in 1981. Although the administration announced that federal income tax reforms would reduce this burden, congressmen again found the issue raised by constituents most often during the 1977–78 winter break was higher social security taxes. Employers whose payroll taxes would increase by similar amounts joined in the chorus of objections to the tax reforms within social security. At the start of the second session of the 95th Congress in January 1978, reform of the tax structure of social security was once more a critical issue.

Considerably less media attention was paid to the changes in the

TABLE 6-5
CHANGES IN SOCIAL SECURITY CONTRIBUTION RATES

Wages Received during Calendar Year	RSDI Rate (percent)	HI Rate (percent)	Combined Rate (percent)	Tax Base*
1977	4.95%	0.90%	5.85%	$16,500
1978	5.05	1.00	6.05	17,700
1979–80	5.08	1.05	6.13	22,900
1981	5.35	1.30	6.65	29,700
1982–84	5.40	1.30	6.70	36,000
1985	5.70	1.35	7.05	38,100
1986–89	5.70	1.45	7.15	40,200
1990 and after	6.20	1.45	7.65	42,600

* Estimated.
SOURCE: Calculated from Table M–5, *Social Security Bulletin*, vol. 40, no. 10 (October, 1977).

benefit schedule (see Table 6–6). The benefit schedule was increased by 5.9 percent in June 1978.

TABLE 6-6
EXAMPLES OF MONTHLY SOCIAL SECURITY PAYMENTS
(EFFECTIVE JUNE 1977)

Benefits can be paid to:	Average Yearly Earnings After 1950 Covered by Social Security						
	$923 or less	$3,000	$4,000	$5,000	$6,000	$8,000*	$10,000*
Retired worker at 65	114.30	236.40	278.10	322.50	364.50	453.10	502.00
Worker under 65 and disabled	114.30	236.40	278.10	322.50	364.50	453.10	502.00
Retired worker at 62	91.50	189.20	222.50	258.00	291.60	362.50	401.60
Wife or husband at 65	57.20	118.20	139.10	161.30	182.30	226.60	251.00
Wife or husband at 62	42.90	88.70	104.40	121.00	136.80	170.00	188.30
Wife under 65 with one child in her care	57.20	125.00	197.20	272.60	304.20	339.80	376.60
Widow or widower at 65 if worker never received reduced benefits	114.30	236.40	278.10	322.50	364.50	453.10	502.00
Widow or widower at 60 if sole survivor	81.80	169.10	198.90	230.60	260.70	324.00	359.00
Widow or widower at 50 and disabled if sole survivor	57.30	118.30	139.20	161.30	182.40	226.60	251.10
Widow or widower with one child in care	171.50	354.60	417.20	483.80	546.80	679.80	753.00
Maximum family payment	171.50	361.40	475.30	595.10	668.60	792.90	878.50

*Maximum earnings covered by social security were lower in past years and must be included in figuring average earnings. This average determines the payment amount. Because of this, amounts shown in the last two columns generally won't be payable until future years. The maximum retirement benefit generally payable to a worker who was 65 in 1977 was $437.10.
SOURCE: Department of Health, Education, and Welfare, Social Security Administration, Washington, D.C., 1977.

Unemployment Compensation

The general purpose of unemployment compensation is to preserve a regular flow of income to normally employed workers during periods of involuntary unemployment. Congress in 1935 established a tax incentive system designed to stimulate state action to create such a program. The current program has its specific legislative origins in the Social Security Act of 1935, but its historic antecedents can be traced much further back.[12] In 1954 former federal employees were extended coverage; in 1958 exservicemen were covered, and in amendments in 1970 and 1971 longer term unemployed persons were provided benefits.

Administering Agencies. This program is administered by divisions in the 50 states, the District of Columbia, Puerto Rico, and the Virgin Islands under the supervision of the Manpower Administration, U.S. Department of Labor. Within reasonably precise guidelines the states, and other jurisdictions, are free to establish their own administrative procedures.

Financing. The apparent desire of Congress in 1935 was to stimulate each state to establish its own unemployment insurance program rather than a single national system, as was the case with OASDHI. The device selected to "stimulate" state action was a tax offset measure. Under this procedure the employer pays a federal payroll tax of 3.2 percent on all wages paid, up to $4,200. Of this payment, 2.7 percent may be offset to fund the benefits paid in an approved state program. The remaining 0.5 percent pays for the federal supervision program and, by congressional authorization, the administration of the state program.

States may set the payroll tax at a rate higher than 3.2 percent; all except 0.5 percent is credited to the state account. States also may charge a rate lower than 3.2 percent if the lower rate is based on the employer's prior experience with unemployment among its employees. This is called *experience rating.* Employees with good employment records are federally forgiven the difference between 3.2 percent and whatever they are actually charged. As a result of this experience rating, tax rates can and do vary within and among the states. There are a number of different systems of rate determination which use different factors and different methods of measurement. Interstate variation in this payroll tax can be an important element in interstate competition for new plant locations. In 1977 the national average contribution rate hovered around 1 percent of taxable payrolls. The ecopolitical issues of experience rating are discussed below.

In 1971, 1974, and 1975, the federal government, using general federal revenues, adopted temporary legislation extending the duration of benefit eligibility in an effort to meet the emergency needs of unemployed in the recession then occurring.

Benefit Schedules. Just as there are interstate variations in the taxes employers pay, there is also interstate variation in the calculation, magnitude, and (to some extent, prior to the temporary federal laws) the duration of unemployment benefits. Typically eligibility is established by a set number of weeks in covered employment and cessation of employment for reasons not related to individual performance. One of the major issues in unemployment is whether or not persons unemployed because of a strike are eligible.

The level of benefit is set at a fixed percentage of the weekly (in five states, annual) wage with minimum and maximum amounts. The usual pattern is to have the benefit approximately equal to 50 percent of the average weekly pay before taxes, not to exceed a maximum amount. Some unions have negotiated supplemental unemployment benefits which bring this up to 90 percent of the weekly wage. Because in periods of unemployment workers are free from transportation and other costs related to working, some find their take-home income actually higher than normal. Although the practice is in fact illegal, workers may be persuaded to accept jobs with the awareness that the unemployment income is really part of the compensation. A student planning to return to school may view the termination of a job on Labor Day as the means for obtaining a "bonus wage." So do other part-year workers who seek compensation from unemployment funds for planned inactivity.

Other Benefits. In addition to the compensation, the state programs are required to have job counseling and job procurement programs. As a condition of eligibility, recipients are required to accept a "suitable" job if one is offered. The idea is that employment at the highest skill level previously held is to be maintained. Pragmatically, the definition of suitable employment can be a political, legal, or bureaucratic issue.

Issues in Unemployment Compensation. In addition to its income maintenance function, a comprehensive unemployment program cushions the shock of economic downturns and serves as a highly significant economic stabilization instrument. It is capable of aiding in the preservation of work skills acquired through expensive training by reducing the pressure to accept jobs at lower skill levels. Careful designs of the tax incentives structured into the experience rating may encourage (or discourage) employers in regularizing their hiring and layoff policies.

Because of these reasons there is a clear collective interest in unemployment insurance, and thus there is a clear need for a public unemployment policy. Disagreement abounds, however, with respect to the objectives, mechanisms, and consequences of current and proposed unemployment insurance programs. The chief controversies at this time are centered on three pivotal issues:

1. How much should the system serve as a hedge against poverty, and how much should it serve more broadly conceived income insurance goals?
2. What restrictions on worker coverage, benefit schedules, eligibility, and disqualification are requisite for program integrity?
3. What are the implications of answers to Question 2 for the manner in which the program is financed?

These broad, pivotal issues are generally debated in response to highly specific policy problems or proposals such as:

1. How should compensation programs operate under conditions of a labor-management dispute?
2. How should the experience rating of employees affect tax liability?
3. Should the benefit schedule be influenced by wealth, other family income, number of dependents, and so on, as well as previous wages?
4. Are separate state programs justified in terms of the contradictory pressure to adapt the program to local political and economic conditions and the need to serve broad national policies?

On each policy issue there are hard choices to be made, and these cannot be intelligently made without a comprehensive view of the ultimate sociopolitical objectives of unemployment compensation.

Workers' Compensation

Workers' compensation programs provide medical care and rehabilitation services, as well as disability and death benefits, to workers and their survivors for job-related injuries. With one exception, these programs are state responsibilities, and there is little uniformity in the benefit levels, mechanism of judging the size of the benefit, method of disbursing the benefits, or how the tax is raised to pay for the programs. Nonetheless, workers' compensation is an important part of this nation's income security system. In 1975, workers, or their survivors, received $4.5 billion in benefits and medical-rehabilitation payments.

In virtually all states the workers' compensation program is funded by a tax on employers only. These funds are used to establish a state workers' compensation trust fund. Work-related injuries are defined by both case law and statutory legislation. Long delays between the injury and the benefit are the rule rather than the exception. Calculating the benefit to reflect actual loss is difficult to accomplish. Whether the loss of a limb should be compensated the same for active and sedentary workers, for example, is a difficult issue. Increasingly, responsibility for work injuries has shifted to tort law. Employers are often able to escape the tax if they demonstrate they are insured for such damage claims, yet often the insurance proves after the fact to be inadequate. The question of responsibility for occupational illness, as opposed to industrial or workplace accidents, is not resolved. Nor is there agreement regarding the relative responsibility of worker and employer for the safe conduct of work.

The exception to the morass of unstructured state law is the black lung program, whereby a federal program of taxation, inspection, and benefit disbursement was instituted for coal miners disabled by a tubercular illness common to, and almost exclusive to, individuals who had worked for a long while in underground coal mines. It is funded by a tax on mining itself paid by mine owners. It has been labeled by some as the model of future worker compensation programs, reflecting the shift from insurance to tort procedure in income security for industrial and occupational disability.

Social Insurance Programs: A Concluding Note

Increasingly, social insurance is part of a national income security system that exists apart from an antipoverty or minimum income security program.[13] The insurance versus assistance debate has long ago given way to the question of how well a particular program redistributes income from one income or demographic class to another, and what welfare objectives are thereby accomplished. Social insurance programs seem to be destined to be the principal machinery to be used to "insure" that a worker or the worker's family will have some predictable share of real purchasing power preserved at retirement or if wage income is disrupted by death, disability, or temporary unemployment. Social insurance is indeed the income security program of those who participate in the mainstream of the American economy. Public assistance, discussed below, provides income security for those on the borderline of the economy.

PUBLIC ASSISTANCE PROGRAMS

Aid to Families with Dependent Children

Aid to Families with Dependent Children (AFDC), the largest public assistance program, was adopted to provide for the care of dependent children who are deprived of the support of two parents because of the death, divorce, disability, or desertion of one parent when insurance (public or private) is absent. Increasingly, it has become financial aid for single parenthood. The key is that unlike OASDHI and unemployment compensation, in AFDC eligibility is based on status, a single-parent family, and established need. The program provides financial and in-kind assistance to meet some of the consumptive needs of the family. In addition, the program has a legislative mandate to provide such help as is necessary to assist the family to attain, regain, or retain a capability for self-support.

Though the concept of direct relief in the client's own home or that of a relative (outdoor relief) may be traced back to the poor laws of 1601, it was not until 1911 that the first programs of outdoor relief specifically for single parents were adopted on a statewide basis (see chapter 8). The extant program was first legislated in 1935 as Title IV of the Social Security Act. In 1950 aid was extended to cover the consumptive needs of the parent or other caretaker with whom the dependent child was living. In 1961, aid was extended to two-parent families if income support is unavailable because of incapacity or unemployment of the non-caretaker parent. This program operates separately as the AFDC-U program.

In 1962 added emphasis was placed on the rehabilitation programs. In 1967 the conditions of financial aid were altered to facilitate and encourage recipients to seek and retain jobs, and a separate subprogram, the Work Incentive Program, was initiated to provide work training and employment services. First in 1950, but again more stringently in 1975, amendments were passed which strengthened the role of federal and state governments in collecting support payments from parents, typically fathers who were not contributing to the support of their children.

Administering Agency. In 1978, the Assistance Payments Administration of the Federal Department of Health, Education, and Welfare administers federal grants to the states for the purpose of this program. The states in their turn either administer the program directly or supervise its administration at the county level.

Financing. States are free to select between two methods of reimbursement for their cash payments. Under the AFDC formula, the federal government pays five-sixths of AFDC payments, up to $18 times the number of recipients, and a variable portion in excess of $18 but less than $32. The variable portion is called the *federal percentage;* this is set according to the states' relative per capita income with the formula:

$$1 - 0.05\left(\frac{\text{State per capita income}}{\text{U.S. per capita income}}\right)^2$$

States bear the entire cost of monthly benefits in excess of $32 per month per person. In addition, states must pay 50 percent of the cost of administering the program and 25 percent of the cost of providing social services which are aimed at the rehabilitation of clients.

An alternative formula for reimbursement of cash payment is:

$$1 - 0.45\left(\frac{\text{State per capita income}}{\text{U.S. per capita income}}\right)^2$$

for the entire money payment. This will be no less than 50 percent nor greater than 83 percent of the total state expenditures for cash payments in AFDC. The federal share of administrative and social service expenditures remains the same. As grants have increased and the $32 limit has remained static, the attractiveness of the latter (the "Medicaid") formula has increased; over 35 states now use it. One consequence of the changed formula for the federal share of the cash payments is that over the past few years not only have costs increased, but the federal portion has also increased from 44 percent in 1950 to 51 percent in 1960 to 65 percent in 1975, and the federal proportion has continued to rise at about 1 percent per year. This growth was compounded by the fact that it was perceived by federal administrators and Congress as being uncontrolled. Expenditures, once incurred by the states, forced federal appropriations. Thus, federal legislators were required to respond to state decisions.

Calculation of Benefits. There are in the federal AFDC system 54 welfare jurisdictions: the 50 states plus the District of Columbia, Puerto Rico, Guam, and the Virgin Islands. Administrative authority is further delegated to the counties by 22 states, while 28 states have programs administered by state agencies. The great diversity of administrative structures naturally leads to considerable variation in administrative practices, making both generalization and interstate comparisons difficult.

There is something called *total basic need* for each applicant family which takes into account individual needs at a level of detail that is staggering. The actual rent paid, whether or not the family has to travel to do its laundry, what the reasons are for a telephone in the home, in what grade level the children are, are only some of the factors that influence the family's "total basic need."

If "total basic need" is less than *countable income*, the family is eligible. Countable income, like total basic need, is determined in accordance with the varied administrative procedures of the 54 jurisdictions. Basically, a family's gross income is established, and from that amount some income is "disregarded"; gross income minus the disregard determines countable income. If a family has no other income, the benefit equals all or a portion of the need for that family. While federal legislation requires each jurisdiction to have a needs standard, it does not actually require a state to pay that amount. Most states (40) have a maximum payment schedule which is the amount a family with no income actually receives; this was $60 per month in Mississippi in 1972 and $350 per month in Michigan the same year. For families with income from nonemployment sources, often called *unearned income*, the benefit in most cases is reduced dollar for dollar. Income "earned" by children in school is disregarded, as is the first $30 plus one-third of adult earnings. Certain costs of employment—uniforms, transportation, day care—are also disregarded.

There is a great deal of evidence to suggest that there are profound differences in the way all of these calculations are made,
even within one jurisdiction. Because of this social workers at the
line level, by their unique interpretation, really control the preservation or promotion of incentives to seek work. Some social workers allow recipients to keep a large fraction of their benefits as
income increases, while others allow them very little. One problem
that has been particularly troublesome is that the rules often work
differently for determining eligibility and determining benefits.
Thus the head of a family on welfare can obtain a job and still
receive substantial help, while a second family, never on welfare
but otherwise in identical circumstances, is not eligible for any aid.
Because of such apparent inequities in the administration of
AFDC, which appear to be inherent in the structure of the program, the pressure for its replacement remains strong.[14]

Issues in AFDC.   In a very real sense the current AFDC programs
continue to exist simply because would-be reformers cannot agree
on the shape of reform. There are few defenders of AFDC as we
know it; presidential aspirants as diverse as George McGovern
and Ronald Reagan have agreed that the program ought not to be
amended and corrected, but fundamentally restructured. Both of
these candidates suffered severe political losses because they
dared to propose a direction for the reform effort. At the core of
the reform problem is the fact that virtually everyone's second
choice is to retain AFDC rather than move reform in the "wrong"
direction.

In 1977, 94 percent of AFDC benefits went to those who otherwise would have been poor. For the 11.2 million individuals (3.6
million families) on AFDC, the program meant the difference
between extreme deprivation and marginal subsistence. This assumes, however, that the program itself is behaviorally neutral.
/ Critics argue that the structure of aid encourages family breakups,
withdrawal from the labor force, diminished savings, unplanned
migrations, and a whole host of behavioral patterns to which the
program then responds. Others argue that such charges are sim-
plistic. Policy options to encourage work, discourage family
breakup, promote savings, and so on are severely limited, and
blaming AFDC programming dodges the critical issues. If we wish
to encourage work, we must raise the disregards and help more,
not fewer, persons. Extending aid to male-headed (i.e., two-parent) families is very expensive, but perhaps desirable. However, it

is unlikely to have much impact on marriage and marriage dissolution patterns.

This program more than any other has become the symbol of a need for reform. AFDC has become the culprit in the "welfare mess," but to some this mess means insensitive bureaucracies, inadequate benefits, laggard efforts to seek out and meet the needs of female-headed families; to others it is a program which is growing uncontrollably, encouraging the very behavior to which it responds, taxing the worthy poor to aid the unworthy poor. The debate over AFDC from 1965 to 1978 is reviewed in Chapter 10.

Supplemental Security Income

Conceptually, Supplemental Security Income (SSI) started out as a simple, straightforward notion. The concept was of a new federal program for the adult categories (aid to the blind, the disabled, and those over 65) funded by the general revenues of the federal government, administered by the Social Security Administration. The program would establish nationally uniform standards of eligibility and provide a single national benefit schedule. The benefit reduction schedule would also be precise and clean. Intergovernmental funding conflict would disappear, interstate differences in benefit would vanish, and the intercase differences created by caseworker-determined "basic need schedules" and "countable income estimates" would no longer plague welfare administrators. The measure would, in addition, provide fiscal relief to the states. A program of such promise had to disappoint some persons, and it did.

The legislation detailed a national minimum benefit of $130 for a single individual and $195 for a married couple (raised in 1976 to $157 and $236, respectively). It was originally thought that this benefit would replace the food stamp subsidy for aided individuals. The first $20 of income from any source would be disregarded. In addition, the first $65 of employment income would be disregarded. Of remaining income, 50 percent of employment income and 100 percent of income from other sources would be counted against the benefit (see Table 6–7). Sixty-five years was established as the eligibility age for both men and women, and precise, federally specified and nationally uniform definitions of blindness and disability were also provided by the statute.

Rather specific tests of wealth were set in the statute to deter-

TABLE 6–7
BENEFIT SCHEDULE FOR SINGLE SSI RECIPIENT WITH EARNINGS
OR UNEARNED INCOME

Earnings*	Benefit	Unearned Income†	Benefit
0	$130	0	$130
65	130	20	130
85	130	85	65
105	120	150	0
205	70		
305	20		
345	0		

*For an aged, blind, or disabled worker with no unearned income.
†Unearned income, with trivial exceptions, refers to income from any source except employment.
Note: A recipient with $85 in unearned income *and* $85 income would receive a benefit of $55, by this formula:
Benefit = 130 −1.00 (unearned income −20) − .50 (earned income −65)[1]
1.00(−85 if unearned income is zero)

mine eligibility. In 1976, people in their own homes of greater than $25,000 value, regardless of their equity, are not eligible. Bank accounts, cash value of life insurance, equity in automobiles, and "other things of value" have specific dollar limits. Assets over the limits are counted against the benefit; thus an individual with a $100 eligibility and a $2,000 savings account ($500 above the allowed amount) cannot receive a benefit for five months. Stocks and bonds must be disposed of before being eligible; a person with $1,500 in stocks must put it into savings account form in order to become eligible. The variations in administration are such that it is likely that a $3,000 antique chest of drawers would be ignored, but a $3,000 motorboat would have to be sold. The treating of assets under SSI proved to be just as troubling as it had been under the old categorical aids program, or as it is currently under AFDC or General Assistance.

General Assistance

General Assistance is *the* residual program of the income maintenance system. Its function is to provide aid to those not covered anywhere else. Aid is provided in cash and in kind and is typically of short duration. It is virtually impossible to make broad statements about General Assistance programs. There are more than 5,000 units of government operating some semblance of General Assistance programs. Even where there is statewide administration, which occurs in only 15 states, local practice typically means wide discrepancies in intent and performance.

Administering Agency. In 15 states General Assistance is administered by the same agency which operates the statewide AFDC program. In nine of those states, supervision and reporting are the only statewide functions. In 17 states, each locality is required to have General Assistance programs, but their dimension is unspecified. In nine states there is no state responsibility at all.[15]

Benefit Schedules, Financing, and Services. General Assistance is the last operating vestige of the 1601 poor laws. Local programs vary from comprehensive, well-financed, highly professional operations to nonexistent programs. Benefit schedules, where present, are varied; often benefits are merely the judgment of a local officeholder, from which there is no effective appeal. Services, too, range from highly professionalized human service networks to common cracker-barrel philosophizing on the part of the aid-giver.

Table 6–8 reflects the relative growth of AFDC and General Assistance. The secular trend is very clear; while General Assistance and AFDC were of similar magnitude in 1945, today AFDC dwarfs General Assistance. Despite this, General Assistance remains a critical program in the income security system.

Issues in General Assistance. General Assistance violates nearly all of the criteria for effective income support programs. While it aids only the poor, it fails to reach many who *are* poor. Of the poor it does reach, the program is inequitable across geographic lines. It appears to be corrosive of work effort for those it helps; it encourages migration to obtain relief; it is stigmatic and clearly violates the civil rights of many of those it is designed to aid. No one will defend the program as currently structured, and like AFDC, it continues to exist only because of the failure of comprehensive reform packages.

Manpower and Training Programs

Employment training and direct, publicly stimulated employment opportunities are the third component of the income security system. In 1976, the federal outlays for training, employment, and other labor services reached $6.6 billion, and they were expected to reach $7.2 billion in 1977. This compares with $11.2 billion in assistance payments and $73.1 billion in OASDI and unemploy-

TABLE 6–8
GENERAL ASSISTANCE AND AFDC CASES AND EXPENDITURES,
1945–1975

Year	AFDC Cases (in thousands)	ADFC Expenditures (in millions)	% Growth	GA Cases (in thousands)	GA Expenditures (in millions)	% Growth
1945 274	$149.5	266.0%	257	$86.3	239.3%
1950 651	547.2	11.9	413	292.8	−26.9
1955 602	612.2	62.4	314	214	49.3
1960 803	994.8	65.3	431	319.5	−18.4
1965 1,054	1,644.1	195.4	677	260.6	142.7
1970 2,552	4,857.2	64.5	1,056	632.4	80
1975 3,553	7,990.8	16.9*	977	1,138.1	−.9*
1976 3,571	9,348.9	8.6*	905	1,127.5	.13*
1977 (est) .3,608	10,155.6		899	1,285.3	

SOURCE: Calculated from various tables, Social Security Bulletin, vol. 40, no. 10
(October 1977).
*Annual rates of growth.

ment insurance payments. This comparison underestimates the
actual dollars spent by all governments in employment and training programs, but it is fair to say that in recent years these expenditures have lagged behind assistance expenditures by about 25
percent. However, the gap is being rapidly closed.

The increasing emphasis on a jobs strategy raises some fundamental issues about manpower policy. The population in need of
manpower services includes some persons who are well educated
as well as those with very limited education; it includes the handicapped as well as the able-bodied. It includes victims of discrimination and those who lack a skill that is marketable on the labor
market. The policy target of manpower policy is diffuse. It includes (1) a response to the problems of structural unemployment, (2) a response to the problem of aggregate unemployment,
and (3) specific aids to those disadvantaged in employment security by virtue of handicap, discrimination, low skills, inadequate
training, and a large number of personal and structural factors
that stand in the path of full-time employment at a poverty-free
wage.

The U.S. federal government's direct involvement in manpower policy can be conveniently dated to the passage of the Manpower, Development, and Training Act of 1962. Earlier legislation, going back to the New Deal work relief programs, contain the idea of linking income security and job opportunity policy. In the New Deal legislation, employment policy was not as important as relief policy and economic stabilization policy. The Manpower Development and Training Act was the first clearly manpower policy. It was originally conceived as a response to structural unemployment, and the program's early emphasis was on experienced workers whose skills had become obsolete. Helping to upgrade the skill of the handicapped and disadvantaged had a lower priority. Providing employment skills and opportunity to the welfare-dependent poor was a very minor aspect of the Manpower Development and Training Act.

The economic recovery of the mid and late 1960s, with its corresponding low unemployment, led to a shift of focus. Under the Economic Opportunity Act of 1964 and the Public Assistance Amendment of 1967, a number of programs were adopted: (1) JOBS, (2) Job Corps, (3) WIN, and (4) CETA.

JOBS. Job Opportunities in the Business Sector was principally aimed at the able-bodied but long-term unemployed. Coadministered by the Manpower Administration and the National Alliance of Businessmen, the program provided contracts to private firms to hire and train the chronically unemployed. Basically targeted to low-skill jobs, the program operated as a subsidized employment program, with the subsidy going to the employer. This program has been largely replaced by Title I of the Comprehensive Employment Training Act of 1973.

Job Corps. The target population of the Job Corps was poverty youth who were not in school. Trainees were taken to Job Corps Centers, where they received basic education, employment training, and job counseling. The trainee's allowance was structured to encourage completion of the program. Now operated by the Department of Labor, the program is expected to provide approximately 22,000 training slots each year.

The program has suffered a bad press because the start-up cost of the various centers appeared to be very high. Cost/benefit studies have generally suggested that these programs are not very cost effective, and the program seems destined for extinction.[16]

WIN. The Work Incentive Program was authored in 1967 as an amendment to the AFDC title of the Social Security Act. The program offered both a carrot and a stick to encourage mothers of school-aged children to reenter the labor market. Some success has been claimed for the program, and massive failure has also been asserted. At the time the legislation was adopted, the effective tax rate in general AFDC was also changed, making it difficult to assess the impact of WIN.[17] One of its major functions was to track AFDC recipients back into the labor force. However, only 30 percent of the adults receiving AFDC track through the program; the remaining are either not screened (approximately 30 percent or are screened out (approximately 40 percent).

The program, now called WIN-two, has shifted its emphasis from training to job placement, but it continues to experience difficulty in producing a cost/benefit ratio in excess of 1. This program also appears targeted for extinction if the Carter program for jobs and income is adopted (see Chapter 10).

CETA.   The Nixon-Ford administrations were somewhat committed to the proposition that welfare-oriented manpower policies were destined to failure, but they were inclined to support a broader conception of manpower policy. A congressional appropriation for a public employment program was tied to legislation which would coordinate these disparate programs. In 1970 Nixon's veto message revealed a desire for coordinating training and placement programs but a disinclination to fund public jobs. Two years later, in an election year and with unemployment going over 6 percent, Nixon did sign an emergency employment act which provided $2.25 billion for public jobs.

This was modified in 1973 into CETA, which had three separate titles, two of which have become significant. Title I provides on-the-job-training in public and nonprofit corporations for persons without employment skills, and Title VI provides Public Service Employment (PSE) for persons with skills but no employment opportunities. Such persons are given jobs in local governments which are federally funded. Both Title I jobs, called CETA jobs, and Title VI jobs, called PSE jobs, are for limited duration. That is, one person may not remain on such a job for more than one year. PSE jobs, unlike CETA jobs, have no family income eligibility test.

Early evidence does not support charges of failure or claims of success for CETA. It is clear, however, that CETA functions more like a system of revenue sharing than a manpower policy. This is to say that CETA programs, currently financed at $2.1 billion, have not dramatically altered employment practices of local governments.

Dissatisfaction with specific manpower policies remains high—revenue sharing and decentralized planning of CETA seem to have been oversold. Categorical programs have had difficulty in demonstrating their success. The allure of jobs as an alternative to direct income support remains high.

IN-KIND PROGRAMS

A thorough review of the income security system must pay attention to those programs that provide goods or services in kind in lieu of cash payments to the individual. In-kind programs increase a household's opportunity for consumption, but they do so in a restricted way. The general argument for provision in kind rather than in cash is that certain goods and services are so essential that the government must make extraordinary efforts to ensure that everyone has at least a minimum. Three conditions are frequently cited for direct provision rather than simply providing cash to let people buy what they think they need. The conditions are: (1) defective choices by the consumer/recipient, (2) problems in ordinary market procedures, and (3) the desirability of expanding social controls.

Food, shelter, and medical care are obviously critical for the support of life. It is sometimes argued (though the empirical support is weak or nonexistent) that some persons, left to their own devices with cash alone, will squander their money on beer and color television sets, leaving too little to buy the essentials. Provision in kind assumes that essentials will be available even if recipients squander their cash resources.

Not all goods and services trade on the open market with equal facility. Even if low-income families suddenly had moderate incomes, they might not be able to purchase goods and services such as housing and medical care because the market could not respond rapidly enough to the new demand. Because of technological and other kinds of delay on the supply side, the new demand for housing, for example, would only force up prices, leaving the low-income family in the same housing, but paying more rent. Not only to bypass ordinary market adjustment delays, but also to avoid unintended windfall profit to providers (landlords, doctors, etc.), the government provides the good directly.

It is by no means clear that public provision really solves these problems. The economic theory of public provision of consumer goods outside the marketplace has been heavily criticized by people of all political persuasions.[18]

One thing is reasonably clear: In-kind provision of directly consumable goods and services by welfare populations enhances the social control of the program. If society wishes to extract a price in the form of control for the provision of welfare, in-kind transfers are the way to do it. In-kind regulation can be quickly written to force new modes of behavior by both recipient and provider. If we do not wish the poor to have access to abortions, we simply strike that service from the list of approved medical procedures; if we wish the poor to live on the east side we build the housing project there; if we wish to make dependency visible we ask people to buy their food with stamps rather than with cash. Readers of this text might object to any of these purposes, but that does not mean that in-kind provisions are purposeless.

When the growth in assistance programs leveled off in the mid-seventies, a new growth sector, in-kind aids, continued to transform the shape of the American income security system. The three major in-kind aids restricted to low-income households are the: (1) food stamp, (2) medical care, and (3) public housing programs. Table 6-9 reflects the growth patterns of these means-tested programs. Collectively, these programs account for nearly one quarter of the real growth in domestic public expenditures, but they amount to considerably less than 1 percent of the gross national product. Nonetheless, there is a widespread perception that in-kind aids are a jumble of overlapping and inconsistent benefits which treat people in similar circumstances unequally.

Food Stamps

Giving food to the poor is hardly a modern innovation. The charity basket and the soup line were once the symbols of poor relief. Contemporary food programs have as their ostensible intent to improve the nutritional quality of diets of low-income families. In fact, the expanding food stamp program has become a major income security program. The federal government entered into the business following World War II with programs to distribute surplus food purchased by the farm price stabilization program. It made simple sense to dispose of these surpluses by giving them

TABLE 6–9
GROWTH OF IN-KIND PROGRAMS, 1965–1974

	Expenditures (in millions)			Recipients (in thousands)		
	Fiscal Year 1965	Fiscal Year 1969	Fiscal Year 1974	1965	1969	1974
Food						
Food stamps	$36	$251	$2,865	633	3,224	13,536
Commodities	213	272	281	2,238	2,544	233
Medical care						
Medicare	—*	6,299	10,680	—*	13,000	16,900
Medicaid	—*	2,275	5,833	—*	9,500	24,279
Housing						
Low-rent public housing	236	352	1,207	30	35	1,109
Public Law 235	—*	1	401	—*	4	419
Public Law 236	—*	—*	519	—*	*	294
Rent supplements	—*	5	249	—*	13	148

*Not in operation.

to the poor. Over the years, however, farm price stability programs adopted other methods than direct purchase of food commodities. In addition, surplus foods were not necessarily nutritious foods. Problems of corruption and administrative malfeasance further darkened the reputation of the commodities program. An Edward R. Murrow television documentary, "Hunger in America," further heightened awareness of the paradox of "the bread basket of the world" not providing adequate food to all of its citizens.

After a series of false starts, the food stamp program in its present form was adopted in 1964. At that time it was not required of the states; they could choose to participate in the food stamp program or remain in the commodity surplus program. They could not do both, but they were free to do neither. Standards of eligibility and levels of aid were basically discretionary with the states. It was not until 1971 that national eligibility standards were set, and the program did not become mandatory until 1973. Since that time funding has been open ended; the federal government pays the entire cost of the coupons and 62.5 percent of salaries and related expenses of operating the program.[19]

Unlike other welfare funded by the federal government, the program is open to all with incomes below stated lines, and aid is provided to households (including unrelated individuals) rather than being limited to families. The household makes an application unless it is already receiving AFDC or SSI, in which case it is automatically eligible. The household receives an authorization to purchase a sufficient supply of food coupons to cover its minimum needs. If its income is zero, it pays nothing for the stamps. For every $3 of income above $30 a month, the household must pay $1 for its full allotment. Thus, a family of four would be eligible for $150 per month of food stamps. It would pay for these stamps according to the schedule in Table 6–10.

The program has had a curious political history. The principal objections are to its high administrative cost. It costs approximately 13 cents to deliver a dollar's worth of food stamps, while direct cash payment costs almost half this amount. It is also objected to because it forces the recipient to reveal a dependency status to the supermarket clerk and others in the checkout line. The procedure of requiring individuals to purchase the food stamps rather than just receiving a food stamp bonus is both burdensome to the recipient and troublesome to the administering agency. Stories of college students and strikers receiving food stamps are seen as politically embarrassing, although such persons are clearly eligible. In 1975 a work requirement, basically symbolic, was added. Fathers out of work temporarily had to register for employment; mothers did not. If the father were unemployed and the mother working, the family could deduct child care expenses while the father looked for work; the same privilege was not extended to the mother. Despite these objections, food stamp aid to the working poor was politically acceptable while cash aid to the working poor remained politically unobtainable. In 1978 Congress authorized a procedure to eliminate the purchase requirement. Therefore, instead of paying, for example, $100 for $150 worth of stamps, the family would simply receive $50 worth of stamps.

Medical Care

It is sometimes asserted that this nation does not have a national health program. Such is clearly not the case. As Table 6–11 clearly reflects, the public share of this nation's health bill has dramatically increased. The decade 1965–75 particularly witnessed a period of great growth in the federal government's role in the provision of health care to low-income persons.

Among all of the Great Society programs, those devoted to

TABLE 6-10
Food Stamp Program Monthly Coupon Allotments and Purchase Requirements, Effective July–December 1974, in 48 States and the District of Columbia

	Number in Household							
	1	2	3	4	5	6	7	8
Monthly allotment	$46	$82	$118	$150	$178	$204	$230	$256
	Monthly Purchase Requirement							
Monthly net income:								
$0–$19.99	$0	$0	$0	$0	$0	$0	$0	$0
$20–$29.99	1	1	0	0	0	0	0	0
$30–$39.99	4	4	4	4	5	5	5	5
$40–$49.99	6	7	7	7	8	8	8	8
$50–$59.99	8	10	10	10	11	11	12	12
$60–$69.99	10	12	13	13	14	14	15	16
$70–$79.99	12	15	16	16	17	17	18	19
$80–$89.99	14	18	19	19	20	21	21	22
$90–$99.99	16	21	21	22	23	24	25	26
$100–$109.99	18	23	24	25	26	27	28	29
$110–$119.99	21	26	27	28	29	31	32	33
$120–$129.99	24	29	30	31	33	34	35	36
$130–$139.99	27	32	33	34	36	37	38	39
$140–$149.99	30	35	36	37	39	40	41	42
$150–$169.99	33	38	40	41	42	43	44	45
$170–$189.99	36	44	46	47	48	49	50	51
$190–$209.99	36	50	52	53	54	55	56	57
$210–$229.99		56	58	59	60	61	62	63
$230–$249.99		62	64	65	66	67	68	69
$250–$269.99		62	70	71	72	73	74	75
$270–$289.99		62	76	77	78	79	80	81
$290–$309.99			82	83	84	85	86	87
$310–$329.99			88	89	90	91	92	93
$330–$359.99			94	95	96	97	98	99
$360–$389.99			100	104	105	106	107	108
$390–$419.99			100	113	114	115	116	117
$420–$449.99				122	123	124	125	126
$450–$479.99				126	132	133	134	135
$480–$509.99				126	141	142	143	144
$510–$539.99					150	151	152	153
$540–$569.99					150	160	161	162
$570–$599.99					150	169	170	171
$600–$629.99						172	179	180
$630–$659.99						172	188	189
$660–$689.99						172	194	198
$690–$719.99							194	207
$720–$749.99							194	216
$750–$779.99								216
$780–$809.99								216
$810–$839.99								216
$840–$869.99								216

Note: For each person in excess of 8, add $22 to the monthly coupon allotment for an eight-person household.

SOURCE: Joint Economic Committee, *Studies in Public Welfare,* 93rd Cong., 1st Sess., paper no. 17.

TABLE 6-11
AGGREGATE AND PER CAPITA NATIONAL HEALTH EXPENDITURES,
BY SOURCE OF FUNDS, AND PERCENT OF GROSS NATIONAL
PRODUCT, SELECTED FISCAL YEARS, 1929–1976

Fiscal Year	Gross National Product (in billions)	Health Expenditures								
		Total			Private			Public		
		Amount (in millions)	Per Capita	Percent of GNP	Amount (in millions)	Per Capita	Percent of Total Expenditures	Amount (in millions)	Per Capita	Percent of Total Expenditures
1929	$101.3	$3,589	$29.16	3.5	$3,112	$25.28	86.7	$477	$3.88	13.3
1935	68.9	2,846	22.04	4.1	2,303	17.84	80.9	543	4.21	19.1
1940	95.4	3,883	28.98	4.1	3,101	23.14	79.9	782	5.84	20.1
1950	264.8	12,027	78.35	4.5	8,962	58.38	74.5	3,065	19.97	25.5
1955	381.0	17,330	103.76	4.5	12,909	77.29	74.5	4,421	26.47	25.5
1960	498.3	25,856	141.63	5.2	19,461	106.60	75.3	6,395	35.03	24.7
1965	658.0	38,892	197.75	5.9	29,357	149.27	75.3	9,535	48.48	24.5
1966	722.4	42,109	211.56	5.8	31,279	157.15	74.3	10,830	54.41	25.7
1967	773.5	47,879	237.93	6.2	32,026	159.15	66.9	15,853	78.78	33.1
1968	830.2	53,765	264.37	6.5	33,725	165.83	62.7	20,040	98.54	37.3
1969	904.2	60,617	295.20	6.7	37,680	183.50	62.2	22,937	111.70	37.8
1970	960.2	69,201	333.57	7.2	43,810	211.18	63.3	25,391	122.39	36.7
1971	1,019.8	77,162	368.25	7.6	48,387	230.92	62.7	28,775	137.32	37.3
1972	1,111.8	86,687	409.71	7.8	53,214	251.50	61.4	33,473	158.20	38.6
1973	1,238.6	95,383	447.31	7.7	58,715	275.35	61.6	36,668	171.96	38.4
1974*	1,361.2	106,321	495.01	7.8	64,809	301.74	61.0	41,512	193.27	39.0
1975*	1,452.3	122,231	564.35	8.4	71,361	329.48	58.4	50,870	234.87	41.6
1976†	1,611.8	139,312	637.97	8.6	80,492	368.61	57.8	58,820	269.36	42.2

*Revised.
†Preliminary.
SOURCE: U.S. Department of Health, Education, and Welfare, *Research and Statistics Note*, No. 27, December 22, 1976.

health care provided both the largest share of the budget and the largest amount of political attention. The great growth in public expenditures reflected a game of catch-up for the United States, which had, until 1965, lagged far behind other affluent industrial societies in share of the gross national product spent on public medical care programs. The heightened attention was due to the fact that health care reform had the dramatic potential of involving all citizens, not just the poor. Unlike other Great Society programs, these programs were intimately tied up with the overall delivery of a need: health care. The major public changes in the decade were the adoption of Medicare and Medicaid, the creation of publicly funded neighborhood health centers, and a very significant expansion of the maternal and child health programs.

These health programs represented a multifunctional approach to the problem of limited access by poor persons to the medical care system of this nation. Less attention was paid to other medical care policy issues, such as the containment of costs and the assurance of quality health care when the care is available. The rapid escalation of medical costs, particularly, led to widespread dissatisfaction with the ability of public programs to respond to a crisis in health care. The burden of new health program expenditures led to a belief that quality health care for the poor was being purchased at the expense of quality health care for middle-income Americans. The validity of such beliefs must await an examination of the programs themselves.

Medicare and Medicaid. On the 30th of July, 1965, President Lyndon Johnson traveled to Independence, Missouri, to sign amendments to the Social Security Act which established a new departure in the federal role in the delivery of health care. This legislation was seen as the culmination of a 20-year debate on the role of the federal government in the direct provision of health care.[20] The legislation, which turned out to be as much a start as an end, established two separate health care programs. The first, Medicare, is a national health insurance program for persons receiving benefits through the OASDI program; the second, Medicaid, provides for a federal role in the direct payment of health care for the indigent.

The Medicare features of the legislation provided a basic health insurance plan as part of the basic benefit structure for virtually all aged persons and a significant number of widows and the physically disabled. The health insurance package provided hospitalization, plus a specified list of posthospital care and a more strictly limited set of diagnostic and home care programs. Benefits were conditioned on the payment of a certain deductible amount and co-insurance. Under present rules, the patient pays the first $84 of hospital care plus $10 per day after the 61st through the 90th day. Funding for the program was through the social security tax. In addition, OASDI recipients could choose to purchase an additional supplemental medical insurance package to provide for physician care outside of the hospital as well as certain drug coverage. An individual may purchase this program but is not required to do so. At a cost of only $6.30 per month, however, it is heavily subsidized by government payments. The coverage itself is operated by private insurance carriers who contract with the federal government.

At the time of the adoption of Medicare, Congress also created the Medicaid program. It was perceived in 1965 as a relatively minor extension of the Medical Assistance for the Indigent Aged Act of 1961. Under the 1965 legislation, recipients of Aid to the Blind and Aid to Dependent Children and, at the state's option, any medically indigent persons were also included. The program provided comprehensive diagnostic, physician care, hospitalization, and posthospital care to those below an established income line, provided they did not own too many assets to prevent eligibility. The program was to be operated by the state, but the costs of operation were reimbursed to the state by the federal government under a system whereby the federal share was inversely related to per capita income in the state.[21]

The adoption of Medicare and Medicaid was a significant shift in the financing of the health industry. Yet thousands of decisive but detailed decisions were left to be resolved via administrative law. Billing procedures, pattern of reimbursement, quality control methods, eligibility to participate as a provider or patient had to be worked out. All the while, medical practice and utilization were experiencing revolutionary stimuli from other sources. The great infusion of dollars into the health care system is detailed in Table 6–11 above. A shift in medicine since 1960, from solo physicians being repaid by a fee for service at the time the service is rendered to the complex clinic practice, with multiple funding, compounds the issue. One thing is certain, however; the public sector is now the big spender in medicine.

Public Housing

Public housing policy is the certain backwater of domestic public policy. Millions of Americans live in substandard, overcrowded, or dilapidated houses. The problems, often intensified by congestion in urban areas and isolation in rural areas, contribute rather directly to many of our other serious social problems. Public efforts to make available to every American something as simple as an airtight, watertight, heated, and properly ventilated dwelling have largely, but not entirely, been accomplished. But housing is not conceived of so narrowly. It is thought of today as some minimal mixture of healthful shelter; privacy; access to schools, employment, and health care; and some semblance of recreational opportunity. In attempting to provide this to all Americans as a right, we have pursued a jumble of mixed strategies, all of which, once tried, appear to be inadequate. In a number of separate acts since 1937 the nation has created an "alphametric soup" of programs, too often with little consideration of the relationship of one to the others.

Strategies for public housing have included the Housing Act of 1937, which provided for federal amortization of private loans to public and to private nonprofit local housing authorities for the construction of low-rent housing, to which tenants are admitted on the basis of their income and pay a low rent not to exceed 25 percent of their net income. Often called instant slums, these "projects" concentrated the urban poor and thereby intensified the social problems, while being largely unresponsive to inadequate rural housing. By the mid-sixties, after many well-publicized failures—the most infamous being the Hewett-Packard project in St. Louis, which had to be destroyed a few years after it was built—the project strategy was largely replaced.

Various direct subsidies to builders were designed to encourage the construction of multi-income-level projects via subsidized mortgages to nonprofit corporations, which resulted in a very high rate of mortgage assignments and foreclosures. This project was known under various titles, but principally as 225 D-3 after the appropriate paragraph in the Housing Act of 1961. This approach was popular from the mid-sixties to the early seventies.

Since the early seventies the new emphasis has been on direct rent and purchase subsidies to low-income dwellers who find their own accommodations and then receive either a purchase subsidy, or more usually a rent subsidy, of the difference between the rent or mortgage they must pay and 25 percent of their net income. The early evidence on this approach is mixed, but it is feared in some quarters that by increasing the demand on a fixed stock of housing, the beneficiaries of subsidized rents are the owners, who realize a higher average rent.

One of the great hopes of housing policy was the notion that by subsidizing middle-income housing, through tax subsidies and other stimulants to the housing industry, a larger stock of adequate used housing would become available to the poor, who would occupy the homes vacated by the mobile middle class. This strategy seems to have been frustrated by housing and mortgage rate inflation which plagues newly formed families, even with relatively affluent means.

The overriding fact is that while in 1972 tax expenditure subsidies for housing to middle- and high-income Americans cost $6.2 billion, more than 94 percent of all low-income Americans received no direct form of housing assistance.

CONCLUSIONS

The structure of American income security turns out, on examination, to be minimal. Rather, it is a curious mixture of ad hoc programs designed to respond, to varying degrees and at varying levels of rationality, to ad hoc political movements and demands. The present income security system is clearly not a system in which interacting elements have unique goals which are designed with sensitive awareness of the goals to be achieved by other elements of the system. Such a system, with insurance, assistance, manpower, and in-kind programs structured around some larger goal, such as maximum income security consistent with maximum preservation of work and family stability incentives, would require a complex set of prioritized goals. The problem is that income security as a social goal conflicts with other primary social goals. The subunits of the income security system attain their own form of political integrity and rigidity, and this makes reform all but impossible.

The next chapter describes the alternative structures of income security which are available if we could just begin with a clean slate.

NOTES

1. Robert H. Haveman, *A Decade of Federal Antipoverty Programs* (San Francisco: Academic Press, 1977), p. 57.
2. President's Commission on Income Maintenance Programs, *Poverty Amid Plenty* (Washington, D.C.: U.S. Government Printing Office, 1969), chap. 1.
3. Hugh Heclo, "The Welfare State: The Costs of American Self-sufficiency," in R. Rose, *Lessons from America: An Exploration* (London: MacMillan Co., 1974) p. 259.
4. Sar Levitan and Robert Taggart, *The Problem of Greatness* (Cambridge, Mass.: Harvard University Press, 1976).
5. Robert Plotnick, "Social Welfare Expenditures and the Poor: The 1965–75 Experience and Future Expectations," Institute for Research on Poverty Discussion Paper 443–77 (Madison: University of Wisconsin, Madison, 1977). Also see Alfred M. Skolnick and Sophie R. Dales, "Social Welfare Expenditures, 1950–75," *Social Security Bulletin,* vol. 39, no. 1 (January 1976).
6. Irwin Garfinkel, "Memo on Carter's Welfare Reform Effort," Institute for Research on Poverty, Madison, Wisconsin, 1977.
7. Stephan K. Bailey, *Congress Makes a Law* (New York: Columbia University Press, 1950).
8. It was originally known as the Economic Security Act, but its name was changed during congressional debate because it was thought that the expression *economic security* had Bolshevik overtones. Arthur M. Schlesinger, *The Age of Roosevelt* (Boston, Mass.: Houghton Mifflin Publishing Co.). For a summary of the legislative history of this legislation, see Part III.
9. Edward Cowan, "Background and History: The Crisis in Public Finance and Social Security," in M. J. Boskin (ed.), *The Crisis in Social Security* (San Francisco: Institute for Contemporary Studies, 1977), p. 3.
10. Martin Feldstein, "Social Security," in Boskin, *Crisis in Social Security,* pp. 17–31.
11. Cowan, "Background and History," p. 8.
12. See Chapter 5 of this text.
13. Martha N. Ozawa, "Income Redistribution and Social Security," *Social Service Review,* vol. 50 (June 1976), pp. 209–23; Sheldon Danziger, "Income Redistribution and Social Security—Further Evidence," *Social Service Review,* vol. 51 (March 1977), pp. 179–83.
14. Ibid.
15. President's Commission on Income Maintenance Programs, Background Papers, *Poverty Amid Plenty,* p. 279 ff.
16. Levitan and Taggart, *Problem of Greatness,* chap. 7.
17. Institute for Interdisciplinary Studies, "An Evaluation for WIN," Welfare Models Project, Minneapolis, Minn., 1971.
18. Edward Fried et al., *Setting National Priorities, The 1974 Budget* (Washington, D.C.: Brookings Institution, 1973), chap. 4.

19. Joint Economic Committee, *Studies in Public Welfare*, 93rd Cong., 1st Sess., paper no. 17.
20. Karen Davis, "A Decade of Policy Development in Health Care for Low-Income Families," in Haveman, *Decade of Federal Antipoverty Programs*.
21. Ibid.

CHAPTER 7

OPTIONS FOR REFORM IN
INCOME SECURITY

A comprehensive view of welfare reform must consider the implications of the reform effort for many factors: overall tax policy, social security, the social service delivery system, national health policy, educational policy, and the low-wage labor market policy. The income security system described in Chapter 6 is, in fact, a complex of more than 40 separate programs, each with its own structure, rules of operation, and politicoeconomic objectives. The very presence of multiple welfare programs is a reflection of the political condition which prescribes that different classes of households in need are to be treated differently.

Among the problems encountered in the administration of welfare, none is more serious than the sheer number of income security programs in operation. Each program is tailored to a specific problem created by income security (or the lack of it), a specific approximate cause of income insecurity, or a specific subpopulation group in need. The result is not an income security system with rationally interacting and reinforcing elements, but a crazy-quilt pattern of programs, with gaps and overlaps. To the scholar, the public official, the taxpayer, and the recipient alike, the set of programs appears to be a confused tangle because in fact it *is* a confused tangle. Programs rationally structured to respond to one condition often function to frustrate the objectives of a second program. The confusion is not the consequence of incompetence or deviousness on the part of income security planners.

The explanation of the confusion and conflict in welfare objectives constitutes an important core body of literature on the political economy of welfare.[1] Among the reasons most frequently cited are these:

1. Given a pluralistic political structure, each interest group, with a single-minded devotion to achieving its own income security goals, will attempt to maximize its own goal. This diminishes the funds available for other welfare objectives.

2. Given multiple centers of decision making and planning in this nation's federal system, programs are frequently designed and implemented without proper regard for programs that are the responsibility of other units of government.

3. Welfare programs do not have a high priority in the American complex of political objectives, and welfare objectives are frequently set aside to achieve other public ends.

4. There is a limited consensus (and perhaps none at all) on what the priority of goals ought to be in the nation's welfare system.

None of these explanations is of much help in suggesting a design for coherence in the tangled set of programs that is euphemistically grouped together for political rhetoric reasons as "the welfare mess."

The consequences for recipients of the jumble of contradictory and often competing programs are far more specific. Since individual households do not neatly fit into the political economic typology, some households find themselves recipients of aid or eligible for aid from more than one program, while others with no less need find themselves eligible for no aid at all. Individual households are sometimes able to opt for the most generous program by behavior that is socially and perhaps individually destructive. For example, if a state does not have an AFDC–U program, or if unemployment benefits are for some reason not available, male family heads are implicitly encouraged in real or feigned desertion of their family so that their wives and children might be aided.[2] More generous aid in one state can encourage uneconomic migrations. To some persons, at least, one of the most serious consequences of multiple programs is the fact that each program reduces the magnitude of the benefit partially, in response to the availability of other income. The cumulative effect of these separate reductions is that the household cannot raise its real income by seeking work. Finally, separate rules of eligibility too frequently produce catch–22 conditions in which the very eligibility for one program contradicts that for another. Multiple-program operation also increases considerably the administrative cost of social welfare.

To the extent that these diverse programs do have similar programmatic objectives, there is at least the potentiality that they could be redesigned into a comprehensive plan which would reduce administrative cost, complexity, and conflict. The trouble comes when there is an attempt to specify politically the prioritized goals that the comprehensive system ought to achieve. In Part III the somewhat gloomy history of that political search for consensus is recounted in detail. Reform options are too often placed forward in the same sort of political isolation that has generated the programs they would replace. Advocates of particular reforms often do not cite the context in which the reform would be viable. Thus Congress finds itself choosing among options where no choice is required and making choices which are mutually exclusive, or at least counterproductive. It is, nonetheless, useful to sketch out the programs, program goals, and goal conflicts that must be considered in any effort to redesign a welfare system.

GOALS OF WELFARE REFORM

Robert Lampman has identified four conflicting goal sets which motivate political actors to consider welfare reform. Lampman's goal sets highlight the complex relationships between ends and means in the redesign of welfare. They are: (1) minimum provision, (2) replacement of income loss, (3) horizontal and vertical equity, and (4) efficiency of investment.[3]

The minimum provision mentality has traditionally guided the assistance programs. It also guided public housing, social service, and medical care programs that are exclusively for the poor. By its nature it is crisis oriented, responsive rather than proactive. It comes into play as a consequence of some exogenous failure in ordinary family and market processes. The primary emphasis is on the assurance that certain minimal standards of consumptive opportunity are preserved, regardless of what else occurs. The replacement-of-loss mentality finds its expression in public and private insurance programs. Here the goal is to preserve some fixed proportion of income without regard to need. The vertical and horizontal equity goal focuses attention on the flow of income from governments to individuals by asking if all persons in similar circumstances are treated equally. This goal is often seen as one of producing a greater degree of income equality within a polity. It normally finds its expression in proposals for various forms of negative income taxation or universal benefit and tax structures. The fourth goal, efficiency, focuses attention on the long-term costs and benefits of alternative reform efforts. It is concerned not with short-term need, income loss, or interincome class equity but rather with the long-term effects on the productivity of beneficiaries, particularly the interaction between work and income received. None of these mentalities described by Lampman is unmindful of the goal set of the others; the problem is simply that of *primacy* of goals. The priorities of each group are significantly different.

The multiple programs which collectively comprise the welfare system respond to these alternative sets of goals. Only a few political actors concern themselves with the overall goals of the system and the limitations based on scarcity of resources. Individually, the programs have a political rationality; collectively, there is no coherence.

Criteria for Evaluation of Income Maintenance Programs

With each group having a single-minded devotion to its own goal set, it is nearly impossible to identify a prioritized set of goals, that is, one which reflects a considered compromise among the competing and sometimes conflicting objectives. There are, nonetheless, several criteria which are more or less commonly used in the evaluation of alternative programs. It should be emphasized that these are not goals to be achieved by each and every program; rather, they are benchmarks to be used in the comparison of alternative strategies to respond to the mulifaceted problem of income security. These criteria are described below.

Adequacy. An income security system should be designed in connection with the employment system and the insurance system, so that all will have access to a minimally adequate income.

Agreeing to this is easy; defining a minimum adequate income is difficult.

Responsibility. The attainment of income adequacy for all must be achieved in such a fashion that there is no diminution of the incentive to save and insure oneself against future needs. Nor should there be a diminution of interfamily responsibility for sharing income between husband and wife, parent and child, child and parent. Agreeing to the concept is again easy; defining the realistic limits of responsibility is difficult.

Effectiveness. Effectiveness in income security is a complex problem because socially no money is lost when individual A is taxed to provide income for individual B. There are four interrelated measures of effectiveness:

1. *Inclusive effectiveness.* This is the measure of the degree to which benefits intended for a target population reach all members of that population. If A represents the target population and B the target population aided, then $B \div A$ is the measure of inclusive effectiveness. The number of persons in the target population not aided is represented by U. Some persons not intended to receive aid do receive it.
2. *Exclusive effectiveness.* This is the measure of the degree to which benefits intended for the target population do not spill over to other persons. If C is the number of persons aided and B is the target population aided, then $B \div C$ is the measure of exclusive effectiveness. X is the number of persons not targeted, but nevertheless aided.
3. *Administrative effectiveness.* This is the measure of the dollars spent in the delivery of the program in relation to the benefits provided. If D equals the total dollar cost of goods and services provided to the target population, and E is the cost of delivering or providing the service and benefits, then $D \div D + E$ is the measure of administrative effectiveness.
4. *Gap effectiveness.* This is the measure of the degree to which a program of income security closes the gap between prebenefit income and the poverty line. If the target population is represented by A (all poor children) the target population aided is represented by B (poor children aided), the target population unaided is represented by U (poor children unaided), the population aided is represented by C (persons aided), and the untargeted population aided is represented by X (persons aided who are not poor children), then:

$$X + B = C$$
$$B + U = A$$
$$X \neq C, \ U \neq C$$
$$B \leq C, \ B \leq A, \ A \leq C$$

Ideally, if we wished to create a program to bring all poor children up to the poverty line in a perfectly effective program, every child would be brought up to that line, with no aid provided to children at or above the poverty line, and no administrative cost would be incurred. Obviously no program can be perfectly effective, but we can compare the relative effectiveness of alternative programs. As a general rule, efforts to ensure greater effectiveness on one dimension cause poorer performance on at least one other dimension.

Work Incentives. In a society such as ours, it is expected that individuals and families will provide for their needs through the work of one or more members of the household. The income security system should encourage this self-sufficiency by ensuring that persons who work have higher incomes from work than they would have if they dropped out of the labor force and were dependent on welfare.

Family Stability Incentives. The income security system should be so structured that it minimizes the incentive for formation of new families. It also should not create an incentive to break up existing families. At the same time, the program should be responsive to income needs generated in the event that new families *are* created or old ones *are* broken up.

Civil Rights, Liberty, and Stigma. The program should so operate that families dependent on the income security program are not stigmatized. They should not lose any of the civil rights and liberties they would have were they not dependent on the program.

Responsiveness to Changing Conditions. The program should be so structured that it responds to changed conditions within individual families and within society as a whole.

Political Accountability. The program should be so structured that the responsible public officials can be held accountable for its operation.

Minimum Cost. All of the above criteria are to be met with the least possible expenditure of public dollars.

All political actors do not agree on the relative desirability of these criteria. Alternative programs maximize different ones. It is difficult to compose programs when, in effect, they are structured to achieve different objectives. The admittedly partial list of criteria presented here does, however, make possible a more comprehensive dialogue about alternate programs.

COMMON CHARACTERISTICS OF REFORM OPTIONS

Though deliberate or unintentional legislative obscurantism might mask it, all cash transfers have three common features:

1. A specification of an eligible population—the aged, children deprived of parental support, persons without support from any other source, all persons within a given polity.
2. A guaranteed minimum level of income to be provided to all persons within the eligible population, though the precise mechanism for establishing the guarantee can be highly varied in both interprograms and intraprogram characteristics.
3. A mechanism which reduces the net benefit of the program as incomes from other sources increase.

These three universally present characteristics of a cash transfer plan determine other derived characteristics, such as the social cost of the program, the degree of equality (or inequality) it produces, and the real incidence of costs and benefits in the program. These derived characteristics in turn elicit a set of responses to the program, both in economic behavior and broader social behavior. The expected and unexpected behavioral responses produce a political constituency to support the policy, and/or a different constituency opposing it.

The behavioral response might also produce a different political balance. The selection, political brokering, and implementation of cash transfer programs is a dynamic process, in a constant state of politicoeconomic flux. This is illustrated in Figure 7–1.

There are, as we shall see, a number of proposals for providing income to persons or families by way of a government payment.[4] Such payments from the government to the individual are called *transfer payments.* They are not made in payment for a good or service. All transfer payments are ultimately linked to tax payments.

Using the tax system and the welfare system in tandem to eliminate or reduce income poverty in a polity is hardly a new idea. The necessary and precise relationship of taxes based on income, and

FIGURE 7-1
THE PROGRAM FLOW

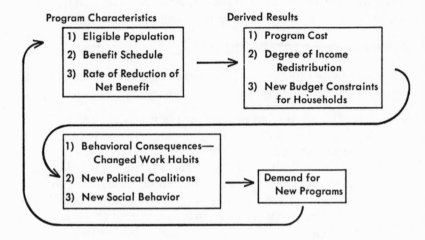

welfare payments based on income, has, however, only recently been articulated.[5] In the simplest form of welfare, W, the government pays to the individual the difference between some established need level, N, and available income, Y.

$$W = N - Y . \tag{1}$$

In the simplest form of taxation on income, T, the individual owes to government some portion of his or her income. The proportion owed is set by the prevailing tax rate, R.

$$T = R \cdot Y . \tag{2}$$

The individual owes government if $T > W$, but the government owes the individual if $W > T$.

If the need standard is thought of as a guarantee, G, the individual's welfare transfer, WT will be positive or negative, depending on the size of his income, the size of the guarantee, and the tax rate:

$$WT = G - R \cdot Y \tag{3}$$

A positive transfer can be seen as a negative tax, and conversely, a negative tax is a positive transfer.

In Figure 7-2, there is one guarantee, *OG*, and one tax rate, 1 — tangent of *a*. Persons with income below *OB* receive transfers, and those with income above *OB* pay taxes. Under real-world conditions, an individual receives a guarantee from multiple sources (e.g., social security, unemployment, welfare, veterans' administration) and pays a different tax rate on different sources of income. Thus, the individual's transfer situation is very complex. It could, at one point in time, be reduced to a single expression:

$$TW_{ij} = G_{ija} + G_{ijn} - r_1 Y_a - r_2 Y_b,$$

where TW_{ij} is the welfare transfer (or tax) to individual i in state j. This individual receives more than one guarantee, $G_{ija} \dots G_{ijn}$ and pays a series of different tax rates on the different income streams, r_1 on Y_a, and so on. No longer can the individual look just at his wage to know his take-home income. He must also know the guarantee for which he is eligible and the tax rates he must face.

FIGURE 7-2
THE TAX-TRANSFER RELATIONSHIP

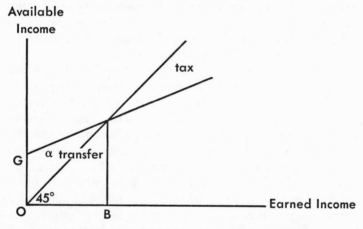

A thoroughly hypothetical but not unreal illustration is given below. The individual is eligible for a food stamp program of $1,000 per year, but this is reduced 33 cents for every dollar earned. He is also eligible for a family income payment of $2,500, which is reduced 67 cents for every dollar earned above $300. The income from these sources is not otherwise taxed. All earnings are subject to a 10 percent social insurance tax. Those with income below $4,000 pay no income tax. Above $4,000 the tax rate is 25 percent, and above $5,000, 50 percent. The individual primarily concerned with take-home income will look at his effective tax rate (i.e., 1.00 minus the change (Δ) in take-home pay divided by the change in income. As the effective tax rate approaches 1.00, the individual does not better his take-home package by earning more. If the effective tax rate exceeds 1.00, the individual actually takes home less by earning more. The actual operations of current programs have produced results essentially similar to those in the hypothetical illustrations in Table 7–1.

NEW PROPOSALS FOR INCOME SECURITY PROGRAMS

Because of the anomalies in current patchwork welfare plans, completely new proposals for guaranteeing minimum incomes are under discussion. The government has available to it a variety of welfare reform proposals which could accomplish the end of providing cash income to low-income persons. It is assumed that social service and social insurance programs will continue to operate, though they will surely be modified, if there is reform of the low-income security system. The reforms under consideration are thus reforms that would replace or supplement the traditional welfare programs: AFDC, AFDC–U, food stamps, Supplemental Security Income, and General Assistance.

Though it is difficult to compare the options in reform with precision, we must start with some schematic categorization of them. We will begin with two forms of the most universal programs: a negative income tax and a credit tax. This will be followed by a discussion of the issue of categorization and the examination of one categorical aid program which is frequently advanced in discussions of welfare reform: children's aid programs. Then we will examine various suggestions that have been made to accomplish reform in income security by the creation of jobs programs.

Most pragmatic reform options proposed to Congress contain elements from each of these approaches to income security. This will be illustrated by a review of the Carter welfare reform package of 1977 in the final section of the chapter.

UNIVERSAL PLANS

The problems generated by an unmindful proliferation of tax system and welfare payments have led some to believe that a basic

TABLE 7-1

EXAMPLE OF IMPACT OF TWO TAX AND TWO TRANSFER PROGRAMS ON FAMILY INCOME

(1) Earned Income (Y)	(2) Transfer for Food Stamp (1,000 − 0.33Y)	(3) Transfer for Family Income [2,500 − 0.67 (y − 300)]	(4) Social Insurance Tax (0.10 × y)	(5) Income Tax*	(6) Net Transfer [(2+3)−(4+5)]	(7) Home Income (1 + 6)	(8) Effective Tax Rate $[1 - \frac{\Delta 7}{\Delta 1}]$
0	+1,000	+2,500	0	0	3,500	3,500	0.43
100	+967	+2,500	−10	0	3,457	3,557	0.43
200	+933	+2,500	−20	0	3,413	3,613	0.43
300	+900	+2,500	−30	0	3,370	3,670	1.10
500	+834	+2,366	−50	0	3,150	3,650	1.10
1,000	+669	+2,031	−100	0	2,600	3,600	1.06
2,000	+333	+1,361	−200	0	1,494	3,494	1.03
3,000	0	+691	−300	0	391	3,391	0.34
3,500	0	+356	−356	0	0	3,560	0.13
4,000	0	+21	−400	0	−379	3,621	1.00
4,032	0	0	−403	−8	−411	3,621	0.64
5,000	0	0	−500	−250	−750	4,250	0.60
6,000	0	0	−600	−750	−1,350	4,650	

*Tax rate: 0% Y>0<4,000
25% Y>4,000<5,000
50% Y>5,000

SOURCE: D. Lee Bawden et al., "The Family Assistance Plan: An Analysis and Evaluation," Institute for Research on Poverty, Discussion Paper no. 73–70, 1970.

restructuring could occur with either a refundable tax credit or a negative tax plan. The essential principles underlying a refundable tax plan and a negative tax plan are identical:

1. Each family is guaranteed a basic benefit. The guarantee, G, is related to the family's living situation. The guarantee could be varied by only family size, as is the usual case, or by other facts as well.

2. The actual benefit paid, B, is reduced as income from other sources increases. The guarantee is systematically reduced by a reduction rate, R, applied to other income, I. If so desired, the first 30 or 100 or whatever dollars could be exempted from the reduction rate. Thus:

$$
\begin{array}{ccccc}
B & = & G & - & [R \times (I - E)] \\
\text{Net benefit} & = & \text{Guarantee} & - & \text{Reduction} \times \text{Income less} \\
 & & & & \text{rate} \quad\quad \text{exemption}
\end{array}
$$

3. At some income point, depending on guarantee, reduction rate, and exemption, B falls to zero. This income point is known as the break-even point. Above that point the family would presumably pay ordinary positive taxes.[6]

Negative Tax Plans

Any system of income security contains implicit guarantees, reduction rates, and exemptions. Negative tax plans simply make these explicit. The President's Commission on Income Maintenance Programs in 1969 proposed a simple universal negative income tax, with a guarantee for a family of four set at $2,400. The reduction rate was 50 percent, and exemptions, except for work-related expenses, were zero. Thus a family of four would receive benefits from the program up to net earnings of $4,800. The PCIMP plan would have replaced categorical welfare but left the then-extant social insurance, unemployment compensation, and all tax laws in place.

As envisioned by the planners of the program produced by PCIMP, the federal government would establish a new unit of government which would calculate benefit schedules and provide payments to individuals based on the schedule in their proposal. The commissioners of PCIMP refused to consider specific implementing proposals, preferring to recommend a grand scheme and leave the details of implementation to legislative and administrative politics.[7]

The effectiveness scores of this grand scheme were very good. This effectiveness was, however, purchased at a great price. The inequities of the existing welfare/tax system were kept in place, and the system was rationalized only at the lower end of the income scale. The benefit schedules were perceived by recipients as being too low, while others perceived the tax rate as being too high. It was suggested that the 50 percent reduction rate on the top of existing income and social security taxes would produce massive withdrawals from the labor market by low-wage workers.

Under present welfare/tax laws, the relationship of disposable income to earned income is anything but precise. A negative tax system goes part of the way toward rationalizing the system, and, in comparison to public assistance, it goes a long way. A particularly attractive feature of a negative income tax (NIT) is its automatic quality. As low incomes rise, payment to individuals falls; when incomes decline, families become automatically eligible. There is no need for individual case finding. The procedure is as nonintrusive to a family's private affairs as is the current positive income tax system. The program prevents the manipulation of welfare benefits to encourage or discourage particular behavior. The universality of the program eliminates the stigma associated with welfare. It is also automatically countercyclical; falling income automatically generates public spending, and when income rises, public transfers are automatically reduced. Since the sole criterion is relative need, payments are made on the basis of family size and income. If these are seen as the only valid measure of need, then, by definition, families with need receive payment, and families without need do not.

Disadvantages of the Negative Income Tax. While conceptually precise, there are a number of technical problems in making an NIT operational. The resolution of these technical difficulties often serves to obviate the supposed advantages of such a program. In operation, NIT programs are not obviously different from traditional welfare plans.

First, there is the problem of frequency of payments. Under the positive income tax system, payments to government are made by deductions from paychecks, with an annual reckoning. Persons dependent on NIT income would need to receive payments biweekly or at the most monthly. This would enormously increase the cost of administration.

Second, very difficult problems of definition would have to be dealt with—what constitutes a family unit, what counts as income, how separated families are to be dealt with are only a few of the problems to be addressed. These issues have plagued welfare administration and would be no less difficult under an NIT plan.

Uneven flows of income would generate problems. For example, would a high-income but part-year worker, such as a professional athlete or Great Lakes ship operator, secure benefits when not working? Problems of wealth not currently producing income are ignored in the positive tax system; would we wish to ignore them also in a negative tax system? These problems have plagued the tax system for years and would become no less difficult in an NIT plan.

Credit Tax

Since an NIT combines the problems of welfare and taxation, it has been suggested that welfare reform should not be done piecemeal, as is likely in an NIT program. Rather, there should be one overarching, comprehensive reform. Rather than payments only to the poor, all individuals would receive a single tax credit (e.g., $1,000), with all individuals paying one tax (e.g., at a 33 percent rate). Thus tax benefit (positive or negative) or liability (positive or negative) would be strictly a function of income. The cost of the program in real GNP terms would be zero. Taxes would, of course, have to generate enough income to pay the benefits plus the other costs of government. In fact, to the extent that a comprehensive tax/welfare reform would generate work and investments, its cost in real GNP terms could actually be negative.

Whatever its conceptual advantage, the financing of a credit tax system at a level to replace welfare programs would require substantial revision of current tax and social legislation. No doubt such a change would be welcomed by many, but it would mean that the incumbent president (or candidate) would have to fight simultaneously for tax and welfare reform. The many millions now enjoying an advantage due to the laxity of our tax welfare laws make that route highly unlikely.

CATEGORICAL PROGRAMS

Since multiple welfare programs reflect the political belief that different classes of persons in need are to be treated differently, it makes sense from a planning perspective to tailor the program features of an income security system to the particular needs of the target population. Status as a single parent produces particular income needs, but this need may, and probably does, differ, depending on the proximate cause of single-parent status. The income needs and the program needs of the widow are different from those of the divorcee, the deserted mother, or the unmarried mother. The needs of intact families experiencing long-term unemployment are different from a similarly situated family temporarily out of the labor force. The aged poor constitute another demographic class with distinct income and program needs. There is no limit to the number of groups that could be identified as needing unique programs. That is why we have so many categorical programs.

There are two fundamental problems associated with categorization. First and most fundamentally, once a group has been selected out for program planning, it is also separated out for purposes of political action. Favored groups—widows, the aged, etc.—can and do campaign for generous programs for themselves, leaving unfavored groups more vulnerable to demeaning and stigmatic treatment, if they receive any help at all. Second, people with need are capable of self-selecting themselves into the program with the most favored treatment. Categorical programs can encourage the very behavior to which they have been designed to respond. Universality has a nice sound, but few want to aid one who has voluntarily dropped out from the economic system with the same level of generosity accorded a truly helpless person.

Children's Allowance Programs

All of the currently operating programs, except food stamps and General Assistance, are clearly *narrow* categorical programs. Categorical programs need not be limited to the poor. However, among the categorical programs offered as a kind of welfare reform, the one most frequently cited is called the *children's allowance.* Under such a plan, families with children would receive a direct payment from the government. They would, of course, pay taxes under the ordinary system, so that, in operation, the program may be little more than a tax credit limited to families with children. This point is frequently overlooked in the literature which extols the virtues of a children's allowance, or family allowance, as it is sometimes called.

Particular programs for children's allowance, like proposals for a negative income tax or credit tax, differ fundamentally in detail. The variance in program detail is usually far more significant than difference in program type. Children's allowance programs have been adopted in 62 countries, including most of Western Europe and the former nations of the British Commonwealth. These programs accomplish a wide variety of program objectives, and though none is a significant replacement for the welfare system in those nations, they frequently are an important element of it. In most cases, the children's allowance is given only to families where there is at least one adult in the labor force. In some nations there is a means test associated with the children's allowance, making it a near functional equivalent of our own AFDC and AFDC–U programs.

Particularly during the late 1960s, a number of proposals for this type of program surfaced in the United States. Benefits ranged from $10 to $50 per child per month. All proposals specified that the payments would be made to all families, regardless of their income. One, by Harvey Braizer, had a complicated recovery rate feature which combined the features of a children's allowance with those of a negative income tax. Most of the proposals would have eliminated the children's exemption of the ordinary income tax system.[8]

In 1969 it was estimated that the gross costs of such a program that could pay a $50 benefit for each child would have been $42 billion. Of this amount, $13.5 billion would be recouped by taxes. The gross payments would have gone to 144 million children, but 45 percent of them would have been in families where the net benefit would be zero or less. Of the families receiving net benefits, only 1 in 4 would have been poor without the benefit, and only $6 billion of the $28.5 billion net costs would have gone to poor families.[9]

Evaluation of Children's Allowances. The type of children's allowance that has been discussed in the United States,[10] that is, a proposal which is deemed as a substitute for AFDC, requires a benefit schedule of larger magnitude with even greater slippage. Smaller universal children's allowances may well be useful for other policy objectives, but that is not the topic here.

It is argued that a children's allowance to substitute for AFDC programs would be less stigmatic than AFDC by virtue of its universality, the elimination of a means test, and the fact that the gross benefit would go to rich and poor alike. There would be no scrutiny of a person's personal or financial conditions as a condition of aid. Further, regular payments from the government to the individual would guarantee that the benefit is regular and is received automatically, not only after need has been established. This assures certainty of aid, something that is clearly absent in programs that go to the poor alone. Since the recoupment is at the rate of ordinary taxation, the program would have fewer work disincentives than either AFDC or a negative income tax. And the lack of strict eligibility rules would reduce the administrative costs of disbursing benefits.

While some of these advantages are found in a credit tax, the children's allowance would have the added advantage of targeting aid to families with children. The program would also reduce the perverse incentive of welfare migration and family splitting which plagues current welfare. The critical disadvantage is that it is not target efficient.

EMPLOYMENT SUBSIDIZATION

Employment subsidization programs respond to the very strong notions about work which present themselves in most discussions about welfare. The notion is to provide jobs to those poor who are able to work, and income to those aged, disabled, and young mothers who by no personal volition are excluded from the labor force. Others, namely one adult in two-parent families, one adult in childless couples, and individuals not disabled and without dependents would receive benefits only through some work-related system.

Job training, which assumes that individuals are willing to work but untrained for available jobs, is one approach to employment subsidization. A second approach is the use of various micro- and macroeconomic inducements to create the supply of available jobs. This approach assumes that there are too few jobs, and public activity is required to create a sufficient supply.

Employment subsidization has a somewhat distinct rationale. It assumes that there are many workers whose productivity is such that they cannot be absorbed into the labor market without some restructuring of the traditional labor market. Those who favor an employment subsidy place their emphasis on higher rewards from work for persons with lower productivity. Because it ties benefits to work, the program is thought to be superior to a negative tax or a credit tax in that it has much stronger work incentives. This not only reinforces the work ethic; it overcomes one of the fundamental political objectives to most welfare reforms.

While it is strongly inducive to work, there are two fundamental problems with employment subsidization. First, unless tied to traditional employment training and job creation programs, employment subsidies would provide no aid to those honestly seeking work but unable to find it. Second, employment subsidization, by making low-wage work more attractive, could, in fact, subsidize the *employer* of low-wage workers rather than the low-wage worker.

The theoretical principle behind employment subsidization is that the government has a responsibility to make work available through job creation, possible through job training, and rewarding through employment subsidization. In other words, the government ensures that individuals have the opportunity to work at a wage sufficient to care for their own and their families' needs, and an individual who refuses the opportunity has no further claim on the government for support.

Though these proposals differ in technical and fundamental detail, there are in general three types of employment subsidization proposals: (1) a wage rate subsidy, (2) an earnings subsidy, and (3) a wage bill subsidy.

Wage Rate Subsidy

A wage rate subsidy guarantees to individuals a level of compensation for their work, without producing the unemployment that is thought to be generated by high minimum wages. The government subsidizes workers for some proportion of the difference between the wage rate they can command in the market and some established target wage. If, for example, the proportion is 50 percent and the target wage is $4 per hour, the individual who can command a $2 wage rate would be subsidized $1 for each hour of work: WRS = 0.50 (target minus actual wage). The total subsidy received by the individual would depend on the number of hours worked.

The subsidization of low-wage work would make work more attractive to unskilled persons or those with low skills. By providing an incentive for low-skilled persons to enter the labor market, the program would also encourage employers to provide jobs, much in the same way that exemption of teenagers from minimum wage requirements is believed to stimulate employers to hire teenagers. For this same reason it is strongly opposed in many quarters. A wage rate subsidy is perhaps the least politically feasible of all income security proposals being offered.

Earned Income Tax Credit

Since 1973 this nation has had a modest earned income tax credit: workers receive a tax credit of 10 percent on all earnings up to $4,000. For earnings in excess of $4,000, this credit is reduced by 25 percent, and all the credit is exhausted for workers who earn $5,600. This is the normal positive tax entry point for a family of four. Figure 7-3, using the 45° line as a point of reference, shows how the individual receives returnable credit for earning up to $5,600 and pays taxes beyond that point. The tax entry point is C, and the disposable income line is ABC.

An earnings credit alone cannot replace welfare, but in conjunc-

FIGURE 7-3
RELATIONSHIP OF DISPOSABLE INCOME TO EARNINGS IN AN
EARNED INCOME TAX CREDIT PROGRAM

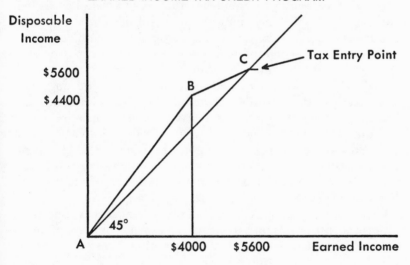

tion with a minimal guarantee it could accomplish similar ends. This is what the Carter proposal envisions.

Wage Bill Subsidy

A third proposal to achieve a higher level of income security through employment subsidization is a wage bill subsidy. To attack the problem of an unintended subsidy to the employer resulting from either a wage rate subsidy or an earned income tax credit, the wage bill subsidy makes the employer subsidy highly explicit. In this proposal the employer would agree to hire a certain number of workers with specific characteristics or to hire workers off of certified lists containing the names of only low-income, low-skilled workers. The employer would agree to pay a wage which is presumably higher than the rate the worker could negotiate for himself, based on his current productivity. The employer would then receive a tax credit based on some proportion of the difference between the actual wage paid and the worker's productivity. Presumably, over time, as the worker's productivity became enhanced by experience, the proportionate subsidy to the employer would fall and ultimately reach zero.

Theoretically, a wage bill subsidy indirectly encourages income security by encouraging employers to hire and train low-skilled workers. By establishing eligibility for the subsidy based on family characteristics, the program would accomplish the objectives of income security. Wage bill subsidies tend to be favored by employers in industries that are labor intensive and reliant on low-skilled workers. Recent experience with variations on wage bill subsidization through the Comprehensive Employment and Training Act for the public sector has shown that such programs are administratively expensive, have low target effectiveness, and do not do well in their promised goal of raising the skill levels of workers so employed. As of this writing, employment subsidization through wage bill subsidization has little support in the academic community or among welfare reform groups.

Welfare reform proposals seldom reach Congress as conceptually precise proposals for a universal negative tax or a comprehensive children's allowance system. They normally are presented as a package of reform options which are more or less integrated with one another. Generally, reforms are presented with considerable fanfare, but when the proposals are followed in detail it usually becomes obvious that there is even less reform than meets the eye. Programs are shifted around and renamed, and budgets are reallocated, but finding what is new and different in terms of the criteria mentioned above is normally quite difficult.

Such was the case with Richard Nixon's Family Assistance Plan (see Chapter 10), and such is the case with Jimmy Carter's Program for Better Jobs and Income. It is clearly impossible to provide a critique of any welfare proposal without a political bias. Those who prepare such critiques may, perhaps unaware, hide their bias in an analytical frame of reference, but by virtue of criteria used in the evaluation, the results of the evaluation are foreordained.

CONCLUSIONS

This chapter has focused on the structural dimension of broad-scale substitutions for our present set of income security programs. Issues of adequacy, universal vs. categorical eligibility, work requirements, and the like create distinct political groupings, either in favor of or in opposition to specific plans. The incumbent administration traditionally attempts to create a winning coalition by welding together several features of the various "pure form" welfare reform proposals. The discussion of the strengths and weaknesses of these alternatives in this chapter can be applied to the specifications of particular proposals.

Three kinds of questions should be asked of each program as it is put forth. First, what does it do for the poor? Does it raise their incomes compared to present programs; does it offer opportunity for reduction of dependency; does it reduce the stigma and other socially dysfunctional components of present plans? Second, who is going to pay for the program, and how much it is to cost? Care should be exercised to ask and answer the cost questions with a precise frame of reference, such as, how is the gross cost of the program to be offset by savings from old programs being phased out and new tax revenues? Cost questions should also pay attention to the final redistribution of income under the new plan as opposed to the old. In short, does the program foster equality? The third class of questions should focus attention on the political feasibility of the program proposed. Programs with analytical precision but limited political appeal are unlikely to either aid the poor or promote equality. There is little that is precise in the estimation of political feasibility. A useful place to start, however, is with the political history of current programs, the topic of the Part III.

NOTES

1. Theodore R. Marner, *Poverty Policy: A Compendium of Cash Transfer Proposals* (Chicago: Aldine-Atherton, 1971); Daniel P. Moynihan, *The Politics of a Guaranteed Income: The Nixon Administration and the Family Assistance Plan* (New York: Random House, 1973); Henry Aaron, *Why Is Welfare So Hard to Reform?* (Washington, D.C.: Brookings Institution, 1972); James Welsh, "Welfare Reform: Born 8/8/69; Died 10/4/72," *New York Times Magazine*, January 7, 1973; Theodore R. Marner and Marty Rein, "Reforming the Welfare Mess: The Fate of F.A.P.," in Allen P. Sindler (ed.), *Policy and Politics in America* (Boston: Little Brown, 1973); Elinor Graham, "Poverty and the Legislative Process," in Ben B. Seligman (ed.), *Poverty as a Public Issue* (New York: Free Press, 1965).
2. John Bishop, "Jobs, Cash Transfers, and Marital Instability: A Review of the Evidence," Institute for Research on Poverty, Special Report No. 19 (Madison, Wisconsin, 1977).
3. Robert J. Lampman, *Ends and Means of Reducing Income Poverty* (Madison, Wisc.: Institute for Research on Poverty, 1971).
4. The idea of a universal transfer scheme appeared long before the current welfare crisis. Outside of the United States, the idea of a universal transfer program dates back at least to the Speenhamland system of relief inaugurated in Berkshire, England, in 1795. In 1920, A. C. Pigou discussed the idea of a minimum-income support program and its possible impact on aggregate outputs. He did not formulate a specific plan of a taxation transfer scheme but clearly indicated that the notion of negative tax rates was practically possible, though he deemed it undesirable.

There was considerable discussion of negative taxation programs outside the United States in the immediate post–World War II years. There is evidence that there was some discussion during the 1940s in the Division of Tax Research, U.S. Treasury Department, but no evidence that a specific paper on the topic was then developed. The evidence that the idea was under discussion is a statement in a 1946 paper by George Stigler that "there is great attractiveness in the proposal that we extend the personal income tax to the lowest income brackets with negative rates in these brackets."

In 1956, Milton Friedman suggested the idea of negative rates taxation as a replacement to direct welfare subsidies in health, housing, and public aid in a series of lectures at Wabash College. This proposal was reiterated in his book, *Capitalism and Freedom*, published in 1962. Liberal critics of the welfare system also began to suggest similar forms of income redistribution schemes at about the same time. One of the early proposals was made by Robert Theobald in *Free Man and Free Markets*, published in 1963. Edward E. Schwartz of the University of Chicago's

School of Social Work published a highly specific transfer-by-taxation scheme in the July 1964 edition of *Social Work*. The most comprehensive early proposal was made by Robert J. Lampman in "Prognosis for Poverty," an address delivered to the American Economic Association in December 1964. The economists were treating the question as an aspect of tax reform, while Theobald and Schwartz focused their attention on welfare reform.

5. Joseph Heffernan, *The Development of the NIT Concept*, unpublished paper prepared for National Science Foundation.

6. D. Lee Bawden et al., *The Family Assistance Plan: An Analysis and Evaluation*, Discussion Paper No. 73–70, Institute for Research on Poverty.

7. President's Commission on Income Maintenance Programs, *Poverty Amid Plenty* (Washington, D.C.: U.S. Government Printing Office, 1969).

8. Harvey Braizer, "Tax Policy and Children's Allowance Programs," in *Children's Allowances and the Economic Welfare of Children*, Eveline Burns, Citizens Committee for Children (New York, 1968).

9. John B. Williamson et al., *Strategies Against Poverty in America* (Cambridge, Mass.: Schenkman Publishing Co., distributed by Halsted Press, 1975).

10. Williamson, *Strategies Against Poverty in America*, chap. 3.

PART III

A CONCISE POLITICAL HISTORY OF INCOME SECURITY PROGRAMS

CHAPTER 8

A HISTORICAL PREFACE TO

WELFARE REFORM

The structure of the social welfare system of a polity is the product of many fundamental forces. It is also the product of unique incidents which occur at portentous times. A full historical description of the evolution of American welfare institutions would require a study of enormous scope and detail.[1] The task of this chapter is considerably more modest; it is to set the stage for a political analysis of the contemporary welfare debate by illustrating the reluctance with which governments have accepted the responsibility of providing a minimal standard of aid to persons who would otherwise be poor or in need. The focus of attention is on the public response to income poverty.

In the main, however, the history of income maintenance institutions is not fundamentally dissimilar to the development of social welfare institutions responding to the particularized needs of the aged, children, the mentally ill, or the mentally defective. In each instance public programs develop in response to an effective articulation of want, available resources, and public acceptance of responsibility.

PUBLIC WELFARE, 1607–1932

Colonial Welfare

For the first 320 years or so of this country's political history, from the first colonial settlement to the Great Depression, welfare programs remained incredibly rigid, almost frozen in time. For this broad sweep of American history, the essential framework created by the English poor laws shaped public welfare programs. This legislation was given a national dimension in 1601, when for the first time, a nationwide system of relief was established, based on the principle that the state is responsible for the care of dependent persons, and a clear plan for providing the resources to meet the needs of those who are indigent.[2] The major provisions of this important piece of social legislation can be summarized[3] as follows:

1. Specific individuals, called overseers of the poor, were charged with the responsibility of seeing to it that the needs of the indigent in their county were met. These individuals were to include church wardens and from two to four substantial property owners.
2. Able-bodied persons who had no means of support were to be set to work by the overseers of the poor.
3. Funds necessary for putting the act into operation were to be raised by "taxing" every householder.
4. Overseers were authorized, with the consent of two justices, to bind out poor children as apprentices.
5. Local authorities were required to erect work houses, the cost of such buildings to be borne by the parish.
6. Legal responsibility for maintaining parents, grandparents, and children was clearly written into the law. The mutual responsibility for parents to support children was extended to grandfathers and grandmothers.
7. Justices of the peace were authorized "to commit to the House of Corrections or Common Gaol, such poor persons as shall not employ themselves to work, being appointed thereto by the overseers."[4]
8. Beggars were to be returned to their point of domicile.

This act was to be of crucial significance in that it established the guiding philosophy of public assistance legislation in England until 1834 and in the United States until 1935. The important aspects of the law[5] which should be established in this connection are the establishment of:

1. Clear governmental responsibility for those in need.
2. Governmental authority to force people to work.
3. Government enforcement of family responsibility.
4. Responsibility to be exercised at the local level.
5. Residence requirements.

The English experience with relief was not without its social critics. Thomas Malthus, Daniel Defoe, John Locke, and Nassau Senior lent their voices to strenuous criticism of the relief practices of 17th-century England. Each asserted in his own way the desire to free the poor from the shackles of servitude that had been imposed on them by the structure of the relief system. Only Malthus and Defoe went so far as to demand complete abolition of relief programs. An examination of these critiques reveals a concern with the impact of relief on incentive to work, as well as the relative responsibilities of the various levels of government and the "need" for guidance and rehabilitation of the working poor.[6]

It is difficult to obtain reliable estimates of the magnitude of public welfare in colonial America. One important fact was that the presence of an indentured servant system rekindled in this country a replica of feudal welfare. In the indentured system of the middle colonies and the slavery system of the southern colonies, there was a clear lack of freedom for the pauper class. Often overlooked, however, was the existence of a set of harsh laws—reasonably enforced up until the time of independence—which required masters to meet the basic survival needs of servants and slaves. (Almost half of all colonists came to this country as indentured servants.) Ironically, as the economy matured from plantation to artisan and preindustrial in character, there was also an increase in its uncertainty. The result was that public relief was the largest expenditure in the public budgets of most major cities at the time of the Revolution.[7]

Concomitantly, the rigid restraint of the poor-law philosophy was thoroughly consistent with the fact that the colonial economy was one of extreme scarcity. Colonial law stressed the provision of indoor relief, that is, relief given within an almshouse, where paupers could be conveniently segregated and put to tasks which at least paid for their meager keep. The apprenticeship of children reflected a belief in family controls for children and stressed work and training for productive employment. Also, the deification of the work ethic and the belief that pauperism was a visible symbol of sin permitted a harsh response to those in need, as a means of saving their souls.

Antebellum Welfare

Between the American Revolution and the Civil War, several broad patterns of welfare emerged, all of which were thoroughly consistent with the basic tenets of the Elizabethan poor laws. The American separation of church and state forced a severance of the connection between parish and local welfare office. Nevertheless, many states (most, in fact) retained a religious connection with the requirement that at least one member of the welfare board must be a "licensed preacher." Local governments accepted grudgingly the role of welfare caretaker and adopted rigid residency requirements.

The most important shift in this period was from indoor to outdoor relief. Outdoor aid, with its reliance on aid in kind and work-relief projects, was most adaptable to the volatile economics of the first half of the 19th century. This led some to see early American welfare of the public sector as principally an instrument for the regulation of the supply of labor.[8] The contrary evidence, that it is essentially a fiscal choice, stems from the observation that the shift to outdoor relief occurred within places of both labor shortage and labor surplus.

Another significant movement before the Civil War was the shift away from public sector to private sector welfare, or voluntary welfare. The responsibility for welfare was therefore left to charitable or eleemosynary institutions, rather than remaining a public concern.

Postbellum Welfare, 1865–1900

The patterns of dependency and welfare established before the Civil War were almost unique among American institutions in that they survived the war and the Reconstruction era almost unscathed. American relief in this period was subject to its share of criticism, similar to that leveled against the British but without the Malthusian concern for overpopulation. In its stead the concept of personal failure in the face of optimum opportunities was to take hold with a vengeance that has persisted well into the 20th century.

In the second half of the 19th century Social Darwinism dominated in the established intellectual houses of America. While William Graham Sumner enjoyed acclaim as a Harvard professor, his critic, Lester Ward, was unable to attain an academic appointment and supported himself as a clerk in the federal government. Largely because of Sumner, Herbert Spencer had a much firmer place in American thought than he did in England. Social Darwinism, the Puritan ethic, and the Horatio Alger myth were combined in a scientific, moral, and political rationale for policies already in practice. *Noblesse oblige* concepts of responsibility for others had lost their respectability by their use in defense of slavery. While the English critics stopped short of a demand for abolition of all public welfare programs, American critics often cited this passage from the works of William Graham Sumner:

> In our modern state, and in the United States more than anywhere else, the social structure is based on contract.... In a state based on contract, sentiment is out of place in any public or common affairs. It is relegated to the sphere of private and personal relations, where it depends not at all on class types, but on personal acquaintance and personal estimates.... society based on contract is a society of free and independent men, who form ties without favor or obligation, and cooperate without cringing and intrigue.... It follows ... that one man, in a free state, cannot claim help from, and cannot be charged to give help to, another.[9]

Reform, 1900–1930

During the first third of this century, the Progressive movement began to stimulate some adaptations of public welfare institutions to 20th-century reality. Institutional facilities of indoor relief were retained for a class of persons permanently estranged from the labor force, particularly the severely physically and mentally disabled, the orphaned, and to a lesser extent, the aged. Other aged, the temporarily disabled, widows, and "half orphans" became increasingly dependent on public and private programs of outdoor relief. Robert Hunter's 1904 social surveys on poverty focused political attention on a belief that these poor, along with the unemployed and underemployed, experienced poverty because of public, preventable, social, and economic evils.[10] With this perspective, state legislatures began to adopt industrial safety legislation; public health programs, particularly those for maternal and child health; and minimum wage and maximum hour restrictions.

In the area of direct cash transfer programs, workmen's compensation was the first form of social insurance to receive serious consideration in the United States. Crystal Eastman wrote a report in 1910 entitled *Work Accidents and the Law* in which she argued convincingly that as long as the employer escaped fiscal responsibility for industrial accidents, the American rate of industrial accidents would remain unconscionably high. She argued that compensation, even when there was no case of employer neglect or commission, would reduce the rate of industrial accidents. She also made a plea for a payment schedule based not on need but on a fixed proportion of the economic loss which resulted from the worker's injury.[11]

Thirty states set up commissions to investigate the relationship between industrial accidents and employer liability in the three years following the Eastman report. By 1920, 42 states had adopted workmen's compensation laws along the lines she suggested: (1) compensation based on economic loss, (2) employer responsibility for all workplace accidents, regardless of specific responsibility, and (3) a system of public, pooled insurance which employers could voluntarily enter. The laws were imperfect in many ways—occupational diseases as opposed to occupational accidents were not adequately covered, and the benefit proportions of loss were often low—but the principle of social insurance was established. The acceptance in theory if not in fact of a collective responsibility for wage loss due to industrial accidents could be extended to cover income loss for other reasons. If there were systematic programs of social insurance against wages lost from old age, premature death, and unemployment, then the major social causes of poverty would be eradicated.

During this period there was also a fundamental change in perceptions of public responsibility for widows and half orphans. Stimulated by the report issued by the White House Conference on Children in 1909, a movement for mothers' assistance, or mothers' pensions, as they were more commonly called, developed a broad base of support. In 1911, Illinois adopted a statewide program of state fiscal responsibility for this purpose. Colorado,

California, Iowa, and Wisconsin soon passed legislation which recognized a public responsibility for aid to this class of paupers. Unlike compensation, aid was based on need, not loss, and there was an additional requirement that, as a condition of aid, family casework be accepted. Thus there was the beginning of public social work in income maintenance programs.

After workmen's compensation and mothers' pensions, the third movement for a more comprehensive cash transfer program came with regard to the aged. As in the other movements, first came the articulation of a rationale for state action, followed by the development of a political pressure group to press that rationale onto the state legislators. Where a curious alliance of unions and business groups pushed the cause of workmen's compensation, and church groups advocated the mothers' pension, it was the aged themselves who presented the case for old-age security programs under public auspices. The rationale was straightforward. One, the gradual inflation had made it unrealistic for individual workers to put away enough of the dear dollars of their working years to cover their needs during retirement in an age of cheaper dollars. Two, while in an agrarian society old-age security could function as part of the extended family, the extended family was not operating in an urban and industrial community. Third, it was simply cruel to use indoor relief, which forced aged persons from their own homes. Fourth, it was cheaper to maintain the aged on pensions than in "homes."

The movement for the aged was a product of the twenties. Its motivating force was the Association for Old Age Security, led by Abraham Epstein. There was notable success in a few states: Pennsylvania, 1923; Wisconsin, 1925; Kentucky, 1926; Maryland, 1927; but the last two of these were struck down as unconstitutional by the state supreme courts. The climate of prosperity and normalcy of the twenties was a significant force against new adaptations, and the old age security movement did not achieve the success of workmen's compensation and mothers' pensions. Perhaps because the opposition was more intense, the rationale was more significantly developed and was to play a major role in the federal adoption of the Social Security Act in the next decade.

A fourth income transfer reform movement met with even less success. Unemployment was then, unlike now, a major contributor to poverty. Wisconsin was the first state to develop a statewide public unemployment program, and that was not until 1932. Eleven years earlier, Wisconsin economics professor John R. Commons had developed a scheme which would require individual corporations to build a reserve to maintain a portion of employment income for *their* workers while they were temporarily unemployed. The plan was modified by his colleagues at Wisconsin, Edwin Witte and Arthur Altmeyer, and reworked by Harold Groves and Paul Rauschenbush just before adoption in Wisconsin. The plan was somewhat desultorily pushed by the American Association for Labor Legislation in the various states. Even in Wisconsin, the only state to adopt a public unemployment compensation program, implementation was deferred until 1934. The Wisconsin experience was significant because it trained a large group of experts in the technical aspects of social security legislation, and this technical expertise was to have an important impact because of the role that Witte, Altmeyer, and Elizabeth Brandeis Rauschenbush were to play in the federal effort.

Despite these advances in the first third of the 20th century, the structure and financing of social welfare remained much as it had been in the 19th century. Less than one half of 1 percent of the citizens received any form of direct cash aid from a public source, other than General Assistance, in early 1929. By 1976, one third of all families were receiving some form of cash transfer.

DEPRESSION AND RELIEF

The Great Depression of 1929–39 brought with it massive, unprecedented unemployment and poverty. From a "labor shortage" in 1928, the situation deteriorated to 4 million unemployed in 1930, 8 million in 1931, and 12 million in 1932. As long-term structural unemployment replaced short-term frictional unemployment, the proportion of the unemployed needing relief rose. The dominance of 19th-century attitudes prevented federal action. The administration response to the federal relief proposals of Senator Robert LaFollette of Wisconsin was: (1) such action could impair the fiscal credit of the national government, (2) states' rights to deal with relief in accordance with local conditions would be impaired, (3) relief treated only the symptoms of the "recession," and (4) natural recovery, which was imminent, would be delayed by vigorous federal action.

With the federal government *refusing* to act, local governments *unable* to act for fear of in-migrations, and the private charities without funds to act, state governments became the principal institutions for the granting of relief. In most states, the actual administration of relief remained with local government, with the funding responsibility being assumed by the state government. One such state agency was New York's Temporary Emergency Relief Administration (TERA), which Franklin Roosevelt brought, along with its director, Harry Hopkins, with him from New York to Washington. Both Roosevelt and Hopkins were convinced of two propositions: one, that relief per se was essentially a local responsibility, and any federal assumption should be structured for local reassumption after the crisis, and the other that work relief, even if it consisted of digging holes and refilling them, was preferable to direct relief. Roosevelt declared in his Inaugural Address that "Our great primary task is to put people to work"[12] and began this effort with a work-relief program as an integral part of the Federal Emergency Relief Administration (FERA), in May 1933. In November 1933, the Civil Works Administration (CWA), a form of Work Projects Administration (WPA), was adopted.

Within the brief span of time from 1929 to the passage of the Social Security Act in 1935 there was concentrated a rapid succession of events which brought important and dynamic changes in the philosophy, policies, politics, and programs of social work and public welfare.[13] The first warning of the impending disaster appeared in the spring of 1929, when the usual seasonal decrease in relief expenditures did not occur. During the first two years, 1929–31, the private family agencies "made a valiant attempt to carry staggering loads, and under the greatest pressure to justify the faith of their leaders in the superiority of their methods over those of the public 'dole' system."[14] A philosophy based on psychological concepts took over, according to Nathan Cohen:

> Social work had turned to psychiatry for help in developing a method of dealing with the individual who was facing problems of maladjustment. It (psychiatric thinking) took over, however, more than a method of treatment! It took over also a view of the nature of man and his social arrangements. It saw personal anxieties and maladjustments as rooted in the individual and his psychological past to the neglect of 'structural maladjustment—that is maladjustment rooted in quite objective social disorders.' Concern for social institutions

was almost neglected in the naive belief that if one worked with enough individuals, the social institutions would indirectly improve.[15]

Given this inadequate philosophy, the social work profession was ill-equipped to step in and rebuild a crumbling social institution for handling the problem of relief. It was manifestly obvious that those in need had need not because of their upbringing but because the politicoeconomic system had run aground. It was equally obvious that a governmental dole program, based on local financing, was totally inadequate to meet the crushing burden of relief expenditures.[16] Josephine Brown has remarked on the metamorphosis in thinking which occurred between the onset of the depression and the inauguration of Franklin Delano Roosevelt:

> In the midst of, and undoubtedly because of, the losing struggle to raise adequate funds to care for the growing army of unemployed [the social agencies] moved rapidly to an almost complete reversal of position. [It was recognized that] public relief and public welfare had arrived, and had come to stay. Throughout the entire Depression there was a continuous development of public relief agencies, at first, uneven, sporadic and entirely local; later, becoming stronger and more orderly during 1932 and 1933 as one state after another, and finally the Federal Government, went into the business of unemployment relief.[17]

In September of 1931, the Charity Organization Department of the Russell Sage Foundation called a conference of private family welfare agency representatives to discuss alternative ways of meeting the relief demands of the coming winter, which was expected to be the worst yet.[18] The social work publication *Survey Midmonthly* carried a report of these discussions in November 1930 which said, in part:

> If private contributions cannot carry the load, the family agencies should push for the establishment of public departments giving both service and relief. Since it has been demonstrated that good standards can be maintained under public auspices, this seems a logical position for them to take in such circumstances, and is the only statesmanlike way of

forestalling the setting up of temporary emergency relief measures, the results of which have often hampered their work for years after past emergency periods.[19]

In June of 1931 the National Conference of Social Work met in Minneapolis for a symposium on the question of public versus private relief. At that conference, the social work profession finally put its full weight behind governmental activity in the field of relief.[20] As social workers began to recognize the necessity of governmental involvement in relief, there was also a move from local to federal relief. This culminated in the passage of the Social Security Act in 1935.

In the summer of 1930, at the invitation of President Herbert Hoover, a conference of governors was held to explore the problems of relief and unemployment. That October, the President appointed a committee, chaired by Colonel Arthur Woods, to develop a federal program for aid to the unemployed.[21] Shortly after the committee began its operations, Colonel Woods issued a news release which said in part, "Increased funds for local relief and social agencies are needed if human suffering is to be prevented. Various community chests, sectarian and nonsectarian, are financing this direct and indirect burden of unemployment. They should be encouraged."[22]

The method of providing encouragement was not spelled out. Throughout the year, the administration stuck to the notion that the situation was temporary and only emergency methods were needed. President Hoover made this position clear in his annual message to Congress on December 2, 1930, when he went on record favoring still further expansion of the temporary programs. The only mention of extending new patterns of federally subsidized relief was in connection with the drought areas in the Ohio and Mississippi valleys.[23]

Despite the lack of leadership from the presidency, Senator Constigan introduced a bill which provided for federal unemployment aid in the amount of $125 million for the remainder of the current fiscal year, and twice that amount for the following year. These funds were to be administered by the Children's Bureau under a federal Board of Unemployment Relief.[24] Senator La Follette introduced another bill, also calling for federal unemployment aid,[25] and these bills were combined. The consolidated proposed legislation provided for federal relief expenditures up to $375 million,[26] but when the bill came to a vote on February 16, 1931, it failed to pass in a roll call which seemed to shatter party lines.[27]

Throughout both sessions of the 72nd Congress various bills for federal involvement in relief were introduced. These bills either died in committee or failed to pass.[28] Each proposal for a new technique for handling the problem of relief was met with the same stock arguments: (1) the government's credit would become seriously impaired; (2) the age-old principle of family and local responsibility would become impaired, and the government would have to continue giving relief forever; (3) states' rights would be violated; (4) a headless bureaucracy would be created; and (5) federal aid could only be a dole and would never get to the cause of the need.[29] The only real relief bill that did pass—the Wagner-Rainey Bill—provided funds for public works and authorized the Reconstruction Finance Corporation (RFC) to make loans and advances for unemployment relief. This bill was vetoed by President Hoover on July 11, 1932.[30] (Subsequently overridden.)

Thus by the second and third quarters of 1932, public relief expenditures were actually decreasing at a time when the number of applicants for relief was increasing. There appeared to be little chance of additional state appropriations; municipalities themselves could not provide additional funds, as some of them were falling into the hands of receivership, and the appropriated RFC funds were woefully inadequate. It was against this background that Hoover campaigned for reelection with the promise to continue his policies, an option that was summarily rejected by the American people.

The presidential election of 1932 presaged a radical change in the role of the national government in the area of relief. Much has been written about the eventual economic recovery and the reform aspects of the New Deal. Perhaps no legislation passed during those crucial first 100 days of the Roosevelt administration can logically be separated from the total effort to meet the problems of the Great Depression. Attention here is directed to those measures that laid the groundwork for our present public assistance operation.

Chief among these measures was the development of the Federal Emergency Relief Administration. In the spring of 1933, when the Federal Emergency Relief Act was under consideration, some

18 million persons were receiving emergency assistance of one kind or another. In some states 40 percent of the population was on relief; in some counties the rate was as high as 90 percent.[31] The FERA bill which finally emerged and became law in May of 1933 was modeled closely after TERA, which Roosevelt had pioneered in New York. The former director of TERA, Harry Hopkins, became chief of FERA. Unlike the New York program, FERA made no provision for a citizen policymaking board, and the director was responsible only to the President. Partly because of this and because Hopkins was later accused of having had questionable influence on the Roosevelt administration, some observers consider the provisions for lay control of public assistance under the Social Security Act to be excessive.

Under the terms of the FERA bill, $500 million for *unemployment relief* was made available to the states. Unlike the programs under the Hoover administration, FERA made money available in the form of grants rather than loans. Congress enacted almost no substantive legislation concerning the structure, powers, and scope of the new agency, and Hopkins had virtually a free hand. Rules and regulations were promulgated setting forth the conditions of relief administration which the states had to meet in order to be eligible to receive the grants. These were for the most part reflective of the forward thinking of the outstanding representatives of the social work profession of that day.[32] Each state was required to establish an emergency relief authority to receive and disburse federal money, and only public agencies could be employed as administrative units for distributing the funds to needy families. The amount of any grant to an individual or family was to be determined on a "budget deficit" basis;[33] rent was to be paid directly to the landlord, and medical care was to be provided on a "vendor" basis.[34] Discrimination against clients was to be avoided; work-relief projects were to be encouraged. Only trained professionals (social workers) were to be employed in the supervisory positions, and project workers were to receive cash compensation.[35]

Despite what has been considered quite superior administration, two fundamental problems plagued the administration of FERA and continue to plague the Family Service Division of the Social Security Administration. The first problem was that of relative allocation to the various states, and the second was the perennial question of work versus direct relief.

The original appropriation act stipulated that one half of the $500 million was to be distributed on a matching basis, and the remainder was to be distributed at the discretion of the administrator, provided that no more than 15 percent went to any one state.[36] This latter requirement was removed in later appropriation bills, but only Illinois approached the 15 percent figure. Both President Roosevelt and Hopkins seemed firmly convinced that, under normal conditions, the business of relief was essentially a state and local matter. Thus, definite efforts were made to see to it that the states and the lesser political subdivisions paid "their share." At no time did FERA work out any coherent or consistent plan for determining that share, however.

The reasons for FERA's difficulty with the problems of resolving the question of state sharing were quite complex. A few factors in this problem have been analyzed by Hilary Leyendecker, as follows:

(1) A uniform matching formula, applicable to all states, would have been unsatisfactory because there was no direct relation between the degree of need and the ability to raise funds. Thus, if the national government had matched state and local appropriations, the state that could raise the most money would receive the largest federal grant, even though its dependency rate might be much less than that of other states.

(2) The rather obvious political problem of getting a bill through Congress where each state did not perceive itself as getting its own fair share.[37]

The second problem, that of work relief versus direct relief, was equally complex. It was not primarily a question of choice between the two approaches, for everyone seemed to agree that work relief was preferable to a dole.[38] The problem arose in making a distinction between a work-relief program and a public works program.[39] In fact, these two highly similar recovery-relief operations became enmeshed in a power conflict between Harold Ickes and Harry Hopkins.[40] Further, when, by terms of the FERA Act, funds were cut off from direct relief and channeled into work relief, the unemployables would again become the sole responsibility of the states, as they had been under the poor law. The federal government was assuming responsibility only for the unemployed, and their needs were to be met through work relief. It proved administratively impossible and impractical, however, to make a distinction between an unemployed man and an unemployable man.

FERA was superseded by the Work Progress Administration and, to a lesser extent, the Public Works Administration and passed from the scene. Its ghost remains, however, because the defects and the problems of FERA strongly influenced the type of public legislation we now have in the Social Security Act.

THE PASSAGE OF THE SOCIAL SECURITY ACT

As the Great Depression continued, it became apparent that many of the problems associated with public dependency were long-range issues that had to be dealt with by means of continuing programs of assistance. President Roosevelt declared, on June 8, 1934, that in the next session of Congress the administration would present a bill to provide security against several of the great unsettling factors in life—especially those related to unemployment and old age.[41]

It is instructive to note that the factors mentioned by the President were later incorporated in the bill under the insurance rather than the assistance principle. Edwin E. Witte, who served as the technical director of the citizens' committee which drew up the bill, pointed out that uppermost in the minds of those who worked most closely with the administration in developing the bill was the notion of an insurance approach to the problem of insecurity.[42] The President seemed to prefer a total insurance approach,[43] and the assistance provisions were placed in the social security bill only after it was decided that the insurance approach did not afford an effective means to deal with the problems of dependency arising out of forces other than temporary, involuntary unemployment or old age.[44] According to Arthur Altmeyer, the assistance provisions were thought of as temporary in nature, soon to be replaced or made redundant by the expanding insurance system. The entire bill was thus drawn up with this in mind.

Initially, the technical staff responsible for administering the program did not include any social workers.[45] A social worker was appointed to the President's Advisory Committee on Economic Security only as an afterthought so that there would be one member who had some daily contact with the poor.[46] Thus, in contrast to the insurance provisions of the bill, the sections dealing with

public assistance were not subjected to extensive study and deliberation by experts. In fact, during the very intense discussion and
careful scrutiny of the bill both before its introduction and during
congressional debate, the assistance part received very little attention.[47]

There is no need to recount here extensively the factors affecting the passage of the Social Security Act. That job has been done
in great detail elsewhere.[48]

The social security bill was born in the depression. The depression gave the impetus to the bill and ultimately made its passage
possible, but it also created opposition to the bill and made its
passage difficult. The depression so channelized the forces of
reform that major features of the bill were almost predetermined.
Both the administration and the Congress were reluctant to add
tax burdens or to increase governmental deficits, particularly at
the state and local levels, as Witte has noted:

> It was these considerations that resulted in the low begin-
> ning social security tax rates and the step-plan of the intro-
> duction of both old-age and unemployment insurance and
> also in the establishment of completely self-financed social
> insurance programs, without government contributions—to
> this day a distinctive feature of social insurance in this coun-
> try.[49]

The major bloc to passage of the bill was the Townsend Plan,
which proposed.an automatic pension of $200 a month for every-
one over 60, with the sole provision that the recipient spend the
money each month. Originally the plan was to operate only in
California, but it gained so much momentum in 1934 and 1935
that members of the technical committee feared it would block
passage of the entire Social Security Act. The technical committee
headed by Ernest Whitte served as a source of guidance on both
technical and political issues. Support for the Townsend Plan
spread like wildfire, as Townsend Clubs were created all over the
country, and support of older people for the social security bill was
threatened. While there were few in Congress who felt the Townsend Plan was feasible, many were reluctant to oppose it or to
support the administration's much milder bill for fear of earning
the enmity of older citizens.[50] Dr. Townsend became a very important national figure. His first appearance before the House Ways

and Means Committee considering the social security bill was widely advertised in advance; it attracted the largest audience of the entire hearings and received front-page publicity in newspapers throughout the country. Witte characterized Townsend's appearance in these terms:

> Dr. Townsend and his witnesses did not so much attack the economic security bill as champion their own plan as a substitute for the titles on old age security in the Administration's bill. They were given unlimited time and treated courteously, but the committee members subjected them to a merciless questioning to bring out the weaknesses in their plan. Dr. Townsend and his witnesses made many damaging admissions, which encouraged many members of Congress to come out openly against the Townsend Plan.[51]

The widespread publicity surrounding the Townsend Plan has often detracted from the examination of opposition to the bill from other sources. One of these proposals, the Lundeen bill, was directly critical of the administration's proposal. This bill proposed unemployment benefits at prevailing wages for all workers, to be administered by commissions composed of rank-and-file members of workers' and farmers' organizations. The Lundeen bill became the focus of radical demands,[52] with the principal statement in its behalf being made by Herbert P. Benjamin, the secretary of the National Joint Action Committee for Genuine Social Insurance. According to Witte's account, Benjamin was very insulting to the House Committee and was finally ejected by a policeman. Earl Browder, executive secretary of the Communist Party of America, described the Lundeen bill as the principal method of propaganda of his party.[53] Mary Van Kleeck, the author of the bill, made a much more dignified statement, but the net effect of the testimony on the Lundeen bill was to identify it as a Communist proposal.

The more substantive questions had been previously resolved in the confines of technical staff meetings. The principal questions concerned unemployment insurance. A variety of plans were offered, but, aside from essentially inconsequential modifications, there were three basic plans: (1) an unemployment insurance program financed by a tax offset system (the Wagner-Lewis bill), (2) a federal subsidy plan financed by a federal grant-in-aid (the Dill-

Connery bill), and (3) a wholly national approach financed out of general revenues.[54]

By the spring of 1934, both the Wagner-Lewis and the Dill-Connery bills had developed momentum. It was clear that if the administration did not take action soon its hand would be forced. The President's advisors were divided on the question of unemployment insurance, and at the insistence of Rex Tugwell the decision on this matter was postponed for further study.[55] The arguments swayed back and forth throughout the life of the technical committee. The Advisory Council, headed by Frank Graham of the University of North Carolina, voted 9 to 7 for the subsidy plan, but by this time the technical committee had finally settled on the Wagner-Lewis approach. To add further complications, some of the outstanding experts, like Abraham Epstein, Paul Douglas, I. M. Rubenow, and Eveline Burns, favored the national system. Political activists of considerable power, like Rex Tugwell and Henry Wallace, also favored a national system. However, President Roosevelt clearly favored a state system, because he doubted that a bill reflecting any other approach could pass, and because he had very real questions about the constitutional vulnerability of the national approach. The President said that whatever approach was considered, the administration must have a final version ready for Congress by January of 1935. On November 9, 1934, the advisory and technical committees decided to abandon the thought of an exclusively federal approach, and one month later they wrote into the administration bill the Wagner-Lewis approach. This portion of the act was passed without substantial change.[56]

As we have noted, the assistance portions of the bill were added without the kind of deliberations that went into the old-age and employment insurance portions of the bill. Because it was felt that the insurance would in time meet all the needs of dependent people, the assistance portions were thought of as temporary in nature.[57]

Thus, in addition to the old-age and unemployment insurance systems, the committee called for a program of grants-in-aid for the states for assistance to the needy aged, the blind, and dependent children. This provision was based on the provisions of the Dill-Connery bill of 1934. Federal grants were also proposed for maternal and child health aid and for child welfare and public health services. The question of a health insurance program was dropped entirely, out of fear that the opposition of the American Medical Association would endanger the entire Social Security Act.[58]

When the bill was introduced in Congress it immediately ran into a jurisdictional fight between the Senate and the House of Representatives. To the embarrassment of E. E. Witte, he was called as the first witness to both committee hearings, which were to proceed simultaneously. For a few days he appeared first at one committee and then at the other, while sending a replacement to the "slighted" committee. Then the Senate postponed hearings until the studies had been completed in the House.

The major question considered by the House Ways and Means Committee concerned the conflict between the administration's insurance approach to the aged, on one hand, and the Townsend Plan and other "hot money" schemes, on the other. The committee concluded its work with an entirely new bill. This bill did not differ very much in content from the original proposal, but it did differ greatly in arrangement and language. The bill was given a new number and even a new title, the Social Security Act; it had previously been termed the Economic Security Act.[59]

The measure was then introduced as a committee bill and replaced the old Doughton and Lewis bills, which had previously been submitted as the administration's proposal in the House and Senate, respectively. The committee's favorable report was filed on April 5, 1935, and consideration before the House began on April 11. The bill was given an open rule by the House Rules Committee. The House and Senate were afraid that the bill would be mutilated on the floor of Congress; on the other hand they also felt that it was of such importance that every effort should be made to avoid the appearance that it was being railroaded through by the administration. However, the "word" was passed from the leadership in Congress that all amendments were to be killed. In all, 50 amendments were introduced from the floor, but none ever came close to passage.

Difficulty had been anticipated over a proposal to substitute the Townsend Plan for old-age insurance provisions of the bill. Congressman Greenway of Arizona did propose such a substitution and went directly to President Roosevelt to get support for his revision. The President's refusal to back his proposal was a major factor in the defeat of the amendment. According to Witte, the vote on the Townsend amendment was taken by division rather than by roll call. Members voting for the amendment were listed in the newspapers; in the majority, they were conservative Republicans who had opposed the entire social security bill. Although the supporters of the amendment to substitute the Lundeen bill were not reported, Witte notes that most of them were opponents of the social security bill rather than supporters of the Lundeen bill.

Final House passage came on April 19, by a vote of 371 to 33. The minority was composed of a handful of diehard supporters of the Townsend Plan or the Lundeen bill, and a somewhat larger number of conservatives who were opposed to all social security legislation.[60]

The bill fared somewhat better in the Senate, perhaps because the drive behind extreme alternative approaches had been dissipated in the debate in the House. The conflicts in the Senate surrounded two essentially technical amendments, the Clark and Russell amendments.[61] Because of the inclusion of these two amendments, it was necessary for the bill to be sent to a conference committee to resolve the differences between the House and Senate versions. The committee reported back on July 16. Further deliberation was necessary, and finally a compromise was reached whereby the Clark amendment was to be dropped, with the understanding that a special committee of the House and Senate would meet to draw up a bill which would incorporate the principles of the Clark amendment, and this new bill would be interpreted as an amendment to the Social Security Act at the next session of Congress.

The compromise bill was passed by both the House and the Senate, on August 8 and 9, respectively. On August 14, 1935, the Social Security Act was signed by President Roosevelt and became the law of the land.

It is important to note that the public assistance provisions of the act seemed to glide through both the preparatory stage and the passage stage. Because of this, the federal participation in the public assistance phases was not to be determined until the amendments to the act were passed in following years. How these amendments developed, where their support came from, and how they have affected the structure of the contemporary public assistance agency is discussed in the next Chapter.

NOTES

1. Some of the most frequently cited book-length historical works are the following: Philip Klein, *From Philanthropy to Social Welfare* (San Francisco: Jossey-Bass, Inc., 1968); Blanche D. Coll, *Perspectives in Public Welfare* (Washington, D.C.: U.S. Government Printing Office, 1969); Samuel Mencher, *Poor Law to Poverty Program* (Pittsburgh: University of Pittsburgh Press, 1967); and the seminal work, Richard H. Brenner, *American Philanthropy* (Chicago: University of Chicago Press, 1960). Shorter but very adequate historical treatment is found in the first two chapters of Russell Smith and Dorothy Zeits, *American Social Welfare Institutions* (New York; John Wiley & Sons, 1970); and J. Riesenfeld, "The Formative Era of American Public Assistance Law," *California Law Review*, vol. 43 (1955), p. 175 ff. Even a cursory historical note on the early period cannot omit the following works: E. M. Leonard, *The Early History of the English Poor Relief* (New York: Barnes & Noble, 1965); George Nichols, *A History of the English Poor Laws* (London: John Millay, 1854); Helen I. Clark, *Social Legislation* (New York: Appleton-Century-Crofts, 1957); C. R. Steinbecker, *Poor Relief in the 16th Century* (Washington, D.C.: Catholic University Press, 1937); Brian Tierney, *Medieval Poor Laws* (Berkeley: University of California Press, 1959). Of course, note must be taken of Sidney Webb and Beatrice Webb, *English Poor Law History* (London: Longmans Green, 1927).
2. Clark, *Social Legislation*, p. 469.
3. See Arthur Parker Miles, *An Introduction to Public Welfare* (Boston: D. C. Heath, 1949), p. 27; Hilary Moorehead Leyendecker, *Problems and Policy in Public Assistance* (New York: Harper's, 1955), pp. 22–30.
4. June Axinn & Herman Levin. *Social Welfare: A History of the American Response to Need.* New York: Dodd Mead, 1975), p. 10.
5. Ibid.
6. E. M. Leonard, *History of English Poor Relief* (New York: Harper Brothers, 1955); F. M. Eden, *The State of the Poor* (New York: Dutton, 1921).
7. R. A. Mohl, "Poverty in Early America: A Re-Appraisal," *New York History*, vol. 50 (January 1969), pp. 5–27.
8. Elizabeth Wisner, *Social Welfare in the South: From Colonial Times to World War I* (Baton Rouge: Louisiana State University, 1970), p. 23 ff.
9. William G. Sumner, *What the Social Classes Owe to Each Other* (New York: Classroom Reprints, 1964).
10. Robert Hunter, *Poverty* (New York: Macmillan Company, 1905), pp. 63–65.
11. See Robert H. Bremmer, *From the Depths* (New York: New York University Press, 1964), p. 253.
12. Franklin D. Roosevelt, *The Public Papers and Addresses of FDR*, compiled by Samuel Rosenman (New York: Random House, 1938), vol. 2, p. 14.
13. The definitive history of this period, written from a social work perspective, is Josephine C. Brown's *Public Relief, 1929–39* (New York: Henry Holt & Co., 1940). Also see E. E. Witte, *Development of the Social Security Act* (Madison: University of Wisconsin Press, 1962), and Clark

Chambers, *Seed Time of Reform* (Minneapolis: University of Minnesota Press, 1963).

14. Brown, *Public Relief, 1929–39*, p. 63.
15. Nathan Cohen, *Social Work in the American Tradition* (New York: Holt Rinehart, 1958).
16. Brown, *Public Relief, 1929–39*, p. 64 ff.
17. Ibid., pp. 63–64.
18. Ibid., p. 66.
19. JoAnna C. Colcord, "Facing the Coming Winter," *Survey Midmonthly,* November 1930, p. 208.
20. Brown, *Public Relief, 1929–39*, p. 80.
21. Ibid., p. 68.
22. E. P. Hayes, *Activities of the President's Emergency Committee for Employment, 1930–31* (Concord: Rumford Press, 1936), pp. 3–4, as quoted in Brown, *Public Relief, 1929–39*, pp. 69–70.
23. Brown, *Public Relief, 1929–39*, p. 71.
24. U.S. Congress, Senate, 72nd Cong., 1st Sess., 1931, SB 174.
25. U.S. Congress, Senate, 72nd Cong., 1st Sess., 1931, SB 262.
26. U.S. Congress, Senate, 72nd Cong., 1st Sess., 1931, SB 3045.
27. Brown, *Public Relief, 1929–39*, p. 118.
28. Adeline R. Hasse, "Congressional Relief Programs: A Record of Action in the Congress of the United States, 1803–1933." *Congressional Record,* vol. 75, pp. 4016–17; cited in Brown, *Public Relief, 1929–39*, p. 111.
29. Arthur E. Fink, *The Field of Social Work* (New York: Henry Holt & Co., 1958), p. 53.
30. Brown, *Public Relief, 1929–39*, p. 124.
31. Leyendecker, *Problems and Policy in Public Assistance*, p. 69.
32. Ibid., p. 71.
33. The total financial need is calculated for a family on the basis of standards set in a policy manual—so much for rent, so much for clothes per child, and so on. The family monthly income is subtracted from this total amount. The difference is the budget deficit and is equal to the grant.
34. Payment is made directly to the person performing the service (the vendor).
35. Monthly report, *Federal Emergency Relief Administration* (Washington, D.C.: U.S. Government Printing Office, December 1933), p. 39, as cited in Leyendecker, *Problems and Policy in Public Assistance*, p. 71.
36. Ibid., p. 72. Also see Brown, *Public Relief, 1929–39*.
37. Leyendecker, *Problems and Policy in Public Assistance*, p. 72 ff.
38. It is interesting to note use of the term *dole*. Originally it was used during the Great Depression to connote an inadequate assistance grant —one so low that the recipient could not purchase the necessities of life. When work relief projects were begun, the assistance checks of those participating were increased so that people on relief would prefer to work, because their checks would be larger. After a while, the word *dole* became associated with any relief program which was not tied to work. In time *dole* acquired a new meaning—a sum given, regardless of

its adequacy, to maintain a person who does not give any service in return.

39. For an extended discussion of the fundamental differences between these terms, see Leyendecker, *Problems and Policy in Public Assistance,* chap. 13.

40. For an intensive analysis of the Hopkins-Ickes controversy, see Arthur M. Schlesinger, *The Age of Roosevelt* (Boston: Houghton Mifflin Co., 1957).

41. Miles, *Introduction to Public Welfare,* p. 232.

42. Witte, *Development of Social Security Act.*

43. Ibid., p. 18.

44. Ibid., p. 165.

45. Ibid., p. 7 ff. Men like Witte, Altmeyer, and Cohen have since been considered social workers, but they were not identified as such at the time.

46. Ibid., p. 52. A Catholic was also added at this time.

47. Edwin E. Witte, "Birth and Early Days of Social Security in the United States," *Public Welfare,* vol. 18 (July 1960), p. 169.

48. For an intensive account of the passage of the Social Security Act written at the time, see Eveline M. Burns, *Toward Social Security: An Explanation of the Social Security Act and a Survey of the Larger Issues* (New York: McGraw-Hill Book Co., 1936), and Paul H. Douglas, *Social Security in the United States: An Analysis and Appraisal of the Federal Social Security Act* (New York: McGraw-Hill Book Co., 1936). The former is a survey of the economic factors and forces which led to the adoption of the insurance approach. The latter is more concerned with the political forces involved, but it was written while the bill was still under consideration and in many ways was a polemic arguing for its passage. A second edition of this work in 1939 was essentially a popularization of more erudite explanations of the provisions of the Social Security Act. In this sense, it was more of an early form of Arthur Larson's *Know Your Social Security* (New York: Harper & Brothers, 1959), a layman's guide to the benefits of the program.

An earlier work which was also used as a polemic to gain support for the bill was I. M. Rubenow's *The Quest for Security* (New York: Henry Holt & Company, 1934), which presents, again from the insurance point of view, the need for government to assume the responsibility of protecting individuals from financial losses incidental to accident. A review of the decisions involved in the development of the Social Security Act is found in Karl de Schweinitz, *People and Process in Social Security* (Washington, D.C.: American Council on Education, 1948), and Lewis Merriam's *Relief and Social Security* (Washington, D.C.: Brookings Institution, 1946). Both of these works trace the development of the act, discuss its administrative operation, and contrast it with the European, and particularly the British experience. To contrast our experience with the English, the student should examine Karl de Schweinitz's *England's Road to Social Security.*

A great deal of insight into development of various provisions of the bill can be obtained from a reading of Edwin E. Witte, *The Development of the Social Security Act.* This is a memorandum written daily by the head of the technical staff of the President's Committee on Economic Security, revised later, and finally published posthumously. Insight into the political temper of the time of the passage of the bill can also be gained from Schlesinger's *Age of Roosevelt.*

Briefer, but still complete, accounts of the passage of the bill can be found in some of the major social work textbooks. Particularly see Leyendecker, note 3, chap. 3; Clark, *Social Legislation,* chap. 21–23; Miles, *Introduction to Public Welfare,* chap. 10.

Primary material relevant to the development of the act can be found in Edith Abbott's *Public Assistance* (Chicago: University of Chicago Press, 1940), and Sophonisba P. Breckenridge, *Public Welfare Administration in the United States: Selected Documents* (Chicago: University of Chicago Press, 1937).

49. Witte, "Birth and Early Days of Social Security," p. 169.
50. Ibid.
51. Witte, *Development of the Social Security Act,* p. 85.
52. Schlesinger, *Age of Roosevelt,* vol. 2, p. 296.
53. Benjamin Gitlow, by no means a reliable source but a leading figure in the Communist Party in 1935, later testified that Lundeen, a left-wing farmer-labor congressman from Minnesota, was a paid undercover agent of the Communist Party. See Schlesinger, vol. 2, pp. 29–62.
54. Schlesinger, *Age of Roosevelt,* vol. 2, p. 303.
55. Witte, *Development of the Social Security Act,* p. 28. A list of the more important records and memoranda prepared by members of the staff appears in the U.S. Congress, Senate, Committee on Finance, *Hearings before the Committee on Finance, United States Senate,* 74th Cong., 1st Sess., 1935, pp. 323–24.
56. Witte, *Development of the Social Security Act,* pp. 39–62. See also Schlesinger, note 40, vol. 2, p. 306.
57. Ibid., pp. 39–62.
58. J. Douglas Brown, "The Development of the Old Age Insurance Provisions of the Social Security Act," *Law and Contemporary Problems,* April 1936; cited in Schlesinger, *Age of Roosevelt,* vol. 2, p. 307.
59. The term had been coined by Abraham Epstein, and he had given that name—Social Security Administration—to a group of his followers who were pushing for a broader social insurance legislation. As it turned out, social security became something of an "angel" term, while economic security became a socialistically tinged "devil" term.
60. Witte, *Development of Social Security Act,* p. 99 ff.
61. Ibid., p. 106. The Clark amendment, ostensibly technical in nature, would as a matter of fact have significantly altered the scope of the act. By the terms of the Clark amendment, industries that provided an industrial pension would be exempted from the employer contribution to the proposed old-age and survivors insurance fund. Thus, the workers in those plants would not be covered by old-age social insurance. Interestingly, Senator Clark assailed the experts who had drawn up the bill and contended his amendment would make it a congressional bill instead of an experts' bill.

CHAPTER 9

WELFARE REFORM, 1935-1968:

INCREMENTAL CHANGES

INTRODUCTION

Though little debated in the 1930s, the Public Assistance Programs have become one of the most controversial public programs ever legislated. The tensions that were to produce the political conflict were written into the initial legislation. These tensions developed between:

1. Federal direction and local option.
2. The demands of a structured governmental program, and the unstructured traditions of the local philanthropy that the program replaced.
3. A cash strategy of providing income, and a service strategy of providing "rehabilitation."
4. The tailoring of a program to the unique needs of a specific subpopulation of the poor, and the demands for equal treatment of all citizens.
5. A program that is adequate to meet the needs of those who have no other income, and the desire to encourage recipients to seek alternate forms of income.
6. Programs for those who can work, and aid for those who

cannot work. This source of tension proved to be the most significant one.

While all of these tensions were present at the inception of the legislation, they did not become political problems until there were visible interest groups demanding a resolution in a particular direction.

One of the central tensions between the individualized social work approach and the demands of equal treatment was perceptively recognized by Alan Keith-Lucas,[1] who argued that the guidelines for determination of aid were hopelessly vague and thus produced a variance in response that was subject to the slightest whim of local governing bodies or even the personality of the individual's caseworker. He further showed that, unlike in traditional bureaucracies, in social welfare the discretion ceded to the public employee actually was lessened as one ascended the bureaucratic ladder. This made political accountability of the program an almost complete impossibility.

Under the leadership of the professional social work community, at that time a hearty band of perhaps 10,000 persons, mostly middle-class women with master's degrees in social work, public welfare began to emphasize service over cash, discretion over accountability, local option over federal direction, open-ended budgeting at all levels of government, and an intensification of the move to categorize the poor and further to subcategorize the forms of aid.

It had taken a major depression to force the first federal review of public welfare practice, and it was beginning to appear that a catastrophe of similar proportions would be required to produce a reexamination of the central assumptions of the Social Security Act and its related policy paradigm. The public programs adopted by the New Deal to respond to income insecurity and the Social Security Act were designed to fit into a rather neatly ordered, secure political economy, in which the condition of poverty and the political acceptance of poverty were seen as part of the natural order of things. Irv Garfinkel has remarked:

Prior to the 1960's the principal objective of our income transfer system was to reduce economic insecurity. The idea was to replace a *normal* flow of earnings, that, for some unavoidable reason, had been interrupted. If earnings were reduced because of retirement, there was Old Age Insurance; if because of disability, Disability Insurance; if because of the death of the breadwinner, Survivors Insurance; if because of unemployment, Unemployment Insurance. The three federal income-tested transfer programs that were established by the 1935 Social Security Act—Aid to the Aged, Aid to Dependent Children, and Aid to the Blind—were supposed to be small programs that would wither away as the social insurance system matured. It was as if poverty were viewed as just a special case of economic insecurity.[2]

The New Deal consisted of three interrelated sets of public policies regarding income security. The first set focused on the role of government in securing and maintaining a full and stable economy. The federal acceptance of a positive adaptive role to this end evolved gradually over the whole of the New Deal and was not achieved in a single legislative act. A series of policies begun during the first 100 days and continuing today recognized that the federal government has an opportunity and a responsibility to use its enormous fiscal and monetary power to protect workers from violent shifts in the economy as business goes through its normal cycle. Thus sheltered from inflation and depression by a partially planned and regulated economy, able-bodied and prime-age workers were expected to provide for themselves and their families with their wages.

The second set of policies stemmed from a recognition that even in a well-planned and regulated economy pursuing full employment, there would be wage-income disruptions and terminations resulting from disability, ill health, early death, and temporary unemployment. The second line of policy focused on the role of government in supplementing private insurance and savings plans which are used to guard against income insecurity from these forces. This public line of defense against income insecurity was to come from a complicated set of publicly sponsored and administered programs of social insurance.[3] The New Deal programs set up a variety of uniquely tailored social insurance programs to respond to the income insecurity resulting from unemployment, early death of the breadwinner, or retirement. Social insurance programs for wage disruptions from industrial accidents and nonemployment disabilities were established or expanded by the Roosevelt-Truman administration. A prime reliance on social insurance as a protection against income insecurity continued into the Eisenhower years (the administrative operation of these programs is reviewed in chapter 6).

The third defense against income insecurity, a residual one, was a set of federal-state-local plans of public assistance designed, at the outset, to provide a minimum consumptive standard for a subset of the poor population who had somehow fallen through the insurance-work net. Not all persons were to be so protected, and distinct programs for the aged, the blind, the widowed, and the orphaned were established by the federal government. As the public assistance programs were initially conceived, they would wither away as a vigorous economy and a fully developed set of social insurance plans would make them unnecessary.

Rather than wither, these public assistance programs became the vortex of the political conflict, albeit a submerged one. As the public assistance programs evolved, they were subject to two competing claims: One was that public assistance programs should be used as an instrument of social and personal rehabilitation to facilitate reentry into the labor force of those who had become dependent on welfare. The second demand on public assistance was that aid should be expanded to all persons experiencing income poverty, and benefit schedules should be established for those who could not be expected to enter the labor force. The political and programmatic conflicts between a desire to provide adequate benefits to those who cannot work and a conscious system to encourage, or rather demand, reentry into the labor force of those who can helped to produce what was to become known as "the welfare mess."

THE WELFARE MESS

A number of assumptions were central to the welfare system established by Roosevelt's New Deal, continued in Truman's Fair Deal, and allowed to drift during the Eisenhower years. The reality behind the assumptions did not change dramatically during the first 25 years under the Social Security Act. What did change was the political acceptance of these assumptions.

First, and certainly of the greatest importance, was the assumption that poverty is not a significant political problem when the economy is in good health. The federal assumption of a direct relief role was justified by the trauma of the depression. In "normal times," inability to earn an adequate income, except for the predictable lapses being picked up by social insurance, was a sign of individual pathology. Private social work agencies funded by voluntary contributions could best deal with such individuals.

Second, it was widely accepted that the magnitude of poverty was on a rapid decline; supposedly those at the bottom of the economic ladder also should have experienced the recovery that the economy in general realized from 1939 to 1946.

Third, it was assumed that the decline in public assistance evidenced from 1939 through 1946 would continue until a small and insignificant program could be returned to the states.

Any number of persons could have told the economic planners that the third assumption was untrue. To many it was becoming increasingly clear that an adequate wage depended on more than a healthy economy. Employment discrimination against blacks and women produced incomes below a standard of decency for perhaps one-fifth of the population. Inadequate, and certainly unequal, education and training opportunities limited another large segment of able-bodied workers. There also is a population of persons capable of functioning outside an institution but not able to "produce" an income at or above the level of adequacy. A warning about this problem came from William Haber in a 1938 *Survey Graphic* article in which he argued that perhaps three-quarters of the assistance recipients who were not aged or disabled were in need of aid for reasons unrelated to the health of the economy.[4] Haber's calculation did not consider an equally large number of persons in that population who were not on any form of relief and who did not have any real prospect of ever receiving an adequate income via either employment or insurance. The permanently dependent, the *Lumpenproletariat,* were simply not a calculation of the New Deal's welfare policy. Nor did they enter into the calculations of Truman or Eisenhower. The persistence of this benign assumption is illustrated by the testimony of Arthur Altmeyer, Truman's Social Security Administrator, as late as 1949:

> ... this public assistance is a residual program to help needy persons who are not adequately protected by the various forms of contributory social insurance. . . . If we have a comprehensive contributory social insurance system ... in time the residual load of public assistance would become so

small in this country that the States and the localities could reasonably be expected to assume that load without Federal financial participation.[5]

In the decade just preceding the inauguration of Kennedy, public welfare programs were altered only by incremental legislation which was consistent with the assumption that had been expressed by Altmeyer. Expenditures in assistance were thought of as short-run, stopgap efforts to deal with an "unusual" condition. There were efforts to add social insurance coverage to a group "inadvertently" overlooked. One change was the decision by the Eisenhower administration to bring medical coverage for low-income persons under the public assistance umbrella. These changes were reflected in the decisions to add disability to the class of persons covered by social insurance (1950), to provide an assistance program for the permanently and totally disabled not covered by social insurance (1951), to authorize federal expenditures in direct rehabilitation (1956), and to expand significantly the federal role in paying for expenditures incurred in child welfare programs (1959).

Thus the assistance features of the social security package, vis-à-vis ill-conceived assumptions and thoughtless incremental legislation, became a permanent and costly component of the social welfare system. Between 1935 and 1945 the direct public aid cost had been cut to half of its 1935 dollar level; however, since 1945 that figure has steadily increased (see Figure 9-1). Clearly, public welfare was a permanent program.

THE KENNEDY ADMINISTRATION WAR ON WELFARE

As the permanency of the public assistance program became increasingly evident, the "war on welfare" was begun. From 1950 to 1960 the number of assistance recipients increased by 400,000, but the composition had shifted. The decline of 400,000 aged recipients was more than compensated for by a rise of 800,000 recipients of Aid to Dependent Children. A politically attractive constituency was becoming a politically unattractive constituency: grateful voters were being replaced by ungrateful nonvoters, blacks were replacing whites, longer-term recipients were replacing short-term recipients. Costs were increasing more rapidly than the case load; in constant dollar terms, costs were up nearly

FIGURE 9-1
INCOME MAINTENANCE PROGRAMS: EXPENDITURES PER CAPITA,
1935–1960 (IN 1959 DOLLARS)

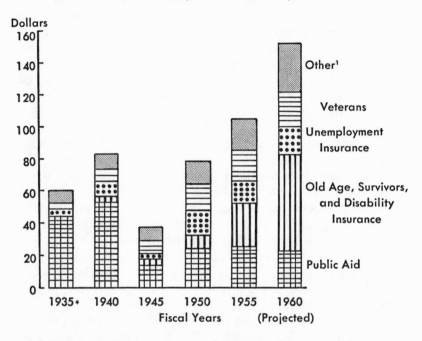

¹Railroad and public employee retirement programs, workmen's
compensation, and temporary disability insurance
*OASDI legislation not yet passed.

SOURCE: *Social Security Bulletin,* August 1960, p. 9.

60 percent. Most significantly, even greater increases were
projected; half a million new AFDC recipients found their way to
the welfare offices in the first year of the Kennedy administration,[6]
and program costs in fiscal 1962, the first full Kennedy year, went
up faster than they had in the entire eight years of Eisenhower's
administration. White House staff were acutely aware of the fact
that welfare policy, unaltered, would soon be a major political
liability.[7]

The first policy response in the Kennedy administration was to
continue the drift by adding yet another subpopulation for a specific categorical cash program. One of the first "legislative victo-

ries" of the new administration was to add a program called AFDC
-U to the AFDC programs, in order to extend coverage to male-
headed families where poverty was visited upon the children because of the unemployment of the parent. This legislation had
been vigorously endorsed by the labor unions and opposed by the
conservative business lobbies. In state legislatures, the power of
the business lobby was stronger and the labor unions' weaker;
therefore the welfare programs did not receive the necessary en-
dorsements to become operative in the states, though they had
been authorized at the level of the federal government.

Thus blocked, the administration tried a new tactic. On February 1, 1962, Kennedy sent to Congress the first message from a
president which was devoted exclusively to public assistance. That
message and the subsequent thrust of the administration was to
back away from the giving of cash aid. HEW Secretary Abraham
Ribicoff had set forth the theme in an intraadministration memo
a few weeks prior: ". . . too much emphasis has been placed on just
getting an assistance check into the hands of an individual. If we
are ever going to move constructively in this field, we must come
to recognize that our efforts must involve a variety of helpful
services, of which giving a money payment is only one, and the
object of our effort must be the entire family."[8] The rest of the
Democratic years would be spent in an effort to locate, pass, and
implement a service strategy. At first the strategy was highly targeted on the poor themselves, but in the ensuing search for a
politically expedient and economically efficient service strategy,
the target base was broadened.

Options, Open and Closed

In the specifications of the options available to a new administration, it is useful to think of alternative strategies as they are located
on two scales (see Figure 9–2). The vertical scale locates programs
as to their exclusivity to those experiencing poverty. At the bottom
of the scale are programs which rely on a means test, a proof of
need. Moving up the scale, there are programs based on pre-
sumed need. These programs are categorical and provide aid to
a subpopulation with a high incidence of poverty, but individual
applicants are not asked to demonstrate their individual poverty.
At the top of the scale are universal programs which provide aid
to all persons within a polity, without regard to their individual

economic condition. In Western Europe in the years after World War II, socialist governments relied on the broadly based programs, while in the United States the New Deal philosophy encouraged the retention of welfare programs that were designed to be administered almost exclusively to persons experiencing a "temporary" income loss.

The second dimension in this artificial typology locates programs in terms of their reliance on direct versus indirect aid. At the left side of the horizontal scale are programs which provide cash and in-kind aid to those who suffer from poverty. Moving to the right, there are programs that seek to deal with primary and secondary causes of economic want. On the far right side of the horizontal scale are indirect macroeconomic policies structured to simulate aggregate demand. Job counseling would be to the left on this scale, and area economic development would be to the right, with job retraining being somewhere between. Early New Deal welfare policies, in the main, would be located on the lower left extreme of this arbitrary scale.

Certain dynamic political implications spring from a program's location in this two-dimensional space. First, categorical means-

FIGURE 9–2
PROGRAMMATIC OPTIONS

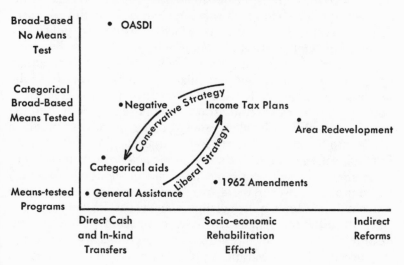

tested programs separate subsets of the poor from the rest of the population of persons experiencing poverty. The homogeneity of the population being aided allows for comprehensive planning and the unique tailoring of the program to the specific needs of its constituent population. This highly specific type of aid creates the appearance, if not the reality, of a donor-donee relationship.[9] Once a population has been singled out for purposes of planning and administration, it also becomes politically separated from the rest of the polity. In the context of American welfare politics, that separation has resulted in a process of stigmatization whereby recipients are blamed for their condition of need. The blaming of the victim leads to a set of programs to reshape the poor, to change their values, to interfere with their practice of child rearing so that the cycle of poverty can be broken. As programs to change the poor are implemented, attention is focused on the problems of adjustment they face and the socioeconomic forces that inhibit adjustment. Corrective action shifts subtly but certainly away from the poor and toward the environment. After a while, the programs are broadened and become broad-based, indirect programs. The programs become captives of the interest groups that have directed the latest transmogrification, and they become increasingly unresponsive to the needs of the original target population. This fuels a need for highly specific categorical programs. There is thus a poverty policy cycle which is self-fueling and repetitive—a process of incremental adjustments which keeps poverty policy in a state of constant political disequilibrium.

A deferral of taxes against assets might be desirable in an aid program for the aged but particularly undesirable for aid to the working poor. Female-headed families have a high incidence of poverty, but their expected escape from poverty is related to the reason the family is female headed. A father's death can plunge a family into temporary poverty, but multiple illegitimate births are frequently associated with a more permanent poverty. It seems to make simple sense to consider this factor in the design of a cash transfer plan. However, there are enormous sociopolitical reasons which mitigate against such planning. In the first instance, categories with different benefit schedules can encourage socially undesirable behavior, such as the feigned desertions associated with the current AFDC program. A politically powerful homogeneous group, like the aged, could well secure preferential treatment, while a maligned and politically powerless group, like unmarried mothers, might be not only unable to press for advantage but also likely to be the target of repression and misplaced moralism.

The Kennedy Effort

John F. Kennedy entered the presidency after eight years of drift in welfare programs toward cash strategies targeted to specific subpopulations of the poor. During the Eisenhower years, adjustments in poverty policy were obtained by adding new groups to old programs, as evidenced by the expansion of AFDC, the creation of new categorical programs (e.g., Aid to the Permanently and Totally Disabled), and the expansion of unemployment compensation to lower-income workers. This was the conservative drift that followed the broader-based reforms that had been adopted by the New Deal under the trauma of the depression.

A series of advisory reports had appeared, all of which called for (1) federal assumption of responsibility for welfare, (2) at least some extension of aid to male-headed families, and (3) a primary reliance on a service strategy to rehabilitate the poor. While task forces within the administration were laying the groundwork for a new federal assistance program, a small town in New York's Hudson River Valley, Newburgh, appointed a new city manager and charged him to reduce city spending. This event helped to shape the public welfare debate.

Actually, the Newburgh welfare controversy had begun shortly after Joseph Mitchell's appointment as city manager of Newburgh in the fall of 1960. At that time a committee of three citizens was appointed to study the rising costs of welfare, with particular reference to the charge that "Newburgh and other Hudson Valley cities had become a dumping ground for the South." The committee's report in early 1961 noted that there was "a possibly more than accidental movement from the South to the North" and that the newcomers were not easily assimilated, had limited education and only a few skills, and were the first to be let go during an economic recession. The committee concluded that the rising relief costs were traceable to the influx of migrant workers.[10] It also found that the average black's weekly take-home pay was $40. Because of their low incomes, blacks had to take what living quarters they could afford, and the resultant crowding in old tenements and houses in the river wards had created "moral" and physical problems: "Normal healthy entertainment at home for teenagers is impossible ... so meetings in bars, street corners, cars are arranged." School officials told committee members that pregnancy among black girls of 12 to 15 years of age was not uncommon and was increasing. Many of the children receiving assistance were illegitimate. The committee found that the inability of the Planned Parenthood unit to advise unwed mothers on contraceptive practice was a factor in illegitimacy, but it appreciated that promiscuity could not be condoned and suggested that the answer lay elsewhere.

The citizens' study committee recommended[11] that:

1. The city investigate the possibility of having the county take over its welfare program.
2. The city consider the possibility of rent control where rentals were being paid by the Welfare Department.
3. The city adopt a "tougher" policy toward relief applicants and a stricter check on changes in status among them.

On June 20, City Manager Mitchell sought to implement the committee's third recommendation. The intent of the Newburgh proposals was not to increase the regulations so as to make chiseling more difficult, but rather to make relief so unpleasant that only the truly destitute would apply.

Samuel Mencher has summarized and characterized the Newburgh proposals in the following fashion:

1. Make assistance as unpleasant as possible through (a) relief in kind rather than money, (b) threat of prosecution, (c) continuous re-evaluation, (d) temporary assistance only, (e) cessation of relief when illegitimacy is involved, (f) removal of children from the home.
2. Make recipients of relief work for the aid given—work assignments.
3. Keep the level of help so low that it will discourage anyone from taking relief in preference to working—no family on assistance to receive more than the lowest paid city employee with a family of comparable size.
4. Prevent outsiders from obtaining help—two weeks the maximum period of aid to newcomers.
5. Encourage remaining on, or returning to, employment— denial of assistance to those voluntarily leaving jobs. Employment must be accepted regardless of its nature.[12]

Eveline Burns examines one other aspect of the policy impasse in public assistance: ignorance about public assistance in the public at large.

One of the fundamental things wrong with public welfare is the fact that people know so little about it. The recent furor over Newburgh, the tremendous outpouring of letters from all over the country, and the debates which the plan has fostered served only to underline this profound ignorance. The frequent references to the supposed policy of supporting the idle and the thriftless in comfort or the allegation that women have illegitimate babies in order to get Aid to Dependent Children could surely never be made if people knew just how modest in our better states, and how gruesome in our poorer states, is the standard of living which is permitted by prevailing assistance budgets. The fear that we are "breeding a population of parasites" and "supporting the shiftless and wayward" would surely be expressed less frequently if people knew about the rigorous eligibility conditions enforced in most parts of the country, or about the fact that some ninety percent of the assistance caseloads consist of the aged, the blind, the totally disabled, and young children and their mothers.[13]

1962 Amendments

Secretary Ribicoff saw in the Newburgh situation a chance to turn the attack on welfare into an opportunity to use it as a flail to justify the administration's reform efforts. In 1956 the professional social work lobby had succeeded in winning a federal authorization, but not appropriation, of federal matching dollars to be used to pay for social rehabilitation programs. Except for occasional demonstration projects, the concept was not used. Now in the glare of Newburgh, an HEW committee board asserted that rehabilitation was the key to the social welfare dilemma. The demonstration projects were said to prove that the rehabilitation expenditures could in the long run save money, but that empirical validation, except in isolated incidents was lacking. Despite this lack of evidence, Congress on February 1, 1962, named the rehabilitation strategy as the prime priority of welfare reform.

A number of books published in the 1960s after the passage of

the 1962 amendments brought forth criticisms of the inadequacy
and intellectual bankruptcy as it was called, of the public assistance
approach. Michael Harrington's *The Other America* was published
in December of 1962. It was promptly reviewed in the *New Yorker*
magazine and is frequently credited with playing a major role in
bringing to the attention of the liberal establishment the persistence of poverty and the inadequacy of public assistance programs. The next fall Edgar May won a Pulitzer prize for a book
written while he posed as a public assistance worker. This work
described in meticulous detail the dysfunctional consequences of
the way state and local bureaucracies were structured for handling
relief programs. In short order a number of similar works, of
varying analytical or journalistic quality, were published. Some of
the more prominent were Elman's *The Poorhouse State;* Gilbert
Steiner's *Social Insecurity* and later *The State of Welfare;* Charles   Silberman's *Crisis in Black and White;* Stein's *On Relief;* and Krosney's
Beyond Welfare. [14] These programs presented a catalog of criticism
about: (1) the arbitrary exclusions of people in need, (2) the stigmatic quality of welfare, (3) the political irresponsiveness of welfare, and (4) the general inhumanity of the welfare system.

When a reexamination of income maintenance programs began, however, it was realized that public assistance, the prevailing
mechanism for providing cash income to the poor, was deficient
in many ways. The program, which was limited to persons in
specific categories, denied aid to many in need. Among those
eligible to receive aid, some were allotted a generous amount,
while others' benefits were meager. The payments made to the
recipients were inadequate to carry out the policy objective—to
raise them to even a minimum standard of living. The criteria of
the program encouraged undesirable behavioral responses, such
as desertion of families by male heads to make the family eligible
for aid. They also discouraged aid recipients from working to
supplement their incomes, by virtue of rules that often left families
no better off by working. Some observers and participants felt that
recipients of aid were forced to trade assistance for some of their
civil rights. Despite these shortcomings, any serious political
review of even elementary accountability of the program's operation was prevented by its complex, divided intergovernmental
structure and responsibility.

The result of this new recognition or reappraisal of the assumptions of New Deal–Fair Deal welfare was the Public Welfare

Amendments of 1962, the first major departure in public welfare policy since the Social Security Act of 1935. The amendments retained the first assumption that those who fall through the work-insurance network are somehow in need of rehabilitation. They emphasized rehabilitation services, the training of staff, and the liberalization of states' discretion. On signing this act, President Kennedy said:

> This measure embodies a new approach—stressing services in addition to support, rehabilitation instead of relief, and training for useful work instead of prolonged dependency. This important legislation will assist our states and local public welfare agencies to redirect the incentives and services they offer to needy families and children and to aged and disabled people. Our objective is to prevent or reduce dependency and to encourage self-care and self-support—to maintain family life where it is adequate and to restore it where it is deficient.[15]

In the first round of the new poverty policy thrust, enormous amounts of discretion were turned over to social work professionals, who developed a legislative proposal that was virtually silent on the salient political tensions of public assistance: the conflict between centralization vs. decentralization in a federal-state program, the tension between federal funding and state responsibility, and the tension between the demands for formal public administration programs and the informal, perhaps antiformal, tradition of social work professionals. The planners of the 1962 amendments pinned all of their hopes on a rehabilitation strategy. The next reform effort would emanate from elsewhere.

THE ORIGINS OF THE ECONOMIC OPPORTUNITY ACT

The passage of the 1962 amendments certified that the goal of public welfare policy was to go beyond the giving of cash, to root out and to deal with the cause of poverty. Recognition of the failure of the social worker rehabilitation strategy was swift and certain. Its assumption that the pathology lay in the individual rather than the system was not directly assaulted, but the belief in the capacity of relational casework to do much about the pathology certainly was. In the next Congress the focus shifted toward the development of "hard services" which would ready employable welfare recipients for jobs. In an atmosphere of bipartisan unity, the Manpower Development and Training Act was written into law and funded at modest levels. But just before his assassination Kennedy was rebuffed by Congress in his attempt to expand job training programs to unemployed youth by a proposal for a youth conservation corps, modeled after the Civilian Conservation Corps of the 1930s. Congress and the state welfare bureaucracies were an impediment to further reform efforts targeted exclusively on the poor. Broader-based programs were the new order of the day.

By the summer of 1963 the forward thrust of welfare reform within the Kennedy administration had definitely been halted. The analysis of poverty, its etiology, prevention, and cure, passed from the social worker to the economist. Robert Lampman, then a staff economist for the Council of Economic Advisers, documented that during the years 1956 to 1961, the years just preceding the welfare reform effort, the progress against poverty had been halted. Lampman demonstrated that in the five-year period in his review the rate of poverty reduction had only been 1 percent, and the numbers of persons actually experiencing poverty as measured by a market-basket yardstick were actually on the increase.[16]

The implicit assumption of the first years of the Kennedy administration, not unlike that of the New Deal–Fair Deal, was that a policy of economic stimulation, coupled with social insurance and a service program to those left out, would eradicate poverty. Given these assumptions, it is not easy to explain why, a scant 15 months after the signing of the Social Security amendments of 1962, the Johnson administration would be heavily into the development of a counterstrategy to combat poverty outside of and even antithetical to the established welfare system.

The task is not easy because there is considerable evidence to suggest that the domestic advisers within the Kennedy administration were reluctant to alter established procedures. Limited cash and in-kind assistance fit well into the prevailing concept of public charity. A program of rehabilitation envisioned by the 1962 amendments was thoroughly consonant with established professional wisdom.[17] There was, however, dissatisfaction. It came from two powerful sources, the Council of Economic Advisers and the Department of Justice. The council staff felt that the current public welfare policy was both wasteful and inequitable. Moreover, there was no coordinating mechanism or concept. In the Justice Department's Committee on Juvenile Delinquency and its counterpart program in the Ford Foundation, there was a feeling that public welfare did little to change the opportunities available to the poor.

Three developments contributed to the shift in popular focus of public welfare from income security to the elimination of poverty. First, there was a journalistic assault on the easy, but false, assumption that poverty in America was on the decline. Among the outpouring of literature which chronicled the magnitude and persistence of American poverty, the most significant was Michael Harrington's *The Other America,* cited above. Harrington wrote an impassioned and highly literate assault on the persistence of the incidence of poverty, despite a growing affluence. Relying heavily on rather dry public documents,[18] he developed the thesis that the American citizen was unaware of poverty because it was physically invisible, hidden away in areas not frequently visited by more affluent citizens.

Second, the incidence of poverty among blacks was four or five times that of whites. The national preoccupation with the issue of civil rights thus helped poverty become, for perhaps the first time in American history, a vital political issue. It is important to recall that public consciousness of poverty as a public policy problem preceded by almost two years the riots that broke out in the black ghettos in the summer of 1964. Though initially begun as a social and political fight, the static generated by the civil rights movement made the unequal economic condition of the black very clear. Paradoxically, it also became clear that poverty is not a function of individual pathology but stems from discrimination on the basis not only of race, but of age, sex, and geographic region. Poor educational opportunities for blacks and women emerged as the principal causal link in the chain of poverty.

The third factor which is cited to explain the abrupt departure in welfare policy is attributed to the vagaries, or chance events, of politics. There is an understandable reluctance to attribute major consequences to random or fluke events, but nonetheless, such events are important. James Donovan reports that the structure of West Virginia Democratic politics forced Kennedy to campaign in areas that had been traditionally ignored.[19] Kennedy was surely aware of the insular poverty that resulted when vast areas of the nation were bypassed by the general economic progress, for he had been one of the early supporters of Senator Paul Douglas's

area redevelopment bill. Kennedy was committed to the concept
of expansion policies which would stimulate aggregate demand.
Also, he readily accepted the notion that a social rehabilitation
program to respond to the personal pathology of the poor would
reduce long-term dependency. However, his contact with the jar-
ring and impenetrable poverty of the West Virginia hollows convinced Kennedy that the traditional strategies of (1) economic
stimulation, (2) area redevelopment, and (3) social rehabilitation
were necessary but not sufficient for the elimination of poverty.

Poverty elimination was a new political goal that had not been
fully explored. There were those on his staff—Robert Lampman,
Walter Heller, Adam Yarmolensky, Robert Kennedy, and Ted Sor-
ensen—who urged a broader approach. Collectively, his closest
advisors were convinced that the HEW–Treasury approach was
simply too narrow. Individually, they did not agree on the direction of the new effort. Heller and Lampman wanted to open the
cash transfer mechanism to the working poor, while Robert
Kennedy and his colleagues wished to experiment with strategies
to alter fundamentally the power relationship at the local level. In
1963 the ferment for welfare reform—now broadened to cover
antipoverty policy—was very strong, but the direction of the reform effort was unclear and unspecified. In June of 1963 Heller
sought to enlist support outside of government. In a speech to the
Communications Workers of America he argued for the necessity
of "opening the exits from poverty," and received an unenthusias-
tic response. Council attempts to enlist journalistic support for a
new antipoverty campaign were similarly unsuccessful. After several skirmishes within the administration, Heller received a go-
ahead from Kennedy to launch a task force to pursue some highly
specific antipoverty proposals to supplement the HEW activity.
The Bureau of the Budget assigned staff the task of coordinating
the more than 100–odd proposals that were submitted to Burt
Weisbrod, a Lampman colleague at the Council of Economic Advisers. A preliminary meeting of staffers was set for November 22,
1963, with a timetable that would lead to legislative proposals to
be submitted after the 1964 Democratic convention. The task
force deliberations were cut short by the news from Dallas of
Kennedy's assassination.

Earlier in the fall the reelection task force had identified poverty
and the problems of suburbia as likely issues or themes for the
1964 reelection effort.[20] The adjourned task force meeting was

one of a series of efforts to convince the president that the central issue or theme should be poverty. Opposition within the administration argued that poverty was a poor issue because (1) backlash effects among low-income whites of any effort to improve the condition of poor blacks should be expected, (2) a presidential recounting of the intractability of poverty would focus too much light on the failure of congressional initiatives to combat poverty, and (3) the clear beneficiaries of the program were nonvoters. Since Kennedy, if re-elected, would have been the first president lame-ducked by the 22nd amendment, there would be plenty of time during the last administration to mount a politically unpopular program. Kennedy had shown a disposition to listen to the advocates and the detractors of a poverty theme for the 1964 election, but he had not indicated a choice.

In the dark and uncertain days following the assassination, President Lyndon Johnson was in frequent contact with Buford Ellington, Director of Emergency Preparedness and former governor of Tennessee. Ellington and Johnson talked of the need for a campaign theme in 1964 that had a distinctive Johnson stamp. Ellington, familiar with the poverty task force, suggested poverty, and Johnson agreed. In his first meeting with Heller, the new President surprised Heller by his unequivocal support for the poverty theme. "That is my kind of program," he is reported to have said, "I want you to move full-speed ahead on it.[21]

The task force quickly assembled the programs that had been submitted earlier to Weisbrod, but each proposal, unique and worthwhile in itself, lacked a comprehensive and coordinating theme. A focal point was clearly a necessity. Sprinkling $1.5 billion worth of new programs among 20 or so government bureaus and departments could hardly be billed as a bold new initiative. The solution came in the form of a proposal for a proposed community action approach whereby each plan would be provided for only after the request had been initiated by a local community action council made up of members from (1) local units of government, (2) the voluntary agencies, and (3) the poor themselves. The "maximum feasible participation" of members of the target population in the selection of efforts would provide the glue to bring together highly disparate and even distinct antipoverty programs. It would also provide the glitter to make this highly disjointed funding of many old programs look like a shining new innovation.

Key persons on the executive office task force which formulated

the legislation to put this program into effect found much to
commend in the community action approach as the centerpiece in
a strategy to inaugurate a program which appeared to have these
advantages:

1. Depending on local initiative, it provided budgetary flexibili-
   ty.
2. It offered wide opportunity for experimentation and adapta-
   tion to local conditions.
3. It strengthened the Executive Office of the President rather
   than the cabinet.
4. The Community Action Council was an effective bypass of
   conservative mayors, Republican governors, state bureaucracies, and sticky technical problems like church-state separation and public-private partnerships, because it established
   a direct conduit from the executive office to local groups
   outside of formal government.
5. The program encouraged participation of diverse and even
   antagonistic groups.

The only question was: Why would congressmen buy a strategy so
clearly beneficial to the President and providing so few political
rewards to traditional congressional constituencies?

This proposed legislation became known as the Economic Opportunity Act (EOA). Some 15 years later, a good history of its
legislative phase has still not been written. The President sent the
bill to Capitol Hill on March 16, 1964. Final congressional action
took place on August 20 of the same year, a lapse of five months
and four days, an incredibly short period for minor, much less
major, legislation. Roger Davidson, a student of Congress, chose
the history of EOA as a prime example of "the executive as legislator." With John Bibby, he wrote:

> The most significant feature of the Economic Opportunity
> Act, from our point of view, was that it was "legislated"
> almost entirely within the executive branch and, indeed, vir-
> tually without prodding from congressional or other 'out-
> side' clienteles. The draft bill that President Johnson sent to
> Congress on March 16, 1964, was the product of almost a
> year of discussions and negotiations among high-level ad-
> ministrators and economists. The process was culminated by

a barnstorming five weeks of work by a special task force headed by Shriver. Ill-prepared congressmen opened hearings a day after the bill was sent to Capitol Hill; and the congressional amendments were, at most, marginal to the substance of the legislation.[22]

Daniel Moynihan wrote of the legislative history in these terms:

A history of the idea of community action has not been written, but it should be. It is an idea that is likely to have considerable effect on American society. It is an amalgam, clearly, of certain theories of social action and social psychology that developed in the universities over the past several decades. There is clearly some carry-over from the idea of community development worked out through the Foreign Aid Program and in various international agencies. Live experiments, as it were, were financed by one of the great foundations in the 1950s. In 1961 the Juvenile Delinquency and Youth Offenses Control Act provided some $15 million to pursue the subject further. An interdepartmental committee headed by the Attorney General sponsored projects in a number of cities, the best known of which is Mobilization for Youth on the lower East Side of New York. Community action was a powerful idea and was supported. When the time came to put together a poverty program, the initial impulse within the second echelon of the government was simply to launch a greatly expanded community action program, following the models already in action. Other considerations led to the establishment of a more diverse program, but community action remains at the center of the present program.[23]

The diverse interpretations of the phrase *community action* in the task-force stage were prophetic. The participation section was to become a kind of ideological litmus test when the program went into action. Some saw it as an unequivocal call for neopopulism, others as an attack on conventional social work wisdom. Mayors perceived it as a ploy in Johnsonian federal expansion, and radicals as a deliberately planted seed of destruction in a symbolic anitpoverty plan.[24] Without Title II, which provided for community action, the EOA was a fairly conventional effort to use the power of government to alter the existing opportunity structure facing the poor.

The first title provided for a series of youth opportunity programs designed to give poor youth the educational experiences, skill training, and job opportunities which were thought necessary to break the cycle of poverty. The principal emphasis was on employment readiness, with programs like the Job Corps for unemployed and out-of-school youth, enhanced vocational programs in ghetto areas, various antidropout campaigns for students, and a work-study program for poor college-bound youth. The third and fourth titles focused on expansion of opportunity in rural and depressed areas through a program of loans and investment tax credits. The fifth and final title focused on job and skill training for adults in welfare programs or likely to become dependent on them. An important section of the last title created the Volunteers in Service of America (Vista), which was to be the domestic counterpart of the Peace Corps. In Vista, nonpoor skilled persons would spend a portion of their time helping the poor to learn and to build viable economic bases in their own communities.

Title II focused not on the opportunity structure but on the political power structure. As ultimately implemented, it did address itself to opportunity structure problems, but in its early days the Community Action Agency boards, made up of one-third from city government, one-third interested citizens and groups and one-third the poor themselves, became the battleground for local antipoverty strategy. Fights for control of the poverty boards were commonplace. In fact, poverty boards *not* racked by conflict were the exception. Title II did allow for quick implementation of programs, and the initial success of the Office of Economic Opportunity (OEO) came from its success in the funding of the Upward Bound and Head Start programs, based on community and private, nonprofit cooperation. In addition, there were day care centers, health care centers, neighborhood legal centers, and the like. In 1965 OEO looked like the most successful policy departure in a decade.

By 1966, however, the program was under attack from mayors, congressmen, social workers, and the poor. Mayors were upset over federal funding of programs in their cities without their consent and, on occasion, even without their knowledge. Congressmen were upset when neighborhood legal offices were used to sue

not slum landlords, but the federal government itself for misman-
agement of welfare programs. Physicians and other professionals
were appalled at the quality and lack of standards in community-
run programs. Charges of ill-conceived programs, mismanage-
ment, and fraud became the order of the day. Vista volunteers
were accused of working as political activists against the established city governments. The poor began to look to OEO as a
source of funding for a fight against city hall and were upset if the
funding was not provided.

In 1967 President Johnson, increasingly preoccupied with the
events of Southeast Asia, was in no mood to defend a program
that was more costly than had been anticipated, did not have an
objective and demonstrable product, and was clearly contributing
to social and political dissension. The mayors brought this battle
to Congress and won for themselves the right to veto projects in
their own communities. By 1968 the thrust of community action
as an alternative source of local antipoverty policy was dead, and
it was only an additional conduit for congressionally funded and
local government-initiated programs that provided a variety of
services to the poor. OEO's existence was to continue for five
more years, but it was evident by 1969 that antipoverty strategy in
America was not to be achieved or directed by an assault on the
local government or the welfare establishments. The new strategy
was to renew a consideration of the ways in which direct cash
payments to the poor could be achieved. It is important to note,
however, that the early funding of new cash payment plans and
experiments did originate in the Office of Economic Opportunity.

NOTES

1. Alan Keith-Lucas, "The Political Theory Implicit in Social Casework
   Theory," *American Political Science Review*, vol. 47, no. 4 (December
   1953), pp. 1076–1091.
2. Irwin Garfinkel, "Toward an Effective Income Support System: An
   Overview Paper," in Michael Barth, G. J. Carcagno, and J. L. Palmer,
   Toward an Effective Income Support System: Problems, Prospects and Choices,
   (Madison, Wis.: Institute for Research on Poverty, 1974), p. 154.
3. James L. Sundquist, *Politics and Policy: The Eisenhower, Kennedy, and Johnson Years* (Washington, D.C.: Brookings Institution, 1968), chap. 9.
4. William Haber, "Relief: A Permanent Program," *Survey Graphic*, vol. 27
   (December 1938), pp. 591–94.
5. *Congressional Record*, 85th Cong., 2nd Sess., 1958, p. 397.
6. In 1960, administratively, ADC (Aid to Dependent Children) was

changed to AFDC (Aid to Families with Dependent Children), reflecting a concern with the family as a whole, as opposed to a concern exclusively with children.

7. Gilbert Y. Steiner, *Social Insecurity: The Politics of Welfare* (Chicago: Rand McNally & Co., 1966), chap. 1.
8. U.S. Congress, Committee on Ways and Means, Hearings, "Public Welfare Amendments of 1962," 87th Cong., 2nd Sess., 1962, p. 161.
9. Leonard Goodwin, *Bridging the Gap Between Social Research and Public Policy: Welfare, A Case in Point* (Washington, D.C.: Brookings Institution, 1973).
10. *The New York Times*, June 11, 1961, p. 71. See also David Franke, "Newburgh: Just a Beginning?" *National Review*, vol. 11 (July 29, 1961), p. 44.
11. *The New York Times*, June 11, 1961, p. 16.
12. Samuel Mencher, "Newburgh: The Recurrent Crisis of Public Assistance," *Social Work*, vol. 7 (January 1962), p. 4.
13. Eveline M. Burns, "What's Wrong with Public Welfare?" *Social Service Review*, vol. 36 (June 1962), pp. 118–19.
14. Michael Harrington, *The Other America* (New York: Macmillan Co., 1962); Edgar May, *The Wasted Americans; Cost of Our Welfare Dilemma* (New York: Harper & Row, 1964); Richard M. Elman, *The Poorhouse State: The American Way of Life on Public Assistance* (New York: Pantheon Books, 1966); Gilbert Y. Steiner, *Social Insecurity: The Politics of Welfare* (Chicago: Rand McNally Publishing Co., 1966); Charles E. Silberman, *Crisis in Black and White* (New York: Random House, 1964); Bruno Stein, *On Relief: The Economics of Poverty and Public Welfare* (New York: Basic Books, 1971); Herbert Krosney, *Beyond Welfare: Poverty in the Supercity* (New York: Holt, Rinehart & Winston, 1966).
15. U.S. Department of Health, Education and Welfare, Welfare Administration, *Major Federal Legislation Affecting Social Welfare, 1961–65* (Washington, D.C.: U.S. Government Printing Office, 1966), p. 6.
16. Robert J. Lampman, "Low Income Population and Economic Growth," Joint Economic Committee, 86th Cong., 1st Sess., Study Paper no. 12 (Washington D.C.: U.S. Government Printing Office, 1959).
17. Gordon E. Brown (ed.), *The Multi-Problem Dilemma: A Social Research Demonstration with Multi-Problem Families* (Metuchen, N.J.: Scarecrow Press, 1968).
18. Lampman, "Low Income Population and Economic Growth."
19. James Donovan, *Politics of Poverty* (Indianapolis: Pegasus, 1973).
20. Ibid.
21. L. B. Johnson, *Vantage Point* (New York: Holt,Rinehart, & Winston, 1971).
22. John Bibby and Roger Davidson, *On Capitol Hill* (New York: Holt, Rinehart, & Winston, 1967), p. 220.
23. D. P. Moynihan, "Three Problems in Combatting Poverty," in M. S. Gordon (ed.), *Poverty in America* (San Francisco: Chandler Publishing Co., 1965), p. 43.
24. Elinor Graham, "The Politics of Poverty," in B. B. Seligman (ed.), *Poverty as a Public Issue* (New York: Free Press, 1965).

CHAPTER 10

WELFARE REFORM,

1968-78:

POLITICAL STALEMATE

INTRODUCTION

The political scientist Charles E. Lindblom has coined a phrase which captures the essence of one of the processes of policy formation: *disjointed incrementalism.*[1] In this context *disjointed* means that evaluation and analysis of current policies and specification of alternative new policies are carried on throughout the polity with virtually no coordination. *Incremental* means that public decision makers consider the alternatives serially, looking only at a small set of the problem at one time. Each change represents only a small modification of the total policy. In welfare, as in other policy arenas, this disjointed set of minor adjustments produces not a welfare system in which each program has a designated function and a rationalized relationship to the other component parts, but a welfare *nonsystem* in which each program has its own rationale and a political constituency to which it responds. The employment securities division, for example, may be structured to secure trained workers for employers who have jobs that need to be filled, while the jobs training section may be structured to create employment skills for unemployed workers. Each bureaucracy seeks to accomplish its unique mission efficiently, without regard for its impact on sister bureaus of government.

There are strong political and institutional inhibitions that mitigate against a comprehensive policy approach. One of these is a result of interest-group politics. Each relevant interest group supports or opposes specific policies in terms of its own perceived self-interest. Policies are thus modified only when a significant number of interest groups (or a single, uncommonly powerful group) perceives a change to be in its net interest. A desire for change alone is not sufficient; there must also be a winning *coalition* capable of shaping the new policy in a specific direction. Countervailing pressure groups will, in most cases, be pushing for other, perhaps antithetical changes. If the demands for change are of near equal balance, a political stalemate results, even though there is no support for the current policy. Figure 10–1 shows the shifting of the policy emphasis in response to changes in the composition of relevant interest groups.

Items are placed on the political agenda because relevant interest groups are discontent with current policies. Items are taken off the political agenda when one or the other interest group "wins." In the case of a political stalemate, all of the relevant political actors are sufficiently unhappy with current policies to keep an issue on the agenda, but none is sufficiently strong to create a policy movement in a specific direction. Policy change is the result of formulating an issue in such a way that a winning political coalition can be mobilized to place the item on the agenda, and sufficient momentum can be generated to bring about a shift in policy. Policy stalemate results when there is sufficient discontent to place the question of change before the public, but the countervailing pressures are so evenly matched that policy change does not result. The issue is kept alive and is a constant irritant to members of both coalitions and to the decision makers. Such was the condition of welfare policy throughout the decade now closing.

THE WELFARE CLIMATE IN 1968

By 1968 the inadequacy of the 1962 public welfare amendments was clear to the relevant political actors. The gigantic hope of the 1964 Economic Opportunity Act had already waned, and there were few around who expected much from jerry-built 1967 public

FIGURE 10–1
POLICY RESPONSES TO POLITICAL BALANCE

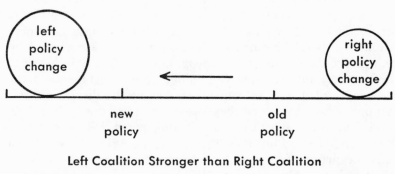

Left Coalition Stronger than Right Coalition

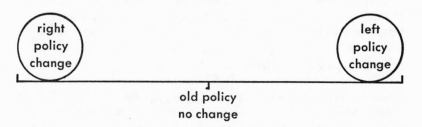

Right Coalition Stronger than Left Coalition

old policy
no change

Left Coalition Equal to Right Coalition

welfare amendments. Public assistance, which had been adopted in 1935 as a temporary program, had been ill-nurtured by a third of a century of neglect. In 1968 it was recognized as one of the most unpopular programs ever adopted by Congress.

There was widespread political discontent with public assistance programs. Taxpayers' alliances fulminated against rising welfare costs, while AFDC mothers picketed city halls for a benefit schedule above the level of destitution. Welfare professionals complained about excessive political interference, and legislators complained that they had no control over the programs' expansion. Legislative hearings are ordinarily not a place where kind things are said about public programs, but the 1968 hearings before the Joint Economic Committee were almost unique in the unanimity of discontent expressed. Among the diverse interest groups which registered their discontent were the National Association of Manufacturers, which complained that the program discouraged entry into the labor force; the AFL-CIO, which felt that the programs should have broader coverage; the National Welfare Rights Organization (NWRO), which wanted higher benefits; the Chamber of Commerce, which felt that the tax burdens of AFDC were unfairly allocated; and the National Association of Social Workers (NASW), which complained that insufficient attention was paid to programs of rehabilitation. The level of discontent, however, was matched by the diverse directions of change suggested.

All of the criticisms focused public attention on what has come to be called the welfare mess. Included in the phrase *the welfare mess* were a number of persistent themes. Some held the belief that welfare recipients are lazy, promiscuous, and dishonest. Communications media focused attention on fraud; stories were written about welfare recipients' "secret jobs"; a hippie commune which reconstituted itself as a "family" of eight and legally received aid of $1,000 a month, and the "deserting" husbands who didn't desert. In Piedmont, California, suburban housewives dramatized welfare waste by driving through the county and easily getting several different "emergency" welfare checks on the same day.[2] A survey in rural areas found that 90 percent of the respondents felt that there were many people on welfare who had quit work in order to receive benefits. More than half of those surveyed felt that the majority of the welfare recipients were lazy, and 87 percent felt too much money was being spent on care of the poor.[3] The personal-fault theme was supplemented by a belief that current welfare programs themselves encouraged withdrawal from the labor force, family splitting, and migration solely for the purpose of receiving aid. The structure of welfare institutions was thus perceived as a major factor in contributing to the excessive cost of welfare programs. The *evidence* that such perverse incentives operated was a simple examination of the growth of welfare caseloads during the 1960s, when the condition of the economy should have specified a reduction rather than an increase which was observed in the AFDC caseload (see Table 10–1).

TABLE 10–1
INCREASES IN AFDC CASELOADS AND CHANGE IN
UNEMPLOYMENT RATES, 1950–1974

Year	AFDC Families (in thousands)		Annual Change Rate in Unemployment $\left(\dfrac{Rate_2 - Rate_1}{Rate_1} \right)$
1950	651		
		−49	
1955	602		
		+199	+0.250
1960	803		
		+113	+0.218
1961	916		
		+16	−0.179
1962	932		
		+22	+0.036
1963	954		
		+58	−0.096
1964	1,012		
		+42	−0.135
1965	1,054		
		+73	−0.289
1966	1,127		
		+170	0.000
1967	1,297		
		+225	−0.053
1968	1,522		
		+353	−0.028
1969	1,875		
		+697	+0.400
1970	2,552		
		+366	+0.169
1971	2,918		
		+204	−0.051
1972	3,122		
		+32	−0.125
1973	3,156		
		+34	+0.143
1974	3,190		

As a consequence of these criticisms there was a demand for welfare reform that was fueled by dislike for the persons receiving welfare, the structural form of current welfare practice, and the method of financing the programs. The impetus for reform was generated by often-exaggerated claims of the work disincentives, family instability, and civil rights and civil liberties violations inherent in welfare programs. Each set of welfare critics was content to redesign programs, without regard for other constraints. Civil libertarians seemed to have no cost consciousness, and those who were cost conscious had little regard for the niceties of constitutional safeguards.

While public aid expenditures moved upward, the national incidence of poverty seemed stagnant. The demand for reform reached nearly universal proportions. The directions of the demanded reform were, however, fundamentally diverse, each with a different but viable political base.

The problem was aggravated because instead of two competing interest coalitions in conflict, there were at least four—none of which was capable of sustained cooperation with any other. One group, initially the most vocal, had poverty elimination as a principal goal. A second group was most concerned with a program that would extend aid to the working poor. A third group was most concerned with the design of a new plan of aid that would encourage labor force participation by recipients of aid, while a fourth group of fiscal conservatives sought a change that would simply put a rigid cap on welfare spending. These diverse coalitions interacted with congressmen, presidential aides, and a collection of executive branch representatives to produce a plethora of welfare reform proposals.

The welfare mess had been one of Richard Nixon's favorite targets in his 1968 campaign. To after-dinner audiences, he often intoned the theme that the time had come to take people off the welfare rolls and put them on the payrolls, indicating his agreement with the third of the four competing groups. As events were later to show, however, Nixon did not know exactly what he did want from welfare policy, but he did know what he did not want. His speeches indicated that he did not want the welfare spending to continue to grow in an unanticipated manner, he did not want welfare recipients to end up better off economically than those who worked, and, most of all, he did not want any growth in the numbers of workers who were serving as "caretakers" of the poor. His rhetoric was sufficiently ambiguous that each reform contingent (except the first) thought Nixon was in their camp, but each discovered that there was no depth to the Nixon administration commitment to reform.

WELFARE REFORM IN THE NIXON ADMINISTRATION

The economic policy of the Nixon administration during his first year in office called for significant cuts in the level of federal spending. Despite all the rhetoric about rising welfare costs, the administration was well aware that reforms would cost more, not less, money. This meant that welfare reform and budget cuts were incompatible goals. One of Nixon's principal domestic advisors in those days was Patrick Moynihan, a maverick liberal who had long advocated some form of universal income guarantee to families with children. Moynihan was not a novice in the art of persuading presidents, having previously played a dominant role in the evolution of Johnson's civil rights program. Moynihan was well aware that Nixon would never buy the conventional liberal arguments for welfare reform. If he tried such an approach it would only cast him in the role of a bleeding heart, eager to help those who refused to help themselves—an approach surely to be rejected, since anyone with Nixon's perception of himself as Horatio Alger would rebel against such an argument.

The argument selected by Moynihan was this: Welfare "waste" was the money spent on fuzzy social programs and bureaucratic tangle. The need was for a program that would go to the heart of the issue. A direct cash payment, provided in a way to create rather than discourage work, would accomplish a threefold purpose; it would (1) end the bureaucratic tangle, (2) encourage work, and (3) provide money to those mired in poverty. Moynihan taught Nixon about the virtues of negative taxation and sold it as being practical, humane, and conservative, in the very best of the Tory tradition. Moynihan met with less success with Nixon's more sophisticated economic advisors, who did not trust the Irishman from Harvard. The President, however, felt that reform was a practical public necessity—he would, by reform, boldly demonstrate how Republican leadership could accomplish things that Democrats could only talk about.

The task of preparing a welfare reform package fell to the newly created and short-lived Council for Urban Affairs. Chaired by Moynihan, the council also included Robert Finch, Secretary of HEW; Charles Schultz, Secretary of Labor; and presidential counselors John Ehrlichman and Arthur Burns. Schultz rapidly emerged as the key vote on virtually all issues, since Moynihan and Finch were typically at odds with Burns and Ehrlichman. Personal as well as ideological differences prevented the group from being a cohesive decision-making body. Its failure to resolve problems in order to present a unified administration point of view appears, in hindsight, to have sealed the fate of the Nixon welfare package at its inception. Arthur Burns, speaking for himself and Ehrlichman, called for only a correction of the most blatant faults of current public assistance—most specifically, raising the low levels of AFDC support in the poorest states. Burns's proposal, dubbed by the administration as the Uniform Standard Benefit (USB), was apparently the President's first option. It was opposed in the Urban Affairs Council deliberations by Finch and Moynihan, whose alternative was initially called the Family Security System. This latter proposal, supported by Secretary Schultz, eventually became the administration's program.

The internal disagreements took some time to be resolved, and the announcement of the presidential welfare reform plan was delayed twice in the spring of 1969. An Urban Affairs Council paper, dated April 4, 1969, expressed support for the skeletal form of a plan that was later to become the Family Assistance Plan (FAP). The paper specifies (or justifies) the need for welfare reform on the following bases:

1. The growth of federal expenditures and caseloads—particularly for AFDC. The number of persons receiving welfare had begun to increase in 1966 and was growing at a rate of 1 million persons annually.
2. The presence of interstate inequities and the inequities among similarly situated individuals, depending on the presence of essentially arbitrary qualifications for eligibility.
3. The uneven distribution of fiscal burden was among the states. Superior efforts in particular states were discouraged by the matching formula then in use.
4. The fact that the current AFDC program was perceived to encourage (a) family instability, (b) withdrawals from the labor force, and (c) undesirable migration of low-income persons—particularly poor blacks.

The first administration proposal would have provided aid to the 6 million AFDC recipients, plus an unspecified number of working poor—perhaps as many as 9 million. An additional federal disbursement of $3.7 billion, of which $0.7 billion would be federal replacement of current state expenditures, was to be necessary. The total payment for a minimum of 15 million recipients was to be only $3 billion more than the current AFDC spending, or only $200 per person. New federal expenditures for new recipients were to be $1.3 billion for 9 million new recipients, or $133 per person. The first administration plan thus sought to buy welfare reform at a rather low dollar level.

The Urban Affairs document proposed a program that "above all . . . would eliminate the much criticized AFDC program." For a family of four there would be a guarantee of $1,600, a guarantee which was lower than the then-operative guarantee in 39 states. The benefit would provide a work incentive of a .50 tax rate to replace the .67 tax rate then specified in law. The states—39 of them—with current guarantees above the Family Security System would be required to continue their AFDC programs, but the committee recommended there be no federal participation in that supplementation. States with even a reasonable guarantee would have faced not a savings but an additional expense.

The Family Security System did not receive sufficient internal administrative support because of its lack of fiscal relief to key states. In April 1969, it was announced in *The New York Times* that the unveiling of the Nixon welfare reform had been postponed until May. It was later postponed an additional three months. A political calendar of the welfare reform effort in the Nixon administration is presented in Figure 10–2.

On August 2, 1969, the general outline of the Nixon welfare reform was leaked to the press, and on August 3, *The New York Times* reported that the Finch-Moynihan plan had won the endorsement of the President. Arthur Burns and Secretary of Labor Schultz had won a commitment for the rigid work test, which was to be a permanent feature of the Nixon reform during the months of congressional negotiations and compromise. When the President formally announced his plan on August 9, cautious support of the reform effort was forthcoming from governors and large city mayors, who thought they saw an opportunity for significant fiscal relief. This proved to be an illusion. When the hearings on the bill opened on October 15, 1969, the administration's efforts were clearly in the direction of shoring up conservative support for the measure. Secretary Schultz emphasized in his testimony the focus on jobs and work incentives. On November 14, 1969, Milton Friedman testified that while the bill was sound in principle, it was defective programmatically. Specifically, Friedman

FIGURE 10–2
A POLITICAL CALENDAR: WELFARE REFORM IN THE NIXON
ADMINISTRATION

8/9/69	Announcement of FAP.
10/3/69	Introduction as HR 14173* by Rep. Byrnes.
1/69–3/70	House Ways and Means Committee hearings on HR 16311.
3/11/30	Redesigned as HR 16311; reported.
4/15/70	Closed rule adopted; vote 204–183.
4/16/70	HR 16311 passes House; vote 243–155.
4/29–5/1/70	Abortive hearings before Senate Finance Committee; report returned to White House.
5/1–6/11/70	Administrative rewrite on HR 16311.
6/11/70	Revised and resubmitted HR 16311 submitted to Senate Finance Committee.
7/22/70	SFC resumes hearings.
10/9/70	SFC rejects FAP; vote 14–1.
11/5/70	Revised versions sent to SFC.
11/21/70	SFC rejects revised revision to social security amendment but approves one-year demonstration.
12/18/70	Senate manipulation of SFC revised revision begins effort to get a vote on FAP.
12/20/70	Senate refuses to vote on liberalized version of FAP submitted by Senator Ribicoff; vote 65–15.
12/28/70	Senate rejects FAP; vote 49–21.
1/20/71	HR 1*, new version of FAP, reintroduced to new Congress in House; goes to Ways and Means Committee.
3/71	Rep. Mills's rewrite of November version reported out of committee and sent to rules committee with request for a closed rule.
6/22/71	FAP given open rule; debate set for 6/22/71.
6/22/71	House passes HR 1; vote 288–132.
6/24/71	Long promises early report on HR 1.
7/29/71	Senate Finance Committee opens hearings on HR 1.
8/19/71	Nixon requests delay in welfare reform in Phase 1 of his economic plan.
8/21/71	Nixon supports welfare work experiment.
9/14/71	Liberal senators plan bypass of SFC.
9/19/71	Civic groups ask Nixon for support.
10/19/71	Three-way talks begin in Senate conferences.
10/20/71	Welfare reform put off until January 1972.
10/28/71	Administration announces it will support Ribicoff group.
1/20/72	SFC revised hearings (evidence of diminished support from administration).
1/28/72	Ribicoff announces withdrawal of support for administration.
2/15/72	SFC concludes public hearings
2/22/72	SFC issues tentative reports on HR 1; fate of FAP title left unspecified, but division now an accomplished fact.
3/27/72	Nixon sends message to Congress asking for action on FAP features.
4/28/72	Outline of Long alternative reported out of SFC.
6/13/72	Long proposal reported in detail.
6/22/72	Nixon sticks to center; refuses compromise with Long except with Ribicoff!
9/12/72	HR 1 with Long feature reported out of SFC.
10/17/72	Compromise bill passes Senate without any FAP reform section it it.

*See House of Representatives Report 91–904.

was concerned with the fact that the real tax rate would be much higher than .50, since recipients would also pay state and perhaps federal positive taxes on gross income.

Following perfunctory public hearings, the House Ways and Means Committee considered the measure in executive session. During the early months of the second session of the 91st Congress, the committee rewrote the administration bill (HR 14173) and reported it out as HR 16311. The redesigned bill strengthened the work requirement features considerably by requiring the work-training participation and employment registration of all recipients over age 16, as opposed to the administration's age 18. The administration rather gladly accepted the changes. Approval by the House Ways and Means Committee came on February 26, 1970. This was an unexpected victory for the administration. Earlier, Representative Wilbur Mills had expressed serious reservations. With Mills's support, the bill cleared the full House easily on April 16, 1970, by a vote of 243 to 155.

On April 29, 1970, the Senate Committee on Finance, chaired by Senator Russell B. Long (D., La.) opened hearings on the House-passed measure. Administration efforts had been concentrated on House action, and it was generally believed that Senate approval would be forthcoming with little opposition. The assessment of Senate passage was made without considering Senator John Bell Williams, a lame-duck Republican from Delaware whose intense opposition to the concept of a nonpunitive welfare system was well known to close students of income maintenance policy. On the second day of the hearing, Secretary Robert Finch was testifying when Williams opened fire. He produced figures which illustrated the micro operations of the program. A family in Chicago, for example, with earnings of $720 would receive $1,600 in FAP payments, $1,628 in a state supplement, $312 in food stamps, Medicaid payments worth $789, and $1,116 in a public housing subsidy. On all this, the only tax liability would be $37 FICA payments; the family's real income would be $6,128 on $720 of earnings. In contrast, an identically constituted family with earnings of $5,560 would receive only the housing subsidy but have tax liabilities of $262 federal income tax, $16 in state income tax, and $289 in social security taxes, for a real income of $119 *less* than the family earning only $720. Finch conceded that the administration was aware of such problems but said that the situation described was unlikely to actually occur. Williams retorted by illustrating a similar outcome in a number of different situations. Finch, obviously stunned by the attack, replied that food stamps, housing, and tax laws were programs proposed outside of his department.

Senator Fred Harris (D., Okla.) then accused Finch of seeking to scuttle the administration program: "With all due respect, gentlemen, this is the most ill-prepared presentation since I've been in Congress ... rumors have been circulating strongly in this room that the administration intends to abandon the bill ... that's why you have made such a lukewarm presentation." Finch strongly replied, "If the Senator wants a categorical denial, I'll be happy to enter it."[4]

The following morning, after 90 minutes of perfunctory hearings, Finch was summoned into executive session of the committee and informed that the committee would not accept the legislative proposal in its present form. The administration requested and received a recess in order to modify the bill and prepare a new presentation. Finch, prepared for defeat, moved to halt speculation that the administration had grown lukewarm in its support of welfare reform. The day after his abrupt confrontation with the Senate Finance Committee he announced that the administration was appointing a top policy team consisting of Ehrlichman, Schultz, Moynihan, Finch, and Budget Director Robert Mayo to revise the proposal in the light of Senate Finance Committee objections. Secretary Finch further stated, "We expect to have proposals ready within a matter of a few days, and I do not expect these further studies to delay significantly the progress of Family Assistance through Congress for enactment this session."[5] That statement turned out to be exceedingly optimistic.

The few days stretched to six weeks. On June 11, 1970, Secretary Finch presented a revised bill to the Senate Finance Committee. The administration report[6] combined the new version of the bill with an announcement of a health insurance program which would be submitted in January 1971, a plan to revise the food stamp price schedule so that the ratchets (drops in consumable income associated with increases in earned income) objected to in the earlier SFC hearing were eliminated, a plan to integrate the housing subsidy with the FAP welfare payments, increased support for social services, and a new way of deciding state fiscal liability.

When hearings were resumed on July 21, Senator Long greeted the newly appointed Secretary of HEW Elliot Richardson (Finch

having been "promoted" to Presidential assistant shortly after the
first Senate Finance Committee debacle) with the following dis-
quieting news:

> The Family Assistance Plan is a massive and costly experi-
> ment which proposes adding 14 million Americans to the
> welfare rolls. In Mississippi, 35 percent of the total popula-
> tion would become welfare recipients. The program would
> cost the Federal Government a total of $9.1 billion—more
> than $4 billion over the Federal cost of the existing system.
>
> It was the hope that the Administration would work to
> improve the bill when the Committee sent it back after three
> days of hearings. In significant respects, the new plan is a
> worse bill—and a more costly one than the measure which
> passed the House.
>
> One important area in which the revised Administration
> Bill is worse than the original concerns the category of unem-
> ployed fathers. Payments to these men in 23 states would be
> cut substantially. The revised bill could result in reduced
> benefits for recipients in 22 states which base benefits on a
> standard of need.
>
> The Administration has not given the Committee any idea
> of what its policy will be and what standards would be applied
> in the numerous areas in which the bill gives the Secretary
> of Health, Education and Welfare discretion to set policy.
>
> The Senate should be, and will be, given an opportunity to
> vote on welfare reform this year. The present welfare system
> is a shambles. With all the faults in the existing system, how-
> ever, the "mind of man is still capable of devising something
> worse."[7]

Committee hearings in July, August, and September did not
give any indication that favorable Senate action would be forthcoming. During the hearing, a number of influential witnesses
expressed criticism of the bill, which ranged from mild to harsh.
These witnesses included:

Mayor John V. Lindsay (R., N.Y.)
W. D. Eberle, Common Cause
Leonard Lesser, Committee for Community Affairs (a commu-
nity organization of poor persons)

Joseph C. Wilson, testifying for Committee for Economic De-
velopment
Harold Watts, Director, Institute for Research on Poverty, Uni-
versity of Wisconsin
Mrs. Ed Ryan, PTA (Parent Teacher's Association)
Howard Rourke, NACO (National Association of County Offi-
cers)
Carl Stokes (D.), mayor of Cleveland, representing National
League of Cities
Karl T. Schletterbeck, U.S. Chamber of Commerce
William C. Fitch, National Council on Aging
Fred Jaffee, Planned Parenthood–World Population
Warren Hearnes (D.), governor of Missouri, for the National
Conference of Governors
Tom McCall (R.), governor of Oregon
Whitney Young, National Urban League

It gradually emerged from testimony that FAP was very "old
wine in new bottles," and aside from expansion of aid to the
working poor—a strategy previously rejected by Congress—FAP
was not a reform proposal at all. As it appeared clear that passage
of FAP in the 91st Congress (1969–70) was unlikely, the Nixon
administration shifted strategy in the fall of 1970 to seek passage
early in the 92nd Congress. First, Nixon sought to secure support
from the conservative senators. He invited to San Clemente, California, the strongly conservative members of the Senate Finance
Committee: Bennett (R., Utah); Fannin (R., Ariz.); Miller (R.,
Iowa); Long (D., La.); and Byrd (D., Va.). Only Bennett committed
himself to support of the President's plan. The President also
sought support of the nation's Republican governors; while he
received a more sympathetic response, the Republican governors
refused to give full endorsement to FAP. Wilburn Schmidt, Wisconsin Secretary of Health and Social Service and Chairman of the
State Welfare Directors Group, reported that FAP had the support
of his group but that only a few directors were willing (or able) to
provide independent political support. After failure to win support in the Senate Finance Committee or the Republican Governors Conference, Nixon attempted to salvage defeat by support of
a plan for a six-month testing of the new welfare, with the program
to become operative unless rescinded on January 1, 1972. Nixon
did not receive conservative support for that compromise, nor

could Senator Abraham Ribicoff, the Connecticut senator who, as a former HEW Secretary, was a leader in the Senate's welfare reform effort, deliver support for FAP. It died in the logjam at the end of the 91st Congress.

Welfare reform was briefly resuscitated in the 92nd Congress. It was given the prestigiously symbolic number of HR 1 and, without difficulty, its second approval in the House of Representatives. The key vote on HR 16311 had been 204–183, but HR 1 passed 288–132, making it appear to some observers that the legislature was now really ready to act. After its passage in the House the reform effort was forwarded to the Senate, where its receipt was "noted."

In July and early August the Senate Finance Committee began its deliberations. Though Senate liberals expressed dissatisfaction with various facets of the legislation, the administrative spokesmen at the hearings equipped themselves well, particularly in contrast to Finch's disastrous performance two years earlier. The bill received strident criticism from the National Welfare Rights Organization, which probably had the effect of securing support for the bill. More important, the lobbyists of the AFL–CIO, Common Cause, and the League of Women Voters supported it, though the League later so qualified its support that it could be described as opposition.

The summer of 1971 was the time when passage of the Family Assistance Plan seemed most likely. Then on August 15, 1971, President Nixon announced his "new" economic policy. At that time the President asked that reform of welfare be delayed until the following year. According to Ribicoff, this announcement sealed the fate of FAP; without presidential prodding there was no one to push the administration's middle-of-the-road position. The Senate Finance Committee then rejected the bill a second time, in November 1971. In early 1972 Senator Ribicoff, believing he had no chance of support for his own liberalized version of FAP, withdrew his program from consideration. On May 28, 1972, the Senate Finance Committee reported its plan of a Senate substitute for HR 1 which bore little resemblance to the administration's plan. Even after Long's plans were announced, the administration refused to compromise.

By summer of 1972 a three-way battle was taking shape in the Senate: Long and the conservatives, Ribicoff and the liberals, and the new, now captainless Nixon team. No legislative action was

possible without a coalition, and there was no compelling reason
for any two groups to join forces. Mitchell Ginsberg of Columbia's
School of Social Work, who served as a bridge between the Nixon
group and the Ribicoff group, reported the last possibility for
joint effort vanished with the arrival of the McGovern option.
McGovern's vulnerability on welfare reform was too great for
Nixon to risk any counterattack by compromising his own position. The Senate liberals had just taken the presidential nomination for one of their own, and they could ill afford to be accused
of not backing McGovern. The Ribicoff-Long forces had no substantive agreement out of which a compromise could be forged.
Ribicoff was not willing to assume any leadership role. A Nixon-
Long compromise was attractive to the Nixon camp, but Long was
content to defeat FAP, and Nixon had no overwhelming desire to
pass his own bill. The chances of a conservative coalition, the only
real chance for welfare option, thus died with the vulnerability of
Senator McGovern on welfare. The origin and fate of that plan are
discussed in the next section. Congress did, however, in 1972
adopt part of the Nixon proposals; that is, they did federalize the
old categorical programs of aid-to-the-aged, aid-to-the-blind, and
aid-to-the-permanently-and-totally-disabled into a single, comprehensive, federal program called Supplemental Security Income Program.

ORIGIN, DEVELOPMENT, AND DEATH OF THE MC GOVERN PLAN

Senator George McGovern had announced his candidacy for the
presidency in the 1972 election earlier than the other candidates,
17 months before the convention. The first stage of the campaign
was characterized by painstaking organization and meticulous attention to detail. Professor Edwin Kuh had been recruited as early
as the summer of 1970 and requested to develop an "economic
brain trust" which could develop an issue slate for the candidate.
In traditional campaigns, intellectuals—and particularly academic
intellectuals—are far removed from the vortex of campaign activity. They normally stand aloof from primary campaigns, reserving
their expertise for the instruction of major party candidates.
Premature identification with a particular candidate diminishes
their issue credibility. Opposition to the war in Vietnam changed

this, and virtually the entire academic community was pledged to McGovern when he was still a very minor aspirant for the nomination. Through the efforts of Gordon Weil, a government Ph.D. from Columbia, an impressive array of committed and talented persons were drawn into the campaign far ahead of the traditional schedule.

The first meeting of the economic staff and advisors took place in June of 1971. Attending a meeting at the home of Blair Clark were Ed Kuh, James Tobin, John Kenneth Galbraith, Robert Triffin, Wassily Leontief, Ray Fair, Bill DeWind, Arthur Schlesinger, and Weil. The focus of the meeting was tax reform, but it was agreed that this subject could not conceptually be separated from welfare reform. In the manner of experts, the notion of welfare reform considered at this meeting was far more comprehensive than the traditional one. Weil accepted the responsibility for the welfare part of the package, and DeWind, the only other nonacademic person present, accepted the responsibility for the tax half. Weil took responsibility for integrating the two parts of the tax-welfare package. Subsequent to this meeting, Leonard Green, of Safe Flight Instrument Corporation, lobbied strenuously for his plan among the McGovern staffers.

Aside from opposition to the war, the McGovern staff were strongly committed to the notion of major income redistribution. Heather Ross, an Urban Institute economist, prepared a specific proposal incorporating the major features of the proposal of the President's Commission on Income Maintenance. This suggestion was rejected by the staff as being too specific, though judged as being in principle correct. Tobin and Kuh were asked to prepare position papers, but neither was forthcoming; Kuh declined on the grounds that such a paper was not in the purview of his primary competence, and Tobin on the grounds that he had already prepared and published a paper in *Agenda for the Nation*. The responsibility thus fell to Weil, who prepared a paper which was presented by McGovern in Ames, Iowa, and submitted in *The Congressional Record* for January 19, 1972.

Weil is not an economist, but he was sensitive to the issues involved in a welfare reform proposal. Moreover, he was aware of the danger of being too specific on such a complex issue. The paper carried a precise disclaimer of commitment of the candidate to any specific plan:

There are a number of methods by which this proposal
could be implemented. Some are discussed here. These
methods require full examination by the best economic tal-
ent available, and the plan chosen must have the support of
the President, if it is to have any chance for adoption. For
those reasons the present proposal is not designed for immediate legislative action. Instead it represents a pledge that,
if elected, I would prepare a detailed plan and submit it to the
Congress.[8]

This was perhaps the most profound statement that McGovern
ever made on welfare reform. The fact that it was promptly forgot-
ten by everybody—including McGovern—goes a long way to explain the failure to adopt welfare reform.

After its delivery in Ames and its insertion into *The Congressional
Record*, the McGovern welfare reform received virtually no attention. Following the New Hampshire and Wisconsin victories,
McGovern became a leading candidate, and the press outstripped
the candidate in detailing McGovern's domestic positions. Try as
he did to address other issues, his supporters forced their candidate to use his exposure time to speak on the war issue. The Ames
speech received considerable play in the Michigan press and *The
New York Times*. Yankelovitch polls reported strong voter resent-
ment to it, particularly among George Wallace supporters. This
led Hubert Humphrey to try his oar at criticizing McGovern on
welfare. The Humphrey staff, the most issue-oriented one in the
primaries, were familiar with the Ames speech and felt it was
perfect for them. They realized that the first-mentioned plan in the
Ames speech was just an illustration, and that when sold as a
specific plan it provoked voter hostility. Thus they felt that an
attack on the welfare plan would bear double fruit. First, it would
show McGovern was not in command of the complexity of domestic policy, and second, when McGovern retreated, as he surely
would, he could be shown to be a vacillator—a jab at the "right
from the start" theme of the McGovern campaign. Humphrey
began to criticize McGovern on welfare in the Nebraska primary,
and, to the surprise of the Humphrey staff, McGovern did not back
down.

A mere recitation of the original disclaimer during the Nebraska primary may have been sufficient to defuse the welfare issue,
but McGovern categorically refused to issue one. Apparently he

felt then that he had to be specific. Unfortunately, McGovern chose to be specific about a plan that was not specific. As the California debates showed, McGovern could not defend a specific position because he didn't have one. The Humphrey staff had fully expected a denial of specificity and were genuinely perplexed by McGovern's ill-considered firmness. On the one hand, they felt that a very little homework by Humphrey would have a large payoff in the California contest, where face-to-face meetings on nation-wide television were already scheduled. On the other hand, some of the older Senate staff hands were reluctant to attack McGovern on this issue, for fear of its impact on Humphrey's already tar-nished image among Democratic liberals whose lukewarm sup-port had cost him the election four years earlier. At the end of a rather acrimonious debate, the decision was reached to press the attack in the California primary, and plans were laid to sabotage McGovern in the first TV contest.

The McGovern staff recognized that they were in trouble, but not soon enough. During the first TV debate Humphrey charged, "Senator McGovern has concocted a fantastic welfare scheme which will give everybody, even Nelson Rockefeller, $1,000, and it will cost the taxpayers $60 or $70 billion, mostly middle-income taxpayers." Humphrey further commented, "A secretary working in San Francisco, making $8,000—a single person—would have an increase in his or her taxes, under Senator McGovern's proposal, of $567." It would have, too! One of the TV panelists most familiar with the issue thought he offered McGovern a life raft with the question, "How much will your plan really cost, Senator?" It was a torpedo instead, for George McGovern replied in his flat, mid-western accent, "I don't know." Later, in a postmortem of the debate, McGovern said of his welfare plan, "I wish that I never heard of the goddamn idea."[9]

Even with the usual dogged optimism that surrounds a political campaign, the campaign director, Gary Hart, with Frank Mankiew-icz, and Gordon Weil, were aware that reform had bombed. The Washington staff phones were soon overloaded with urgent calls from respected economists offering authoritative and contradic-tory suggestions of how McGovern should handle the welfare re-form issue in future debates. Following the debates, McGovern did not recoup. The slapstick handling of the welfare issue con-tinued for days after the first debate. A press conference to further explain the proposal with the aid of a Brookings Institution economist, was characterized by Hart as the high point of a campaign comedy and the low point of campaign strategy.

A decision was made to turn the issue back to "the experts," but by this time welfare reform was a thoroughly discredited issue. One would have expected a major income redistribution plan to be editorially attacked by *National Review* and *The Wall Street Journal*, and it was, but not until after Humphrey had exposed McGovern's weakness in the California primary. It is also significant that the plan was attacked by Tom Wicker in *The New York Times*, Melville Ulmer in the pages of the *New Republic*, and even by his daughter's father-in-law, Herbert Rowan, in the *Washington Post*. The criticism was as imprecise as the proposal, but McGovern's response was that as President he would only propose legislation, and if Congress felt it too radical they could reject it.[10]

The tax-welfare task force was the "expert group" with responsibility for dealing with the welfare issue. The task force was clearly cognizant of the enormity of the task they faced. During the summer of 1972, three fairly consistent positions emerged. The academic economists recommended a respecification of the original plan along the lines suggested by Harold Watts at the St. Louis preconvention hearings. Adrian DeWind, Stanley Surry, and others suggested that the welfare consideration be dropped and that the candidate focus his attention on tax reform. Alvin Schorr and Wilbur Cohen suggested a specific rejection of the earlier plan and the substitution of a more modest welfare reform.

The three options were presented at a meeting at Hickory Hill, Virginia. When the meeting ended the proponent of each of the three positions thought he had converted the candidate. A week and a half later a draft form of a speech to be delivered in New York to a security analysts meeting was circulated. The speech focused on tax reform, with no suggestion of a negative tax plan. In its stead there was a plethora of proposals for incremental change in social security and welfare programs. For the next few days an intricate behind-the-scenes battle ensued, and the negative tax plan was in, then out, in again, and finally out. In fact, the mimeographed copy of the security analysts speech actually contains a large white space in the middle of a page where McGovern had pledged his support to a negative income tax plan but at the very last minute ordered it deleted. Alvin Schorr is willing to assume the credit for the final deletion. He feels that in a late Monday afternoon meeting on August 28 he convinced McGovern of the folly of a guaranteed income proposal. Others close to the scene say that Schorr achieved the deletion by a threat to publicly resign from the McGovern staff of advisors if the section were not deleted. Schorr admits discussing a resignation with Mankiewicz but says there was no threat to make it public, and the question of resignation was not discussed with McGovern as far as he knows.

At any rate, on August 29, 1972, in a speech before the security analysts, McGovern in fact withdrew support from the NIT plan. But he never got out from under it. The drum beat of tension and surrogate speeches built around the $1,000 "gift" continued until the election. Advocates of the NIT were disappointed at this withdrawal of support, and opponents of NIT were unaware of the fact that he no longer proposed it.

WELFARE REFORM, 1972–1976: CONGRESSIONAL INITIATIVE

Though Congress rejected the Family Assistance Plan and did not consider the McGovern reform, it would be a clear and fundamental error to say that Congress was inattentive to welfare reform. The welfare proposals of President Nixon contained, in addition to the family assistance features a set of proposals that would restructure welfare programs for the "deserving poor," that is, the aged, the blind, and the disabled. Without the issues of work effort and family dissolutions to trouble the planners and decision makers, reform of these programs could move with considerably less conflicting pressure. The programs included Old Age Assistance, Aid to the Blind, and Aid to the Permanently and Totally Disabled. In HEW jargon, these programs were lumped together as the "adult programs." Historically, the critical issue in welfare reform of this package of programs has been the relative fiscal and administrative responsibilities of the various levels of government in the delivery of aid.

Persons in these conditions of need were not expected to work, so there was little concern over the impact of a reform of their work effort. Issues of family stability, though substantively present, were simply not raised as planning or political issues. Overwhelming, however, was the fact that people would not become aged, blind, or disabled in order to receive aid. Feigning these conditions is also difficult.

The fiscal/administrative responsibility issue was, by comparison, an easy one to resolve. Paradoxically, the defeat of the family assistance package of the Nixon reform effort created a political climate where the adoption of the adult categories was possible. Congress went even further than the President requested. Just prior to the 1972 presidential and congressional elections, Congress, with overwhelming bipartisan support, created the Supplemental Security Income (SSI) Program. The program went into effect in January of 1974 as a federal substitute for the federal/ state adult-category programs. This established for the first time in this country a guaranteed minimum income for certain classes of the poor. The minimum was set at 75 percent of the poverty line for a single individual and 70 percent for a couple. The difference was put into place to discourage marital splitting of aged couples. States whose previous benefits were higher than the new standard were required to supplement benefits up to their previous standard.

In a remarkably successful effort to reduce the stigma associated with aid, the program was placed administratively under the control of the Social Security Administration. The new program increased dramatically the dollars in aid going to the aged, blind, and disabled, from $2.1 billion in 1972 to $6.3 billion in 1977. Though serious problems of client access, service delivery, and intergovernmental responsibility remain, it should not be overlooked that welfare reform for the aged, blind, and disabled has succeeded beyond the expectations of the early reform advocates.[11]

Food Stamp Reforms

SSI reform aided the nonworking poor who were not expected to work. Aid for the working poor and the nonworking poor who were unable to find jobs remained as critical issues. For the working poor, Congress found an outlet in the food stamp program. Originally conceived of as a small demonstration project with noncategorical aid—that is, aid to all in need without regard to status—the food stamp program grew from $35 million in 1965 to $4.5 billion in 1977.

In the years since 1972, Congress has consistently broadened this program. Federally funded but state administered, the program specifies that no family should spend more than 30 percent of its income on a nutritionally adequate diet. The cost of an adequate diet is established by family size and composition. This cost figure established a food stamp benefit. Up until January

1979, families were able to purchase that dollar level of food stamps with whatever one-third of their available income amounts to. Thus, the food stamp program has an implicit 30 percent negative tax rate. Since January 1979, families have been able to purchase all of the stamps but will be eligible simply to receive the "bonus value" of the stamps by application. Since the bonus value declines in response to increased earnings the 30 percent negative tax rate still applies. Nonetheless, this expansion is expected to significantly increase the costs and the benefits of the program. In fact, the food stamp program does provide a kind of funny-money negative income tax.

Manpower Programs

With SSI for the adult categories and food stamps for the working poor as well as others, the remaining unaided target population was those persons seeking work and not finding it. Frustrated job seekers constitute a category larger than the poor. Congress created complex revenue sharing and job creation programs. Collectively these programs spent in 1974 $3.9 billion, of which $2.7 billion went to households which would have been poor had they not received such earmarked job aid. By the 1978 fiscal year, this expenditure had risen to $15 billion. The expansion of manpower programs is shown in Figure 10–3.

This change in funding reflected a fundamental shift in thought regarding welfare reform in the period from 1968 to the mid-seventies. The thrust of activity was focused on creating a near universal income transfer system conceptually based on a notion of a negative income tax. By the mid-seventies, this central thrust had shifted to focus on a series of categorical (that is, subpopulation-specific) programs bound together with a set of programs to provide jobs rather than direct transfers.

The Ford Interregnum: 1974–1976

Increasingly, the Ford presidency is viewed as a period when the country stopped its forward momentum long enough to recover from the trauma of the impeachment process. Welfare reform, along with other domestic issues, achieved a back-burner status. Two reform proposals surfaced briefly, each reflecting the shift from negative taxation to job creation.

The Congressional Proposals and the Ford Initiative. Throughout

FIGURE 10–3
GROWTH OF MANPOWER PROGRAMS, 1964–1979

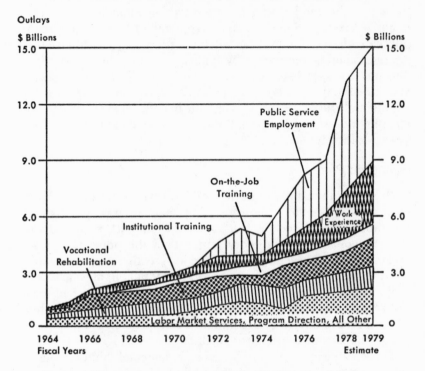

SOURCE: *Special Analyses, Budget of the United States Government* (Washington, D.C.: U.S. Government Printing Office, 1978, p.235.)

most of this period, the U.S. Congress played a reactive rather than a proactive role. Shortly after the defeat of the Family Assistance Program, the Joint Economic Committee charged the Subcommittee on Fiscal Policy chaired by Martha Griffiths to examine the existing welfare reform options and recommend an alternative. This study, undertaken by a small staff, did collect and collate an incredible body of literature regarding welfare reform issues. Its last paper was entitled "Income Security for Americans: Recommendations of the Public Welfare Study."[12]

There were two major provisions to the Griffiths proposal. Under the first part, SSI, food stamps, and AFDC would be folded into a single program which would also provide aid to able-bodied but poor persons with no jobs or inadequate jobs. The basic guarantee for a family of four would be $3,600, which falls at the rate of 50 cents on each dollar of earned income. The program would be federally administered but the individual states would be required to maintain those already on AFDC with a current benefit if such families otherwise would be worse off by the creation of this new program. The second feature of the Griffiths proposal was a modest tax credit program of $225 per person, which would replace the $750 personal exemption. The credit would be deducted from ordinary income tax liability. Should the credit be larger than the tax liability, the excess would be paid to the filer. The estimated net new cost, after deducting for savings from programs phased out or down, would have been $15 billion.

Though Congress did adopt the tax credit concept in 1974 and expanded it in 1978, the Griffiths proposals did not receive much serious congressional attention.

Ford's Income Security Program. At approximately the same time and somewhat, but not entirely, independently, the staff of the Assistant Secretary for Planning and Evaluation of HEW developed a companion proposal. ISP contained no tax credit proposal but was otherwise essentially similar to the Griffiths plan. One important difference was that its report dealt in considerably more depth with the technical and administrative issues associated with the introduction of a negative tax plan. Also, the rhetoric of the report more sharply focused on the need for a jobs program to coexist with any income security reform.

THE CARTER WELFARE PROPOSAL: 1976–1978

The Carter administration inherited a welfare system that had no positive constituency. Recipients, social workers, public officials, and tax-conscious groups agreed only on the inadequacy of the current system. Each of the four constituencies had in the immediate past initiated a welfare reform effort, and each constituency had failed to achieve its reform, largely because of the opposition of the others. Because of the political costs that had come to be associated with welfare reform efforts, there were no knights errant ready to champion a new welfare reform effort. The problems to which previous knights errant had responded were still, however, very present. The rapidly expanding welfare costs in the

Nixon/Ford years, in juxtaposition to the intractability of poverty, made welfare reform an urgent but unpleasant necessity.

Through the offices of the new secretary of Health, Education, and Welfare, Joseph Califano, and Ray Marshall at Labor, an interdepartmental task force was established to propose once again a new welfare initiative.

The congressional initiative of 1974, led by Representative Martha Griffiths, had resulted in a landmark study which increased congressional awareness of the balkanized constituencies and decisional complications which were, collectively, the lion in the path of welfare reform. The Griffiths committee and the studies it spawned revealed that 55 separate federal programs offered various sorts of cash, in-kind aid, and services to various categories of low-income persons. Griffiths' Congressional Joint Economic Subcommittee on Fiscal Policy encapsulated the problem: "They (programs) are expanding in terms of the number of people covered, in terms of benefit levels and in terms of the sheer number of programs. And each such expansion aggravates the problems of high benefit levels, disincentives to work, unfair treatment of many groups and administrative confusion. And each such expansion makes it ever more difficult to bring order to this chaos."[13]

As a consequence, programs uniquely rational functioned in juxtaposition to offend one's sense of justice and equity and to violate a large number of cherished mores. The collective welfare system, while disbursing nearly $50 billion worth of benefits, covered some in need, denied aid to others, and gave aid where the need was less urgent. It provided vastly different amounts of aid to families in highly similar circumstances. It was costly to administer and was so complex that many of the potentially eligible were either denied aid, received less than they were eligible for, or simply did not apply out of fear, shame, or ignorance. On the other side of the coin, benefits were continued to those no longer eligible, overpayments were made, and the opportunities for fraud were rampant. The federal government was spending $400 million, administratively, just to reduce the incidence of fraud, abuse, and error in overpayments alone. More serious was the fact that the program contained adverse work incentives, adverse incentives to thrift, and positive incentives to family dissolution, and it encouraged migration in pursuit of higher welfare benefits.

The interdepartmental task force decided to follow on a course between both schools. Its rhetoric was fundamental reform, but its component parts were clearly incremental. What emerged from the task force's deliberations was a welfare reform initiative that was submitted to Congress in August of 1977. The details of the Carter plan, which was labeled Program for Better Jobs and Income, can best be understood by looking at its four component parts.

First, the Carter proposal asked that $8.8 billion be appropriated to create up to 1.4 million public service jobs. It was expected that 2.0 million persons would hold such jobs in a given year as they are processed through these jobs on their way to regular employment in the public or private sector. Most of these jobs would pay a minimum wage (projected to be $3.30 in 1980) and be full-time, full-year jobs. The job income would thus be $6,600.

In addition, a family would receive an income supplement from· the second part of the program. The size of the supplement would be geared to family size. The jobs would not be eligible for the earned income tax credit of the fourth part of the program; a worker would always have an income incentive to move from the public job to regular employment in the public or private sector. Those eligible for such jobs would be adults—one per family— who are in the "expected to work" category of the second part of the program, but who have been unable to find employment in the regular economy. The job program would replace both CETA and WIN. Care would be taken to assure that public jobs would not replace ordinary public jobs, thus removing the objections to the plan from the labor unions.

On the local level, the jobs program would work as follows:

Intake.   An applicant for employment would enter the employment and training system at the local office of the jobs program.

Job Search and Orientation.   The local employment and training agency would be responsible for helping the applicant locate an appropriate job or training situation. This would include, but would not be limited to, five weeks of intensive job search assistance.

Subsidized Work and Training.   The local employment and training agency would make arrangements with public agencies or nonprofit organizations to create subsidized work and training situations.

Placement in Unsubsidized Jobs.   The local employment and training agency would also be responsible for placing all applicants—including those in subsidized jobs—in private employment as such jobs develop.

Funding.   Funding for the jobs program would be given directly to local prime sponsors under legislation that would authorize a maximum number of job slots. The proposed 1981 budget will request funds to support up to 1.4 million full-time and part-time job slots which, it is estimated, will be sufficient to meet the need. The slots would be allocated among localities according to the number of likely participants. The allocations would be adjusted periodically to maintain a balance between the demand for and supply of job slots and to take into account the ability of the employment and training system to create work opportunities.

The second and most controversial feature of the Carter plan creates an income support system for those expected to have at least one full-time worker: two-parent families, not aged or disabled; single persons; childless couples; single parents with youngest child 14—a rough approximation of the current General Assistance population. Such families would receive during the job search a basic benefit (for a family of four) of $2,300 ($1,100 for second adult, $600 per child). The first $3,800 has a zero reduction rate, while after that the next $4,600 of earning reduces benefits at a rate of 50 cents on the dollar, phasing out at $8,400.

The third feature is designed to federalize AFDC and amalgamate it with SSI. All families headed by an aged, blind, or disabled person or a single parent with a child under 14 would receive a basic benefit of $4,200. Should they have earnings but are not required to work, the benefit would fall 50 cents on the dollar.

Benefits for both schedules phase out at $8,400. Figure 10-4 shows that a family with no expected workers effectively would receive a benefit of $4,200 with a tax rate of 50 percent. With earnings of, say, $3,800, it would receive a benefit of $2,300.

Families in the amalgamated AFDC/SSI program have a lower guarantee but have a zero reduction rate on the first $3,800 of earnings.

The final of the four features is an expansion of the earned income tax credit (EITC), as illustrated in Figure 10-5.

Existing EITC.   Currently, the EITC is a cash credit or rebate of 10 percent on all earnings up to $4,000, for a maximum credit of $400. The credit is phased down by $1 for every $10 of earnings on adjusted gross income over $4,000, and it disappears at $8,000

FIGURE 10–4
BENEFITS FROM CARTER PLAN

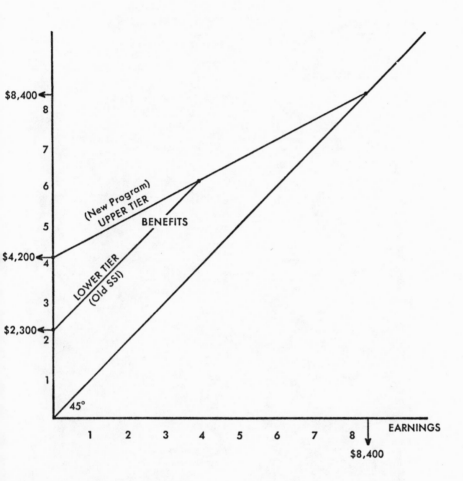

FIGURE 10–5
THE CARTER TAX CREDIT

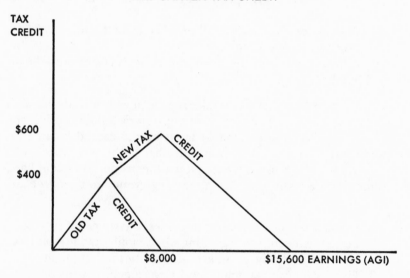

of adjusted gross income. This structure creates a work disincentive for families with earnings between $4,000 and $8,000, many of whom would be receiving cash assistance under the administration's proposal.

The Modified EITC. The proposed EITC would have the following measures:

1. A 10 percent credit on earnings up to $4,000, as under current law.
2. A 5 percent credit on earnings between $4,000 and the point at which a family will become liable for federal income tax under a tax reform proposal to be made by the administration.
3. A phase-out of the credit above this tax-entry point by $1 for every $10 of income.
4. Adjustment of paychecks to reflect the EITC through the tax withholding process.

An incentive for workers to take regular unsubsidized public or private employment, rather than subsidized public service employment, would be created by applying the earned income tax credit only to earnings from unsubsidized jobs.

Compared with the current system, the proposed system has a number of advantages that almost everyone would agree are present:

1. It has a better fit with the federal tax system.
2. Perverse incentives regarding work, family stability, and welfare-induced migration are reduced but not eliminated.
3. Fiscal relief to state and local government is provided.
4. A national minimum for all persons is partly established.

This last point is critically important: Under the Carter proposal, there is a *right* to an income for virtually all Americans, except for a very few—single adults and childless couples who hold minimum-wage jobs would not be covered.

The original cost estimates of the Carter proposal are given in Table 10–2.

WELFARE REFORM: FUTURE PROSPECTS

A series of welfare reform proposals has briefly surfaced, each of which has been consigned to political oblivion because:

TABLE 10–2
COST AND SAVINGS ESTIMATES, PRESIDENT CARTER'S
PROGRAM FOR BETTER JOBS AND INCOME (IN BILLIONS, 1978
DOLLARS)

Current expenditures
  AFDC $6.4
  SSI 5.7
  Food stamps 5.0
  Current EITC 1.3
  Extended unemployment 0.7
  Public jobs (including WIN) 5.9
                                                    $25.0 billion
Tax and other savings
  Decrease unemployment
    expenditures $0.4
  Decrease housing subsidy 0.5
  Increase social security tax
    payments 0.3
                                                            $1.2
      Total Savings ....$26.2 billion
New programs
  Work benefit and income.....................................$20.4
  New EITC 1.5
  Employment training costs 8.8
      Total ....$30.7 billion
      Net New Cost ....$4.5 billion

SOURCE: HEW news release, August 6, 1977, p.19.

1. They have been crowded off of the legislative calendar because of the press of other issues.

2. The cost estimates have been hopelessly optimistic, and even ardent supporters have withdrawn their support when realistic cost estimates are reported.

3. Proposals have been offered with broadly sketched features, and the fine-tune planning efforts tend to turn away both liberals and conservatives who perceive in each new welfare reform proposal their own welfare Rorschach.

4. Most significantly, no plan so far proposed has been able to generate the consistent constituent support that would energize a member of Congress to take up the cudgel, fight the good fight, and make the necessary compromises. To the contrary, those who advocate specific welfare reform proposals risk the ire of the many others who have slightly and sometimes significantly different agendas of welfare reform. Unless and until circumstances or value orientations are sharply modified, welfare reform will remain a shoreline dimly perceived. No one likes current welfare, but numerically and in terms of political resources, too many

believe current offerings are better than specific proposed alternatives.

NOTES

1. Charles E. Lindblom, *A Strategy for Decisions* (New York: Free Press; 1963).
2. Steven C. Charen, "The Politics of Income Maintenance," unpublished paper, Princeton, N.J., 1971, p. 70. See also "Welfare Out of Control," *U.S. News and World Report*, February 8, 1971, and "Welfare—The Shame of a Nation," *Newsweek*, February 8, 1971.
3. "Rural Negative Tax Study," (Heffernan tape) Institute for Research on Poverty, University of Wisconsin, Madison, Wisconsin.
4. *The New York Times*, April 1, 1970.
5. *The New York Times*, April 2, 1970.
6. U.S. Congress, Senate, Committee on Finance, *H.R. 16311 The Family Assistance Act of 1970*, 91st Cong., 2nd sess., June 1970.
7. *CQ Almanac*, 1970, p. 1035.
8. *Congressional Record*, January 19, 1972, vol. 118, p. 3.
9. Gary Hart, *Right from the Start*, p. 190.
10. *Washington Post*, May 16, 1972.
11. The student interested in updating to the present time the developments in SSI should consult the sources outlined in the Appendix at the end of this text.
12. *National Journal*, vol. 6, no. 47, p. 1772.
13. *National Journal Reports*, © 1974, p. 1565.

PART IV

THE ORGANIZATION AND EVALUATION OF SOCIAL WELFARE PROGRAMS

CHAPTER 11

THE STRUCTURE OF SOCIAL SERVICE
PROGRAMS:
AN OVERVIEW

In the first chapters of this text we defined a social welfare program as having three critical components: (1) it articulates a minimum standard of consumption or service, (2) it establishes a benefit schedule, and (3) it defines the boundaries of the population subgroup that is afforded the protection of the standard. A concrete program to deliver that standard to that population is established by legislators incorporating these components. Whatever the defects of this effort to establish boundaries to the field of social welfare, the definition does focus attention on the *product* of social welfare programs rather than the *process* of social welfare efforts.

The programs established to accomplish social welfare objectives are the product of a polity's political and economic system. The structure of a polity's social welfare system and the structure of its basic politicoeconomic institutions coexist in a tension relationship, one to the other. The social inequality to which social welfare institutions attempt to respond is the consequence of dysfunctions within the market system, which grants economic well-being and security to some but not to all. The failure of some persons to respond to economic dysfunctions which place them in a position of need is also a consequence of fissures in the political structure which obstruct the democratic ideal of majority rule consonant with minority rights. In response to these dysfunctions, social welfare institutions are created, and their operation changes the environment that generated them. The new environment generates in turn a need for a new set of social welfare institutions. Diagrammatically, this relationship is illustrated in Figure 11–1.

FIGURE 11–1
SOCIAL WELFARE INSTITUTIONS: PRODUCT OF CHANGE AND
PRODUCER OF CHANGE

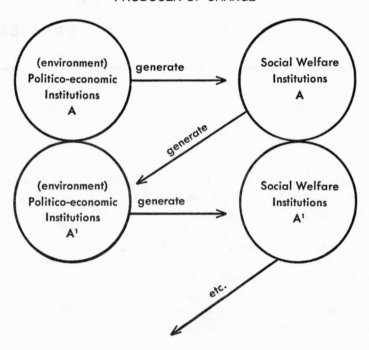

The dynamic tension between the polity's politicoeconomic institutions and its social welfare institutions fuels the controversy surrounding two basic yet competing conceptualizations of social welfare systems. As we noted in Chapter 1, Harold Wilensky and Charles LeBeaux labeled and juxtaposed these two frames of reference: the residual view and the institutional view.[1] The residual position argues that social welfare programs and agencies begin to play their role only when the normal structures of the market, the family, or the political institutions exhibit failure. These are the preferred institutions for the allocation of goods and resources, socialization, and public decision making. Sometimes these institutions fail: depressions occur, families are broken up, and some persons are arbitrarily excluded from the processes of government. When such failures occur, social welfare agencies are activated to right the wrong. Some individuals, because of age or illness, may need specialized help to benefit from the functioning of a just society. In all cases, according to this view, social welfare institutions are basically responsive and corrective. The residual social agency is reactive and withdraws as soon as the "regular" institutions are again working properly.

The alternative view, sometimes perceived as antithetical to the residual conception, is the institutional approach, which sees social welfare programs and agencies as a traditional first-line institution, along with the market and the family. Social welfare is structured as "a system of laws, programs, benefits, and services which strengthen or assure provisions for meeting social needs recognized as being basic for the welfare of the population and for the functioning of the social order."[2] In this conception, it does not require an abnormality or failure to be activated. Institutional social welfare agencies are proactive rather than reactive, creative rather than corrective, and assertive rather than responsive.

STRATEGIES OF INTERVENTION

In real terms, specific social agencies and programs contain elements of both the residual and institutional concepts. The structure, processes, and governance of most agencies and programs contain some blend of both ideas. Usually, social welfare programs and agencies are charged with the responsibility of providing a minimum standard. In the pursuit of that goal somewhat disparate strategies of intervention have been adopted. Social welfare programs can be more precisely classed by their reliance on strategies of intervention rather than on the basis of an institutional/residual conceptual core.

Three strategies of intervention designed to provide the minimum standard through social welfare programs are generally recognized. These strategies, which are based on the perceived source of need, are:

1. The service strategy, which perceives the need to be due to at least some of the characteristics of the recipients.
2. The income strategy, which holds that social welfare objectives are most effectively and efficiently pursued by programs of income distribution.
3. The power strategy, which perceives the need to be due to the political circumstances which shape the institutions that serve, or fail to serve, the recipient class.

These strategies have evolved from different theories of why the minimum is not "ordinarily" available. The service strategy is discussed in a later section of this chapter. The income strategy has been thoroughly covered in preceding chapters and will not be reconsidered here. The power strategy is the topic of the following section.

THE POWER STRATEGY

The power strategy, based on a notion that a class of persons falls into need because they are without the resources to do battle in a pluralistic political environment, focuses attention on the political circumstances which shape the institutions that serve, or fail to serve, the recipient class. While the power strategy is currently receiving new attention and being reconceptualized, it is certainly a part of the early days of social welfare programming in this country. The Hull House concept was fundamentally a power approach. Various groups that were both poor and powerless were helped to organize politically and to achieve power—at least to some extent—by the organization, communication and inculcation of a common identity. This allowed each group to define its own goals politically and to accomplish them.[3]

During the 1940s and 1950s and the early 1960s, the power strategy in social welfare programs took a second seat to the service strategy. Reemerging in the mid-sixties under the auspices of OEO, the power strategy was revised largely as the unintended consequence of a rather vaguely worded requirement of the 1964 Economic Opportunity Act which mandated "maximum feasible participation of residents of the area and members of the groups served."[4] The participation requirement allowed blacks and middle-class white professionals to use the legislation as an instrument to restructure social welfare services and even city politics in general.[5] The goal became to create autonomous, democratic organizations which were not dependent on the local political structure, as the earlier community organization effort had been.[6]

Not surprisingly, the new effort at political organization in pursuit of social welfare objectives met with intense opposition, particularly in the large cities where it had its largest successes. Mayors largely suspected the purity of motives of those who would organize the poor "to break down the walls of the city."[7] At the 1965 Conference of Mayors, a president-elect of the group promised "to take (community participation) out of politics and place it in the office of the mayor."[8] This end was largely achieved in 1967 with the Green amendment, which effectively established a mayor's veto over all initiatives of the community action agencies. With this amendment, the Community Action Program ceased to be controversial. Without the participation requirement, OEO simply was a conduit for federal funding of local service programs. Two years later Nixon was able to disperse the programs to various operating agencies without significant protest.[9]

In addition to the organization thrust, OEO also spawned another power strategy: the Legal Service Program. Originally conceived of as a mechanism to provide lawyer services to poor persons, it soon outstripped its role as a supervisor of divorce actions and mortgage procedures. Instead it became a powerful source of class-action suits to stop proposed cuts in social programs like Medicaid and initiated the enforcement of reasonable due process in a vast number of income security programs. Considerable effort to stop this class-action thrust was exerted in the Nixon-Ford administration. In 1971, the active model of legal services in the late 1960s was reduced significantly. Nonetheless, legal action is today the principal free-standing power strategy.

The thrust to recreate an organization strategy remains alive, with patterns of political activity and influence that are incredibly complex. As Robert Dahl writes:

> Any simple theory about how American citizens influence the conduct of their government is bound to be misleading; any brief statement is even more inadequate. Nonetheless, two general conclusions seem scarcely contestable. First, differences among citizens in their resources, their skills, their incentives, their allies, and their opponents have prevented, and perhaps in some degrees always will prevent, a close approximation to perfect equality among citizens in their

influence on the conduct of government. Second, few groups in the United States who are determined to influence the government—certainly few of any groups of citizens who are organized, active, and persistent—lack the capacity and opportunity to influence some officials somewhere in the political system in order to obtain at least some of their goals.[10]

I would add a third conclusion: Nowhere is the political task more formidable than in an effort by low-income groups to promote a restructuring of the social order that is perceived by the remainder of society as a threat to their privilege. As Robert Merton has shown:

> When social systems have institutionalized goals and values to govern the conduct of component actors, but limit access to these goals for certain members of the society, "departures from institutional requirements" are to be expected. Similarly, if certain groups within a social system compare their share in power, wealth and status honor with that of other groups *and* question the legitimacy of this distribution, discontent is likely to ensue. If there exist no institutionalized provisions for the expression of such discontents, departures from what is required by the norms of the social system may occur.[11]

People tend either to retreat from or to attack forces controlling their lives which they can neither influence nor escape. During the 1960s, there was a rise of what was called "protest politics." With the failure of this effort, the poor appear to have returned to a position of apathy.

There is something curious in the general reaction to the power strategy. When the poor coalesced, or rather attempted to coalesce, as a group in political life, the reaction was to deny the legitimacy of the strategy, though the existence of lobbying or pressure groups is one of the salient features of American politics. There is nonetheless a moral ambivalence to pressure-group politics. One feature of pressure-group politics that is distinctly American is the absence of overt class groups. Whereas in European politics and political thought class conflict is a central element, American politics has not been characterized by class conflicts, and American political thinkers have, with a few exceptions, been silent on this topic.[12] More important, openly class-conscious politics stands in antithesis to the ambience of American politics. This fact goes a long way to explain the force of the reaction to the power strategy.

In addition to power advocates, policy issues are structured by technocrats who serve as full-time representatives employed to work out details. But we find it often happens that skilled technicians in policy formulation will, for example, swing back and forth between employment in the Department of Labor and the AFL-CIO without any serious wrench of ideological conflict, and they find the movement adds to their experience and skill, and, perhaps most important, contacts of friendship and mutual respect between the organizations. To date at least, there is no evidence of shifting between NWRO and HEW. For these and other reasons too numerous to catalog, the poor are dependent on nonpoor and nonagents to press for their demands.

Political Mechanisms of Nonagents

It may be an affront to the professional dignity of some social workers to be told they are not the servants of the poor, but it is clearly historical and present truth. Social workers, at least those who work with the poor, could perhaps be classified as semiagents for the poor. Often, because of their dual and sometimes conflicting commitments, they have clearly done much but not enough to improve the quality of welfare policy. Generally speaking, their task has been to take godawful policy from the legislators and translate it into a practice which is merely awful.

In their interaction with legislators, these activists have tended to utilize a limited number of political mechanisms. These mechanisms are not mutually exclusive and are not intended to imply that any one activist is wholly dependent on one type of mechanism. The three political mechanisms are: (1) conflict reduction, (2) risk taking, and (3) conflict creation.

Conflict Reduction. The reduction approach is typically used by "welfare bureaucrats" who never take a chance: one of these, Wilbur Cohen, once told this author that he never sent a bill up to the Hill without knowing exactly how many votes it had. In this strategy, the mood of the legislature is sensitively and precisely measured. The reductionist and his aides retire to his office and, like generals planning a battle, examine a carefully chartered master plan and decide that this year they'll push for adding a new category or increasing the federal share. While there is a rational policy objective locked away in the secretary's file, the essence of reduction is never to let these broad policy objectives become part of the public record or be the subject of public debate. Thus this policy direction is highly elitist. Cohen is only the master reductionist; he has many fellow practitioners. State and local welfare directors also make use of this device. They enjoy telling academics (or at least they enjoy telling me) how they got this or that policy through the legislature or town council without a word of debate or a single dissenting vote. The entire effort is directed toward slow but steady changes.

The rationale of reductionism in welfare is that the normal process of elective politics and the more or less open contest of interest groups in legislative politics are stacked against the poor. Whether measured in terms of numbers, prestige, influence, access to decision makers, or access to mass media, the poor are at an outstanding disadvantage in any attempt to play the game of politics according to the rule of Madisonian democracy which governs most of American politics. Practitioners of the art of reduction perceive themselves as hardheaded realists, as pragmatists, but also as the only ones who have consistently delivered "the bacon" to the poor (despite the fact that the "bacon" they deliver usually turns out to be fatback).

Risk Taking. The political mechanism of risk taking is rapidly replacing reduction as the preferred strategy of social workers. The practitioners of the art of risking reject the reductionist approach not so much because it is slow and ineffectual as because it is essentially elitist. It leaves the poor permanently powerless and dependent on the welfare bureaucrat—a condition perceived as being politically and psychologically unsound.

The risk approach seeks to bring the present tensions of the current system and the values of a new approach out into the open. When used by the agency administrator, this approach is characterized by aggressive efforts to interpret the agencies' programs and to involve clients, legislators, and good-government interest groups such as the League of Women Voters.

When used by settlement houses and community action centers, this approach involves *pressure* to organize and educate the poor, and considerable effort is exerted to alter the process of policymaking in welfare. This approach seeks to hit at the root cause, the powerlessness of the poor. A reading of the normative literature in community organization reveals that this approach places enormous faith in the capacity of the poor, the workings of the democratic process, and the willingness of well-off citizens to change their stance when they are fully informed. However, journalistic accounts reveal that, to date at least, this approach has achieved *policy* success only on peripheral issues where there was insignificant opposition, such as the location of the local welfare office or free spraying for water bugs in public housing apartments. On larger issues, such as raising grant levels or changing the rate structure in public housing, *policy* success has been conspicuously absent. The psychological goals of changing clients' perception of self and capacity to act on their own behalf have met with much larger success. It should be noted, however, that while a client's perception of self is improved, the policy issue is still lost; this is therapy that can prove to be expensive.

Conflict Creation. The third political mechanism to be discussed, conflict creation, is oriented to the creation of a new tension rather than use of an existing one. Richard Cloward and Frances Piven have argued for the need to *produce* a "welfare crisis." They argue that the traditional technique of advocacy by special-interest groups was clearly not working, and the fundamental legislative reforms of the New Deal were not so much the result of interest-group pleading as the fact that the crisis of the depression had disrupted and destroyed the old regionally based coalitions underlying the pre–New Deal national parties. Thus the "new democratic coalition," heavily based on urban working-class groups, was allowed to pass in order to implement the economic reforms of the New Deal.

Cloward and Piven also argued that today's urban party organizations have become avenues for the advancement of minority political leaders rather than channels for the expression of poor and minority-group interests. The strategy of crisis would expose the latent tensions between ghetto voter and urban party leadership, or it would thrust forward ghetto demands and back them with the threat of defections from those who had been loyal to "establishment liberals." They believed that "a series of welfare drives in large cities would impel action on a new federal program to distribute income, destroy the present welfare system and alleviate the abject poverty which it perpetuates."[13]

THE SERVICE STRATEGY

Of the three strategies of social welfare intervention—service, income replacement, and power—the service strategy is the least conceptually clear. We have used the term *social service* as if its meaning were clear. In fact, few terms are used with less precision than this one. The term clearly takes on different meanings in different political and cultural contexts. The definitions of social service, and the conceptions from which those definitions spring, therefore carry a great deal of ideological baggage.

For social service critics on the radical left there is the perception that social services are band-aids which provide surcease but functionally are a diversionary tactic. They effectively serve to redirect energies from the fundamental goal of a more equitable distribution of income and political power.[14] At the other end of the political spectrum are those who perceive social services as being inimical to the values of the Protestant ethic (thrift, hard work, temperance, sexual fidelity, and so on) and argue that social services, by their "surfeit" of benefits, actually encourage and generate the problems to which they ostensibly respond.[15]

The phenomena which radicals and conservatives alike fear do, of course, occur: youth retraining programs can divert attention from a chronic problem of a shortage of jobs or irrelevant and inadequate programs in secondary education; a postrelease correctional program may serve as a cheap substitute for prison reform; divorce counseling programs often have the effect of increasing the incidence of divorce. Shorn of rhetoric, however, all of these results simply suggest that social service programs are responses to currently observed social dysfunctions.

Liberal social workers tend to reject both the conservative and radical viewpoints. They argue that it is the task of the social service system to respond to dysfunction and dislocations which may well not occur in a more ideally structured political economy but which are all too evident in ours. The social service structure is responsive to present reality conditions and not to some obscure alternative reality. Liberal definitions of social services tend to depend on heavily conceptualized typologies which err in the direction of being classification systems based on "purpose." It has been observed that purpose is an inadequate criterion for the classification of policy, since a particular policy typically has multiple purposes. The same is true for a typology of social service programs.

The search for a definition must conclude on a weak note. It is clear, as Ronald Gilbert has observed, that "The many attempts in the social welfare field to define and classify social services have resulted in minimal pay-off to practitioners and theoreticians. In fact, there is no commonly accepted definition for answering the question, 'what is a social service?' "[16]

It is equally clear that as public and private programs develop in scope and range, the term *social services* has acquired an elastic quality. Once synonymous with poor relief, it now embraces a multitude of heterogeneous activities. There is no consistent principle in the definition of the term.[17]

Finally, it is clear not only that the expression carries a considerable amount of ideological baggage, but that the phenomenon it attempts to describe is in fundamental transition. Both conditions make any effort at definition both hazardous and arduous. There is, however, no shortage of heuristic definitions. To these I now add my own: Social service programs as here conceived are a subset of social welfare programs, as previously defined.[18]

Social service programs are one of the instruments available to bring to a subpopulation a specific standard by employing the interpersonal and intergroup interactions of the professional social worker. These interactions are often accompanied by specific in-kind services and goods, such as day care, transportation to health centers and the like. Such specific services and goods become social services only as they are consciously designed to achieve a more basic welfare objective.

Income security, power monitoring, and in-kind transfer institutions all have objectives which range beyond social welfare objectives. Social service programs do not. Because social service programs lie wholly within the social welfare sphere, whereas the other functions do not, there is a tendency to equate social service with social welfare. That is an unfortunate equation. Social service programs are those sets of goods and services which attempt to modify the characteristics of a recipient of a social welfare program. For example, a day care service is not a social service; it is an in-kind social welfare benefit. A jobs retraining program is a social service in the sense that it is a conscious and deliberate effort to alter the marketable characteristics of the individual in question.

Because of the demands of accountability in both a political and an economic sense, it would be nice if there were a mutually exclusive and easily identifiable set of functions that could be labeled as social service functions. Such is not the case. In a major sense, social services tend to respond to overlapping social dysfunctions and personal troubles. The social service programs respond to these dysfunctions and problems in three ways:

1. Through programs designed to aid individuals and families in coping with acute problematic conditions.
2. Through programs structured to assist families and individuals to gain access to larger community services and programs normally outside of the social welfare sector, and certainly outside of the social service sector.
3. Through therapeutic, rehabilitative, and developmental programs to assist troubled persons to acquire the skills and insights requisite to personal problem solving.

THE STRUCTURE OF DELIVERY

There are a number of ways in which the delivery structure of social services can be subdivided for purposes of critical analysis. Agencies can be categorized by (1) auspices, e.g., voluntary, local government, state government, federal government, mixed; (2) client served, e.g., the aged, the blind, criminal law violators; (3) geographic area served; and (4) principal professional process employed, such as casework, therapy, or group work. None of these works very well, and any typology will have defects. The typology of social services should vary by the purpose of the analysis. That is to say, a typology useful for one analytic goal might prove to be troublesome for some other analytic goal.

There is, thus, no one correct analytic typology. The Council of State Governments staff, however, has developed one overall framework for a grand view of social service programs. At the first cut, services are divided by the principal problem of the client served (e.g., acutely ill, alcoholic, aged, chronically ill). Second, services are subdivided by the locale of the delivery (in institutions, in alternate care arrangements, in offices or clinics, in homes). The CSG group then provides a set of illustrative services and facilities for each category.[19]

This framework provides a quick look at the range and diversity of social service programs. It is also useful to identify omissions or gaps in the service structure in a specific geographic area. In addition, it is useful as the starting point for an organizational evaluation of service delivery systems.

One of the dominant factors of recent years has been the prolif-eration of formal organizational structures and delivery systems being put into place to accomplish social service objectives. At the critical human level, social service organizations are structured to provide the necessary services or resources to restore or establish minimal social functioning, in order to facilitate the highest attain-able level of personal welfare. Specifically, social service institu-tions are people-processing institutions. There are four critical objections with regard to the formal structures and delivery pat-terns. These are:

1. The social service agency system fails to respond to the popu-lation it claims to serve. This is evidenced by a gap between the objective standards set and actual operation; for example, the target population does not receive the legislatively mandated stan-dard.

2. The procedures established to deliver the standard are dehu-manizing and inconsistent with professional criteria. For example, when the service is delivered the process of delivery implicitly violates the goal desired in providing the standard.

3. Social service organizations, even when they deliver the stan-dard in a consistent way, are wasteful, inefficient, and ill managed. The service could, by reorganization, deliver the same standard to the same population at a lower cost to the taxpayer.

4. The target population and the service standard are misspeci-fied in terms of the broader goals of the social welfare system.

The validity of each of these arguments must not be casually accepted or rejected. Empirical evaluation of such social judg-ments is required. The requirements of evaluation are the topic of the final chapter of this text.

CONCLUDING NOTE

A viable social welfare system is always in flux. It contains ele-ments of power, income, and service strategies. None can effec-tively function without reliance on the others. There is an unfortunate tendency for professional and political critics of the welfare system to focus attention on one strategy or another and to forget that changes in one are bound to have some impact—often undesirable—on the other strategies for achieving laudable social welfare objectives.

NOTES

1. Harold M. Wilensky and Charles N. LeBeaux, *Industrial Society and Social Welfare* (New York: Free Press, 1965), pp. 138–47.
2. Walter A. Friedlander and Robert Z. Apte, *Introduction to Social Welfare*, 4th ed. (Englewood Cliffs, N.J.: Prentice-Hall, 1974), p. 4.
3. Sidney E. Zimbalist, *Historic Theories and Landmarks in Social Welfare Research* (New York: Harper and Row, 1977), chap. 5.
4. Economic Opportunity Act of 1964. For a seminal discussion of this topic, see Patrick Moynihan, *Maximum Feasible Misunderstanding*.
5. Paul E. Peterson and J. David Greenstone, "Radical Change and Citizen Participation: The Mobilization of Low Income Communities through Community Action," in R. H. Haveman (ed.), *A Decade of Federal Anti-Poverty Programs* (New York: Academic Press, 1977).
6. Ralph M. Kramer, *Participation of the Poor* (Englewood Cliffs, N.J.: Prentice-Hall, 1969).
7. Michael Harrington, *The Politics of Poverty* (New York: League for Individual Democracy, 1965), p. 18.
8. Personal communication, Mayor Beverly Brieley, Nashville, Tenn., Spring 1967.
9. Haveman, *Decade of Federal Anti-Poverty Programs*.
10. Robert A. Dahl, *Pluralistic Democracy in the United States* (Chicago: Rand McNally & Co., 1967), p. 386.
11. As quoted in Chaim Waxman, *Poverty: Power and Politics* (New York: Grosset & Dunlap, 1968), p. 72.
12. Grant McConnell, *Private Power and American Democracy* (New York: Alfred A. Knopf, 1966).
13. Frances Fox Piven and Richard Cloward, *Regulating the Poor* (New York: Random House, 1971).
14. Jeffry H. Galper, *The Politics of Social Service* (Englewood Cliffs, N.J.: Prentice-Hall, 1975), chap. 8.
15. Joseph Feagin, *Subordinating the Poor* (Englewood Cliffs, N.J.: Prentice-Hall, 1975).
16. G. Ronald Gilbert, *Toward a Classification of Social Service Systems: A Theoretical Framework*, University of Southern California, Regional Research Institute in Social Welfare, 1971, p. iii.
17. Richard M. Titmus, *Essays on "The Welfare State"* (Boston: Beacon Press, 1969), p. 40.
18. See Lawrence M. Friedman, *Social Welfare Legislation: An Introduction*, Institute for Research on Poverty Discussion Papers (Madison: University of Wisconsin, 1968).
19. Council of State Governments, *Human Services: A Framework for Decision-Making* (Lexington, Ky., 1975).

CHAPTER 12

RESEARCH AND EVALUATION NEEDS IN
SOCIAL WELFARE PROGRAMS

In order to assess the effectiveness of a complex social welfare system, some sort of judgmental framework must first be articulated. At one level of analysis, judgments regarding effectiveness are irrelevant. This is the level of political analysis, where we are concerned with an explanation of how a particular program came into being and which economic and political conditions are required to modify the program in a particular direction. If, however, we believe that individual actors can affect the kinds of social welfare programs we have, then judgments are vitally important.

MODES OF INQUIRY

There are three interrelated questions with regard to social welfare choices, and each demands a different mode of inquiry. First, for a given politicoeconomic process and condition, we need to know what choices can occur; this is the realm of the possible. Second, we need to know, for a given set of goals, what choices ought to be made; this is the realm of the prescriptive.[1] The third mode of inquiry which is addressed to the effectiveness of social welfare programs is evaluative research. This form of inquiry is concerned with the development of a transmittable body of knowledge on how we judge the suitability of particular programs, given a particular political condition and a given prescriptive orientation. Evaluative inquiry, as described by Tony Tripodi, is:

> ... the systematic accumulation of facts for providing information about the achievement of program requisites and goals relative to efforts, effectiveness, and efficiency within any stage of program development. The facts of evaluation may be obtained through a variety of relatively systematic techniques, and they are incorporated into some designated system of values for making decisions about social programs.[2]

This chapter will deal with each of these three modes of inquiry and with political analysis, policy evaluation, and program evaluations as three aspects of social welfare evaluation. The chapter (and this text) concludes with a postscript on the role of social scientific inquiry as it focuses on the development of a "better" welfare system.

THE REALM OF THE POSSIBLE

The goal of the mode of inquiry concerned with what choices can occur is to explain, as parsimoniously as possible, the outcomes of the policy process rather than their desirability or effectiveness. In this mode of inquiry, the goal is to explain the path of public policy itself. Here the scholar seeks to identify, with the utmost possible precision, the factors and conditions most likely to produce a given social welfare system. He or she also seeks to identify which of these conditions are mutable and which are not. Such inquiry requires precise modeling of the social choice process and the development of descriptive and historical data to fit these models. There is an effort to specify the causal connection between the environmental systems and the policy outcome.[3]

In the past 15 years or so a large body of literature has been devoted to the exploration of the linkage between environmental circumstances and public welfare policies as they differ in the 50 American States.[4] Attention has been paid to demographic variables such as population density and urbanization, to economic variables such as industrialization and per capita income, and to political variables such as party competition and patterns of voter participation in elections. Members of the various social sciences have developed contrasting explanatory models which emphasize the importance of variables traditionally associated with their own disciplines. Those attempting integration have generally concluded that it is the economic factors which are most closely tied to variation in performance of public welfare programs such as general assistance, unemployment compensation, and AFDC.

The response by political scientists to these findings has generally been that measurement problems, and particularly problems associated with the colinearity of the relevant variables, have produced a condition which underestimates the importance of *political* variables. Their argument has generally been that if the researchers had been more careful and precise in their selection of both dependent and independent variables, and if they had been more sophisticated in their statistical procedures, political variables would regain their proper place as the central variables in the prediction of policy performance in the states of the American federal system. This argument, to say the least, has not found a comfortable resting place in the literature. It is not this author's intention to review the debate, as very adequate summaries and criticism of this stream of research activity are already part of the political science literature.[5] The principal impact of this research stream and the criticism it has spawned is that there is no single answer to the question of how to account for interstate variation in policy output.

One of the unfortunate consequences of the form of the debate over the "determinants" of public welfare performance has been that unique events are treated rather carelessly, as of minor importance. Yet we are intuitively aware of the fact that unique events do dramatically influence the course of public policies. The peculiar commitment of a governor, the stamina and skill of a legislator, the presence of a highly charismatic welfare interest-group leader are also factors in the path of development of welfare programs. However, aside from anecdotal accounts and occasional case studies, there has been little effort to investigate these factors systematically.

THE REALM OF THE PRESCRIPTIVE

Politicoeconomic conditions normally will allow for a number of outcomes. The range of choice among welfare programs is clearly not finite. It has been demonstrated that the constraints of power relationships and the condition of scarcity clearly function to narrow the range of choice. But choice is not totally deterministic: within a range, albeit narrow, there is opportunity for selection. The intelligent exercise of judgment within that range is what professional advice is all about.

During the 1960s the American polity seemed to function in a belief that government should be given a shot at solving all of our social problems—poverty, sexism, inequality, delinquency, and all of the rest. As the chapters above document, much progress has been made, but none of the problems has been "solved," and some of them seem to have been exacerbated. For awhile we seemed to believe that governments could eliminate poverty, end crime, clean up the environment, and guarantee an energy supply, among other accomplishments, if we could only find the "right" policy. There was an apparent failure to accept the notion that some societal forces could *not* be harnessed, even if it were desirable to do so, or that citizens as entities with their own volition would often adapt to policies in ways which would render the policy either useless or, worse, counterproductive. Of course we recognize that, for example, income guarantees may reduce work incentives for the poor, or child care programs can have undesirable consequences for family stability. So long as these dysfunctional consequences are perceived as being real, the focus of attention can be alternate ways of minimizing but not eliminating such responses. Good prescriptive research can yield the basic paradigms for effective evaluative inquiry.

EVALUATIVE RESEARCH

Beginning in the early 1960s and continuing into the present time, governments at all levels in the American polity have spent billions of dollars in preventative, corrective, and remedial programs in an effort to ease the ravages of the social problems which have plagued our society. Principally, the monies were used in the area of health, education, and welfare in various programs aimed at disadvantaged population groups, dysfunctional institutions, and so on. The specific goals of such programs have been aimed at promoting educational opportunities, reducing juvenile delinquency and adult criminality, facilitating and making job training efforts more relevant, redistributing income, insuring health care, and so on. Ostensibly the larger goals of these programs were directed at giving disadvantaged Americans the necessary resources to enter and maintain themselves in the mainstream of our economic and social life.

To date the record of these programs has been mixed. Despite the expenditure of truly significant sums of money, the opportunity structure of our society has not changed much. Statistical indices of most social problems, except poverty and racial discrimination, demonstrate that the problems have become more intense.[6]

Social welfare programs face significantly serious competition for scarce public funds. For the foreseeable future there will be heated competition *between* social welfare programs and other public programs, and *among* social welfare programs, for a share of public dollars. Thus a need exists for some objective method of ascertaining the ability of a particular social welfare program to achieve its objective. Increasingly, agency administrators will have to attach to future funding requests solid evidence of program results. Competing agency administrators can be expected to seek to discredit such "findings."[7]

The Process of Evaluative Research

Evaluation, when competently done, measures the extent to which a program obtains its goals. The evaluative process specifies which among the multiplicity of objectives shall be used to judge the program. It declares that some observable phenomenon constitutes a presumption of success and structures an argument to indicate that the favorable outcome, if there is one, is the result of the policy action or program under consideration. This process is subject to abuse; it has been said, for example, that no program ever evaluated by the operating agency ever fails, or that any program evaluated by an external agency ever succeeds.[8] Evaluative research uses the scientific method as the basic analytic tool in determining program impact. Because real-world conditions do not have the experimental purity of controlled laboratory conditions, however, quasi-experimental designs are used to maximize the likelihood that a political actor can in fact know what the results of a program are. Due to the difficulties inherent in each of the phases of the process, the results are "known" only within a range of certainty. The principal task of the policy evaluator is not to show success or failure but to increase that range of certainty.

Identification of Goals

The evaluative process begins with an identification of the goals to be evaluated.[9] This seems obvious, but it is in fact an inordinately value-laden undertaking. Initially there is the problem of ranking goals in an effort to indicate which ones are intended, and their order of importance, and which are desirable but unintended consequences of the policy action or program. The evaluator also must deal with the problem of overt versus covert goals. If attention is given exclusively to overt goals, then the real impact of the program which results from the symbiotic relationship of many programs operating together is likely to be lost. And the evaluator must frankly and honestly deal with the dysfunctional or undesirable consequences that can occur because of the policy action or program. Social science methodology is often overwhelmed by attempts to measure many goals simultaneously, yet the false reification of a program to a too-small set of objectives may mask its good points and expose its bad points. Care in goal identification is a critical first step in a policy-useful evaluation plan.

Formulation of Operational Definitions of Policy and Program Results

The second critical step is the selection of observable phenomena which are indicative of goal success and program dysfunctions. In some very rare cases, these measurable results will be *both* obvious and tangible. In the worst cases they will be *neither* obvious nor tangible. If the question under consideration, for example, is the work habits of a particular target population, one has to consider such things as employment rate, wage rate, hours of work, and work habits of relevant others. The evaluator has the responsibility of demonstrating that the "observed" changes are both valid and reliable estimates of the objective of the policy action or program. The test of program success must stand up to criticism from the scientific community and the political community. Thus, attention must be paid to (1) the permanency of the impact, (2) the replicability of the observation of the success, and (3) the reliability of the observation.

THE RANGE OF POLICY INVESTIGATIONS

So far in this chapter we have dealt with program evaluation as if it were essentially a scientific or technical process. Policy evaluation, the retrospective view, and policy analysis, the prospective view, are both concerned with the outcome or impacts of policy. In political analysis, the goal is to explain how a particular policy comes about; policy is the dependent variable. In policy analysis and program evaluation the policy becomes the independent variable, and the identification of the real-world consequences of the policy becomes the goal of research. The structure of investigation can be seen in Figure 12–1.

FIGURE 12–1
THE STRUCTURE OF POLICY INVESTIGATIONS

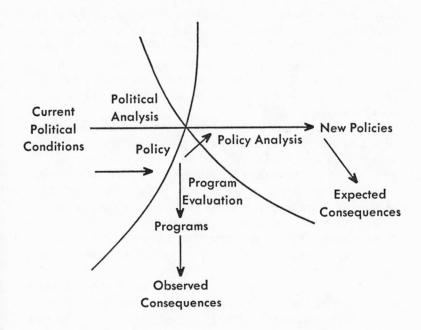

The full range of policy investigations includes political analysis, policy analysis, and program evaluation. All play a part in the explanation of what has occurred or can occur in the realm of social welfare policy. It is important to identify what *can* occur; this is *political analysis*. It is also important to identify what the likely consequences of that occurrence would be; this is *policy analysis.* Identifying the result of policies already in place is called *program evaluation.* Each of these approaches focuses on its own set of investigatory problems. In discussing evaluative research we have been concerned with the problems and limitations of political analysis. In the pages to follow, the problems of policy analysis and program evaluation will be separately examined. This is an unfortunate pedagogic necessity, because in real-world conditions, political analysis, program evaluation, and policy analysis take place as a single evaluative process.

POLICY ANALYSIS

As we have seen from the material examined above, the political system functions to transform desires generated by the politico-economic system into public policies. The shape of that policy is conditioned by the factor of economic scarcity and the prevailing relationships extant at the time the policy developed. Current policy, current economic conditions, current power relationships all interact to yield a set of policy options. The identification of the desirability and likely outcomes of these various options is what policy analysis is all about.

It is not possible in an introductory text such as this to explore all of the ramifications of projected policy analysis. Policy analysis begins with a definition of a social problem to be solved. But problems are merely the perception of an individual or group of individuals. No one perception of the problem is inherently correct, yet we know from common experience that the way a problem is identified often dictates a particular solution. Policy analysis thus has to deal in the first instance with problem specification and provide a rationale as to why the problem so perceived *is* the problem.

Second, policy analysis requires an identification of the resources which are available for the resolution of the problem. Just as the particular perception of the problem implies a particular range of solutions, so does resource availability limit the choices available.

Third, policy analysis requires an articulation of achievable goals and the identification of observable conditions which can be used to judge whether or not the goals so identified are obtainable and by how much.

Fourth, policy analysis requires a suggestion of how the resources will be deployed to resolve the problem in the direction suggested by the goals. This is the planning component of policy analysis; it is by itself a complete field of study.

Finally, policy analysis requires a structured argument to identify and predict the desirable and the dysfunctional consequences of any proposed intervention. Too often policy analysis ignores this aspect of policy. Thomas Dye has developed a useful framework for assessing the net impact of a policy option (see Figure 12–2):

FIGURE 12–2
ASSESSING POLICY IMPACT

	BENEFITS		COSTS	
	Present	Future	Present	Future
Target Groups and Situations	Symbolic Tangible	Symbolic Tangible	Symbolic Tangible	Symbolic Tangible
Nontarget Groups and Situations (Spillover)	Symbolic Tangible	Symbolic Tangible	Symbolic Tangible	Symbolic Tangible
	Sum	Sum	Sum	Sum
	Present Benefits	Future Benefits	Present Costs	Future Costs
	Sum All Benefits		Sum All Costs	
		—		
		Net Policy Impact		

SOURCE: Thomas Dye, *Understanding Public Policy* (Englewood Cliffs, N.J.: Prentice-Hall, 1978).

All these aspects of public policy are very difficult to identify, describe, and measure. Moreover, the task of calculating *net* impact of a public policy is truly awesome. The *net* impact would be all the symbiotic and tangible benefits, both immediate and long-range, minus all the symbiotic and tangible costs, both immediate and future. Even if all the immediate and future and symbolic and tangible costs and benefits are *known* (and everyone *agrees* on what is a "benefit" and what is a "cost"), it is still very difficult to come up with a net balance. Many of the items on both sides of the balance would defy comparison—for example, how do you subtract a tangible cost in terms of dollars from a symbolic reward in terms of the sense of well-being felt by individuals or groups?[10]

The modes of inquiry available to identify the items in the Dye framework are:

1. Demonstration projects, where policy is tried out on a pilot basis and the consequences of the policy are carefully observed, recorded, and reported.
2. Public hearing and examination, where knowledgeable persons testify and provide their best and informed guesses about the expected outcomes.
3. Comparisons of in-place programs with communities of similar characteristics where there is no such program.
4. The construction of elaborate experimental designs structured to fill in the blanks in the framework.

Criteria for Program Evaluation

The shift from descriptive/prescriptive research on policy output to analysis/evaluation of policy input is based on inquiry into three areas: performance, adequacy of performance, and efficiency. The first establishes the link between program activity (an output) and the measurable resources (an input). If, for example, the reduction of criminal recidivism is a program goal and a half-way house is the program operation, then the goal of the program performance evaluation is to demonstrate the causal connection between reduced recidivism and the half-way house. The first research priority is to demonstrate the connection between program activity and desired impact, principally to demonstrate that there is a causal connection and not a spurious relationship between the two.

The adequacy of the performance refers to the quality of the relationship between activity and measured impact. Here the need is to establish valid and reliable measures of recidivism. With performance measures articulated, it is possible to establish performance goals for the program. As the ratio of observed performance (OP) to performance goals (PG) approaches 1 $(OP/PG \to 1)$, performance can be said to be goal-fulfilling and thus successful.

The third aspect is efficiency. This topic (previously covered in the text) refers in reality to the relative standing of performance measured against cost. This approach seeks to compare proposals and programs against a common standard—usually a dollar benefit measure. The purpose is to distinguish between programs on the basis of their relative effectiveness; the goal of efficiency is the accomplishment of the objective with the lowest real social cost.

PROGRAM EVALUATION

Program evaluation has become an important part of the policy process. The principal difference between policy analysis and program evaluation is that the former is *prospec*tive, while the latter is *retrospec*tive. The purpose of programs of evaluation is to provide an assessment within *current* resource utilization; the assessment measures efficiency and effectiveness so that more rational projections and decisions might be made regarding future utilization.

Evaluation is thought of by some as a mechanism for rational social planning, while others view it as a threat to social programs. As a technique it is neither, but it is more usefully thought of as an instrument which will enable administrators to make more reliable decisions, and elected officials to have more complete information regarding social programs. When program evaluation is competently done, it provides the following to decision makers at all levels of the political system:

1. Valid and reliable information about what works for the agency or unit of government in terms not only of activities alone, but how these activities impact on the target.
2. A clear and reproduceable record of the programs' accomplishments in light of program goals, agency resources, and client needs.
3. An important instrument for judging the agency's future needs and staffing requirements in order to maintain current levels of service.
4. A beginning supply of the information essential to determining the realistic costs and benefits of social welfare programming.

The most important result of the heightened use of program evaluation lies in the awareness it has generated about the distinction between policy input and policy impact. The former is a

measure of government activity—dollars spent per capita on a
target population, or the number of specific services actually provided. The latter is a measure of the changes in behavior and
function that reasonably can be attributed to the policy interaction.

THE CHANGE FROM POLICY OUTPUTS TO POLICY IMPACTS

Over the past ten years, as the magnitude of dollars spent on
policy analysis has increased dramatically, there has been an important shift in the focus of investigation. Policy output is the
measure of government activity. For the purpose of political analysis, to describe, identify, and explain the determinants of policy,
policy output measures are important. Policy analysis must go
beyond this and measure the *impact* of policies. That is to say,
there must be an effort to identify and measure real changes in the
environment which are derived from or which compose the sec-
ond-order consequences of the policy changes. An accounting of
the *per capita* dollars spent on social services is a measure of policy
output; the effect on recipients' employability or life-styles is a
measure of policy impact. Measuring the latter is profoundly more
difficult.

The placement of the focus of attention on policy impact demands large changes in the procedure of policy investigation. The
dependent variable is not the policy, but the consequence of the
policy, and the policy outputs, the dependent variables of political
analysis, are the independent variables of policy analysis. The shift
can be seen in Figure 12–3.

The shift in focus to policy-analytic techniques was accompanied by the introduction of Planning-Program-Budgeting Systems (PPBS), first in the Department of Defense and then later
throughout government. This "new" approach was based on the
simple premise that the decision-making process can be effectively rationalized if there is a more effective flow of information. This
was certainly valid for intraagency decision making. In 1965 President Lyndon Johnson directed that all decision-making agencies
should develop central staff for analysis, planning, and programming, with the PPBS chief being directly responsible to the head
of the agency or the principal deputy.

When analysis evaluation processes were introduced into interagency allocation decisions, a number of problems arose. Two
quite prominent problems were the specification of criteria for

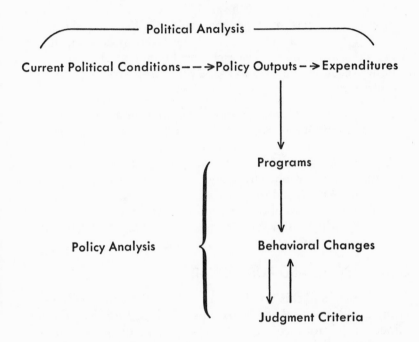

FIGURE 12-3
DISTINCTION BETWEEN POLITICAL ANALYSIS AND POLICY
ANALYSIS

policy evaluation, and the impact of negative evaluation findings
or projections. The political assessment thus was not diminished.

The Impact of Negative Findings or Projections

Those who are involved in policy research are seldom neutral
about the outcome. It is often the case that evaluators, administrators, those who deliver the service, and those who receive the
service find themselves in a political predicament which will not
allow for the risk of failure. These persons, via ideological condi-
tioning or because of circumstances, become committed to specific policy reform by specific techniques. Often the actors in a policy
drama perceive themselves as being trapped in a position of advocacy. Thus, evaluations tend to be structured so that negative
findings are either unlikely to appear or are easily refutable if they
do develop. On the other side of the coin, it is often the case that

the actors, particularly program managers, will seek to use evaluation and projection as a mechanism of legitimization. A program manager who reasonably expects positive findings from a projected study will surely endorse the analytic task as a future instrument of political persuasion rather than an instrument of policy decision. For these reasons, care must be taken in deciding under which conditions policy research may be initiated.

Policy research is most successful when the following conditions are present:

1. There is agreement among the actors on an unambiguous statement of the specific problems that the proposed or evaluated program is designed to solve.
2. There is agreement before the fact and among the actors of the criteria of objectives upon which the impact of the program is designed to be measured.
3. There is a careful delineation of principal program components which allows for some differentiation of alternative programs and alternative components of programs.

CONCLUSIONS AND POSTSCRIPT

This chapter and this text have focused on the conceptual, operational, and technical problems which are associated with the sustained application of a critical appraisal of proposed and operating policies in the area of social welfare. My goal in presenting the material is not to supplant existing patterns of the social worker's intervention, though I would be gratified if the approaches indicated here did supplement traditional approaches. The policy analyst in social welfare will always have to deal with the contradictions of advocacy and analysis.

There are two central problems that remain. One of the difficulties in shaping a conceptual scheme of the social welfare policy process is the difficulty which causes us to misperceive what happened for what we wish would have happened. The second is that analysts become advocates too easily. I hope the orientation introduced here will counter both tendencies.

NOTES

1. The normative question discussed earlier in this text deals with the question of what goals a society ought to have. Prescriptive questions are more narrow; given a goal, what programs ought we to have?

2. Tony Tripodi, Phillip Fellin, and Irwin Epstein, *Social Program Evaluation* (Itasca, Ill.: F. E. Peacock Publishers, 1971), p. 12.
3. Thomas Dye, *Understanding Public Policy* (Englewood Cliffs, N.J.: Prentice-Hall, 1978), chap. 13.
4. Ibid.
5. Ibid.
6. The evidence on this point is clearly mixed. See, however, David Warner, *Toward New Human Rights* (Austin, Tex.: Lyndon B. Johnson School of Public Affairs, 1977), and Boyd Littrell and Gideon Sjoberg, *Current Issues in Social Policy* (London: Sage, 1976).
7. Dye, *Understanding Public Policy*.
8. James Q. Wilson, "On Pettigrew and Armor," *The Public Interest*, vol. 31 (1973), p. 132 ff.
9. Tripodi et al., *Social Program Evaluation*.
10. Dye, *Understanding Public Policy*, p. 314.

CRITICAL SOURCES FOR
THE EXAMINATION OF
CURRENT POLICY DEBATES

By *Barbara Turman*

An exhaustive bibliographic note on current policy issues would require a separate monograph. This note is therefore highly selective. A few journals, magazines, newspapers, and retrieval instruments are particularly helpful. Among the journals that typically contain articles, bibliographic essays, and substantive critiques on current topics are *Urban Affairs Quarterly*, *Public Policy*, *The Public Interest*, and *Policy Analysis*. It is generally agreed that among national newspapers, *The Christian Science Monitor*, *The Wall Street Journal*, the *Washington Post* and the *New York Times* provide the broadest coverage and analysis of current issues. The *New York Times* is the best indexed of these and is typically available on microfilm at most major universities and city libraries.

Increasingly significant ranges of literature are now searchable by computer. The printed index is placed "on line" on computer tape and accessed through a computer terminal. Computer searching is significantly faster and more current than traditional search procedures.

An important guide to the examination of current policy topics,

with regard to substantive content, current status, and recent pub-
lical history, is the fantastic array of government documents. Instruments frequently used in accessing these documents are
abstracted here.

GUIDES TO FEDERAL PUBLICATIONS

The Federal Index. Cleveland, Ohio: Predicasts. 1976–. Vol. 1–.
   Monthly.

The Federal Index covers a broad spectrum of governmental activities. It is divided into two sections: Section A deals with the
concerns and activities of the federal government, including the
president, executive departments, independent agencies, Congress and the judiciary; Section B is concerned with governmental
issues such as the economy, environment, energy, health, education and welfare, trade, services, and state and local governments.
The citations to the source documents collected in this index are
derived from the *Congressional Record,* the *Federal Register, The Weekly
Compilation of Presidential Documents, Commerce Business Daily,* and the
Washington Post. Each citation indexed includes: government
agency involved, abstract of the action taken or proposed, journal
abbreviation, date and page, and additional sources. Access to the
documents is provided through the table of contents or the subject index. The advantage to using this index lies in the fact that
one source may be consulted rather than using each publication's
separate index. This source is available for on-line computer
searching.

Public Affairs Information Service. *Bulletin of the Public Affairs Information Service.* New York, 1915–. Vol. 1–. Weekly.

Useful for current research in the areas of political science,
government, legislation, economics, and sociology, this selective
subject index lists the latest books, pamphlets, government publications, reports of public and private agencies, and journal articles relating to economic and social conditions. More than 1,000
periodicals published in English throughout the world are included. This source is also available for on-line computer searching.

U.S. Superintendent of Documents. *Monthly Catalog of United States*

Government Publications. Washington, D.C.: U.S. Government Printing Office, 1895–. Monthly.

This is the most complete list of both current and retrospective U.S. government publications issued by Congress, the executive agencies, and the different bureaus. Each issue contains a list of documents published during the month, arranged by department. Each publication listed includes basic bibliographic information: author, title, date of publication, pagination, price, and Superintendent of Documents number if available. Beginning with the July 1976 issue, there are four separate indexes: author, title, subject, and series/report. There is also a cumulative annual index. This source available for on-line computer searching.

DIRECTORIES

Encyclopedia of Governmental Advisory Organizations. Detroit, Michigan: Gale Research Company, 1975.

This source is useful for locating information on governmental advisory committees. It includes approximately 2,700 committees: Presidential advisory committees, public advisory committees, and interagency committees. Currency is maintained through a continuing service published semiannually: *New Governmental Advisory Organizations.* This book is divided into ten subject areas, and within each section, committees of mutual interests are grouped together. Entries for each committee include: name, address, telephone number, executive secretary, history and authority, program, membership, staff, and meetings. It contains an alphabetical and key word index.

United States Government Manual. Washington, D.C.: Office of the Federal Register, 1935–. Annual.

This manual serves as the official handbook of the federal government. The programs and purposes of most government agencies and their key officials are described. Also included are the quasi-official agencies and certain international organizations. Contained within each listing of departments and agencies is a summary paragraph describing that organization's role in the federal government. The descriptions tend to emphasize the programs and activities rather than the internal agency structure. It includes name, agency, and subject indices.

Official Congressional Directory. Washington, D.C.: Government Printing Office, 1809–. Irregular.

This is a compendium of useful information on the federal government: Congress, the executive agencies, and the judiciary. Its emphasis is on Congress, with biographical sketches of congressional members; membership of the standing committees and subcommittees, select and special committees, and congressional staffs of both houses; membership of joint committees, commissions, and boards; and lists of Senate and House committee assignments. It contains biographical information on the members of the judiciary branch of government. Officials of international organizations, foreign diplomatic representatives, and consular offices, along with rules governing the press galleries and members of the press entitled to admission are listed. Principal administrative officers of executive departments and independent agencies are also given. The *Congressional Staff Directory* serves as a useful supplement to the *Congressional Directory* for a listing of congressional staffs, subcommittees, and committee staffs.

Washington Information Directory. Washington, D.C.: Congressional Quarterly, Inc., 1974–. Annual.

This source offers a shortcut through the maze of information available in Washington, D.C. Divided into 16 broad subject headings, it contains more than 5,000 entries on Congress, the agencies of the executive branch, private and special-interest organizations which maintain Washington offices in order to follow legislation, government operations, and policy.

In addition to a subject index whose entries are cross-indexed, there is an agency and organization index. Other features include appendices which list members of Congress, addresses, telephone numbers, key staff, committee assignments, and subcommittee memberships, in addition to biographies of each member of the latest Congress.

Each entry contains two paragraphs. The first lists the name of the organization, its address, telephone number, and name, and title of the director; the second offers a description of the work performed by the association.

STATISTICAL SOURCES

American Statistics Index. Washington, D.C.: Congressional Information Service, 1973–. Annual with monthly supplements.

This is a comprehensive compendium of social, economic, business, and natural resources statistics published by the U.S. government. Statistical documents from more than 400 issuing agencies are included. The first annual, the *1974 Annual and Retrospective Edition,* indexes significant publications from the 1960s selectively, and comprehensively for 1970–1973. Each annual thereafter provides comprehensive coverage for the previous year.

American Statistics Index (ASI) is published in two parts: the Index and the Abstracts. The Index is divided into two sections: by subjects and name and by categories. The categories include geographic breakdowns such as city, state, foreign country; economic breakdowns such as income, industry, and occupations; and demographic breakdowns such as race, sex, and age. *ASI* indexes and abstracts current periodicals, annuals, biennials, series, monographs, and all Congressional publications which contain statistical material. At many major libraries, this index is available for on-line computer searching.

U.S. Bureau of the Census. *Statistical Abstract of the United States.* Washington, D.C.: U.S. Government Printing Office, 1879–. Vol. 1–. Annual.

This one-volume work collects statistics on the social, political, and economic organization of the United States. The statistics given in the tables usually cover a period of years so that a comparison of the collected data is possible. Sources of information for all statistical tables are provided, as well as a subject index.

LEGISLATIVE HISTORY

Congressional Information Service/Annual/Index. *Abstracts of Congressional Publications and Legislative Histories.* Washington, D.C.: Congressional Information Service, Inc., 1970–. Monthly, with quarterly index cumulations and final clothbound cumulations in two volumes.

This invaluable source offers brief abstracts for the following kinds of Congressional publications: committee prints and hearings, House and Senate documents, reports, and miscellaneous publications, Senate executive reports, and Senate executive documents. It includes an index of names and names of witnesses at hearings, in addition to an index of bills, reports, and document numbers and an index of committee and subcommittee chairpersons. This is also typically available on-line.

U.S. Library of Congress, Congressional Research Service. *Digest of the Public General Bills and Resolutions.* Washington, D.C.: U.S. Government Printing Office, 1936–.

The *Digest,* published continuously since the second session of the 74th Congress, provides a brief abstract of bills and resolutions introduced each session with any changes during the legislative process. Indexes to the bills and resolutions include: sponsor and co-sponsor, title, and identical bills. It is published during each session of Congress in two cumulative issues, with monthly supplements and a final edition at the conclusion of the session. Although not as timely as Commerce Clearing House's *Congressional Index,* it does provide more extensive abstracts.

U.S. Congress. *Calendars of the United States House of Representatives and History of Legislation.* Washington, D.C.: U.S. Government Printing Office.

Since the *Calendar* is published daily when the House is in session, this is the most timely source available in terms of tracing current legislative histories of bills and resolutions introduced in Congress. It contains information on bills reported to either house or on which later action was taken. For each bill a cumulative history is given showing the dates when an action was taken and the law number if the bill became a law. Arrangement is by bill number, but it also contains a listing of bills in conference and bills through conference. Each issue is cumulative so that the daily status of a bill can be determined. On Monday a cumulative subject index of all legislation of both the House and the Senate is provided.

The final edition of the House Calendar is published after the close of a Congress. It contains the only list of both bills that

become law and those that did not. There is no other official list
of bills which failed to become law because the President withheld
approval of a bill after the adjournment of Congress. It provides
the status of major bills and notes vetoes. It lists bills and resolutions which passed either or both Houses, also pending bills and
resolutions.

U.S. Congress. *Congressional Record.* Washington, D.C.: Govern-
    ment Printing Office, 1873–. Vol. 1–. Daily while Congress is
    in session.

The *Congressional Record* is presumably a verbatim account of the
proceedings on the floor of the House and Senate. However this
is not the case, since members may withhold their remarks for
revisions or editing or submit remarks never delivered. The
Record consists of four sections: the proceedings of both the
House and the Senate; the Extension of Remarks, containing tran-
scripts of lengthy remarks made by Congressmen which may not
be germane to the legislation; and the Daily Digest. The Daily
Digest contains highlights of the session, actions taken by each
house, summary of the committee actions, and committee meetings for the following day. It also includes bills signed by the
president.

The *Congressional Record* is published in two forms: the *Daily
Record* published at the end of each day, and the permanent, bound
Record. The bound *Record* is merely an indication of opinions of
congressional members; it is not a report of words actually spoken
in debate. The pagination of the *Daily Record* does not correspond
to that in the bound *Record.* Therefore, the index to the *Daily Record*
issued every two weeks cannot be used for the bound *Record,* nor
can the complete session index of the bound *Record* be used in
conjunction with the *Daily Record.* Texts of bills and resolutions are
not normally reported in the *Record.* Both the bi-weekly index and
the master index for the bound *Record* consist of two parts: index
to proceedings, including material in the Extension of Remarks,
and a history of bills and resolutions. The bi-weekly indices are not
cumulative. A bill is indexed under a member's name and the
subject at the time it is introduced. The history is arranged by bill
number; and bill number references are cumulative, so that the
latest index will show a complete history for each bill in that session. On-line computer searching is available.

CONGRESSIONAL ACTION

Congressional Index. Chicago, Illinois: Commerce Clearing House, 1969/70–. Weekly.

This service permits quick research on the status of legislation pending in Congress. All public bills and resolutions are listed, briefly abstracted, and indexed, from their introduction to their final disposition. This two-volume set covers the legislative activity for both sessions of Congress, providing constant updates during each session to indicate the changes in the status of legislation. Volume one indexes by subject and authors for both volumes, in addition to providing the status of legislation pending in the Senate. Volume two indexes the House of Representatives. There is also an index for reorganization plans, treaties, and nominations, which are executive documents requiring Congressional action. Also provided is a list of measures that were approved or vetoed, by bill number and Public Law number.

A separate Voting Records Division records how the majority of each political party voted and notes the names of those who did not follow the party line. Other useful features include a list of members of both houses, with biographical data and their memberships in permanent committees and subcommittees.

Although changes are issued weekly while Congress is in session, they are in fact approximately one month behind the actual events in Congress.

Congressional Quarterly Weekly Report. Washington, D.C.: Congressional Quarterly, Inc., 1946–. Weekly.

Providing a capsule summary and analysis of the congressional and political events relating to the U.S. government for one week, the *Weekly Report* shows the status of major legislation for that week. In regard to major bills, the weekly issues include the subject matter of the legislation, sponsors, status in committee, hearings, floor action, and results of conferences. A useful feature is a table showing the roll call votes taken for all members. Measures approved show a Public Law number and the date signed. It also includes the full text of presidential press conferences, major statements, messages, and speeches. Each weekly issue has its own index, with quarterly indices by names and subjects cumulating throughout the year.

The *Congressional Quarterly Almanac* published annually distills the year's activities in Congress into broad subject categories. It pulls together much of the information already included in the *Congressional Quarterly Weekly Reports,* but it does not replace it.

National Journal. Washington, D.C.: Center of Political Research, 1969–. Weekly.

This journal offers systematic coverage of significant topics that shape federal policy. Each issue contains four or five well-researched articles on timely topics, a Weekly Briefing section, a checklist of important actions of the president, Congress, executive agencies and departments, and the judiciary. Also included are the voting records of congressional members for that week. Cumulated indexes include personal names, private firms and associations, government agencies, a geographic index, and a subject index.

STATUTES

U.S. Code Congressional and Administrative News. St. Paul, Minnesota: West Publishing Company, 1950–. 81st Congress, 2nd Session–. Bi-weekly with annual cumulations.

The full text of all Public Laws enacted during a particular session of Congress is included, along with their legislative histories. Proclamations, executive orders, both bills and joint resolutions, and major bills enacted are contained also. There is a popular names of acts index and a subject index. It is published semi-monthly during each session of Congress, and monthly when Congress is not in session.

United States Statutes at Large, Containing the Laws and Concurrent Resolutions ... Washington, D.C.: U.S. Government Printing Office, Vol. 1–, 1789–1845–.

Statutory law as evidenced in the *Statutes at Large* eventually becomes codified in the *U.S. Code.* The *Statutes* provide a permanent, retrospective record of the full texts of all laws passed in the United States during a given year. The arrangement is chronological by date of passage of the act. It is primarily a compilation of public and private laws. Also included are reorganization plans, concurrent resolutions, and proclamations. There is both a subject and individual index.

United States Code. 1976 edition. Washington, D.C.: Government Printing Office, 1977.

The *U.S. Code* contains the general and permanent laws of the United States in force on January 3, 1977, arranged within the context of 50 titles or subjects. New editions are issued every six years, with cumulative supplements issued after each session of Congress. Supplements contain all enactments and repeals subsequent to the latest edition, as well as corrections. A popular name index and a subject index are provided.

United States. *Federal Register*. Washington, D.C.: U.S. Government Printing Office, 1936–. Daily except Sunday and Monday, and days following legal holidays.

The *Federal Register* contains all presidential proclamations, executive orders, rules, and regulations of the various agencies and departments; decisions of federal agencies affecting individuals and corporate bodies; notifications of new rules proposed by administrative agencies pursuant to legislative intent; and a Cumulative List of Parts Affected, which is a numerical guide to the titles and sections of the *Code of Federal Regulations* affected by amendments published to date. Entries are arranged generally by issuing agency. It contains daily, monthly, quarterly, and annual subject index.

Code of Federal Regulations. Washington, D.C.: U.S. Government Printing Office, 1949–.

This represents the codification of all federal administrative rules, regulations, and guidelines, both general and permanent, that first appeared in the *Federal Register*. These are the current rules and regulations in force. It is composed of 50 titles or subjects, which frequently correspond to those of the *U.S. Code*. There is a separate subject index volume.

PRESIDENTIAL PAPERS

Weekly Compilation of Presidential Documents. Washington, D.C.: U.S. Government Printing Office, 1965–. Vol. 1–. Weekly.

This compilation includes all presidential activities for one week. It includes proclamations, executive orders, addresses and remarks, appointments, letters, nominations to the Senate, acts approved by the President, checklists of the White House press releases, messages to Congress, and announcements of resignations and retirements. It does not include promotions of members of the uniformed services, nominations to service academies, or nominations of Foreign Service officers. Each issue, published Monday for the preceding week's activities, has a cumulative index in addition to a quarterly, semiannual, and annual subject index.

NAME INDEX

Adult programs, 255
Advertising, 33
AFDC, *see* Aid to Families with Dependent Children
AFDC-U program, 139, 176, 218
  reform, 170
Affirmative action programs, 75–76
AFL-CIO, 238, 249
Aid to the aged, 156, 191, 193, 211, 255
  preferential treatment, 220
  programs, 255, 256
  welfare reform, 255–256
Aid to the blind, 156, 211, 255
  welfare reform, 256
Aid to Families with Dependent Children, (AFDC), 127, 139–143
  administering agency, 140
  calculation of benefits, 141–142
  childrens' allowance programs, 176–177
  eligibility, 139
  financing, 140–142
  reform, 242–243, 258, 259
  SSI amalgamation, 262
Aid to the Permanently and Totally Disabled, 255
Allocation of goods and services, 32, 71, 75
  distributive effect, 71
Altmeyer, Arthur, 194, 199, 201, 215
American Association for Labor Legislation, 194

American Medical Association, 31, 205
Apprenticeship of children, 188
Aristotle, 84
Arrow, Kenneth, 38
Association for Old Age Security, 193

Bakke case, 75–76
Basic need schedules, 143
Banfield, Edward, 44
Bawden, D. Lee, 171
Benjamin, Herbert P., 203
Beyond Welfare, 224
Bibby, John, 230
Black lung program, 138
Blanc, I., 84 ·
Blind, aid to, *see* Aid to the Blind
Board of Unemployment Relief, 197
Bonus wage, 136
Brazier, Harvey, 176
Brodbeck, May, 47
Browder, Earl, 203
Brown, Josephine, 196
Burns, Arthur, 241, 242, 243
Burns, Eveline, 204, 223

Califano, Joseph, 260
Carter, Jimmy, 181, 257–263
  welfare reform, 259–265
Case poverty, 119–121
Caseworker, 212
Cash transfer payments, 86, 124, 125, 226, 232, 241

311

THE BOOK MANUFACTURE

Introduction to Social Welfare Policy: Power, Scarcity and Common Human Needs was typeset by Autographics, Inc. of Monterey Park, California. The book was printed and bound by R.R. Donnelley, Crawfordville, Indiana. Cover design was by Harvey Retzloff, Chicago. Internal design was by the F.E. Peacock Publishers art department. The type is Baskerville with Helvetica display.